ERATOSTHENES of Cyrene (*c*.285–*c*.194 BC) was a leading scholar, scientist, and poet of the Hellenistic era, who became the third director of the great library at Alexandria, and achieved notable distinction as a geographer. He compiled a comprehensive handbook of astral mythology, the *Catasterisms*, by collecting constellation myths from the previous tradition, altering and improving them as he thought fit, and devising new myths where it was necessary or desirable. This genre of myth, in which stories were put forward to explain how persons, creatures, and things had come to be set in the sky as constellations, was developed at a relatively late period, mainly from the fifth century onward, and the canon became largely fixed after Eratosthenes established his synthesis in the third century. Although his compendium has not survived, much is recorded of its contents in the later summaries translated in this volume, and it was the main source, directly or indirectly, for the astral myths recounted by Hyginus.

GAIUS JULIUS HYGINUS (*c*.64 BC–AD 17) was appointed by Augustus to be director of the Palatine library, and a prolific author who wrote about a wide variety of subjects. Two surviving works are ascribed to him, the *Fabulae*, a collection of tales from Greek myth, and the *Astronomy*, an elementary guide to astronomy which contains the fullest surviving collection of constellation myths. Whether or not the *Astronomy* was actually written by Hyginus, it is invaluable for what it records of the astral myths in the Eratosthenian tradition.

ARATUS of Soloi (*c*.310–*c*.240 BC) was born in Asia Minor, studied at Athens under the Stoic philosopher Zeno, among others, and received an invitation in 276 to come to the Macedonian court, where he wrote his astronomical poem, the *Phaenomena*, which is his only surviving work. It contains, among other things, a full account of the Greek picture of the sky, in which all the constellations are described in due succession.

ROBIN HARD has translated Apollodorus, *Library of Greek Mythology*, Diogenes the Cynic, *Sayings and Anecdotes*, Marcus Aurelius, *Meditations*, and Epictetus, *Discourses, Fragments, Handbook* for Oxford World's Classics. He is the author of *The Routledge Handbook of Greek Mythology*.

OXFORD WORLD'S CLASSICS

*For over 100 years Oxford World's Classics have brought
readers closer to the world's great literature. Now with over 700
titles—from the 4,000-year-old myths of Mesopotamia to the
twentieth century's greatest novels—the series makes available
lesser-known as well as celebrated writing.*

*The pocket-sized hardbacks of the early years contained
introductions by Virginia Woolf, T. S. Eliot, Graham Greene,
and other literary figures which enriched the experience of reading.
Today the series is recognized for its fine scholarship and
reliability in texts that span world literature, drama and poetry,
religion, philosophy, and politics. Each edition includes perceptive
commentary and essential background information to meet the
changing needs of readers.*

OXFORD WORLD'S CLASSICS

ERATOSTHENES and HYGINUS

Constellation Myths

with

Aratus's 'Phaenomena'

Translated with an Introduction and Notes by
ROBIN HARD

OXFORD
UNIVERSITY PRESS

OXFORD

UNIVERSITY PRESS

Great Clarendon Street, Oxford, OX2 6DP
United Kingdom

Oxford University Press is a department of the University of Oxford.
It furthers the University's objective of excellence in research, scholarship,
and education by publishing worldwide. Oxford is a registered trade mark of
Oxford University Press in the UK and in certain other countries

First published as an Oxford World's Classics paperback 2015

Impression: 10

Published in the United States of America by Oxford University Press
198 Madison Avenue, New York, NY 10016, United States of America

British Library Cataloguing in Publication Data

Data available

Library of Congress Control Number: 2014954273

ISBN 978-0-19-871698-3

Printed and bound in Great Britain by Clays Ltd, Elcograf S.p.A.

CONTENTS

INTRODUCTION

THE night sky is an alien environment, filled with countless points of light set in no kind of order. It is rare for any group of stars to form any obvious pattern which might encourage people to think that they are looking at a plough or wagon, perhaps, or a cross or crown. In spite of this, a natural tendency has always existed for human beings to try to domesticate the sky by identifying groups of stars with earthly things, even if that task often requires some effort of the imagination. It is not essential that the group should form a unified image—a star-cluster like the Pleiades might be thought to be a cluster of nymphs, maidens, or animals—but larger patterns of stars are fancied to form a picture, or forced into some kind of picture. Homer refers to our Plough not only as the Wagon, but also as the Bear, although the latter resemblance is far from obvious; and he identifies a gigantic figure further south as being Orion, a mighty hunter from Greek legend. This process of identification starts through a spontaneous impulse of the imagination, in relation to stars and asterisms which are of practical use to farmers or navigators, or to groups of stars which bear a more or less obvious resemblance to what they are supposed to represent; but the process is extended as a result of deliberate effort, as astronomers set to work to map out the sky in its entirety through methodical observation. By the fourth century BC, the sky was pictured as being filled throughout with constellations, some forty-six in number. The figures represented either persons, or creatures, or else things of varied nature, ranging from an arrow to a ship or river. Almost all were given names that assigned them to general categories, as opposed to proper names, and by and large, these constellations did not inherently have any closer connection with the world of myth than the modern ones created since the Renaissance. Our Hercules was known as yet merely as the Kneeler, and our Pegasus[1] merely as the Horse. Another constellation whose

---

[1] In the Latin titles of the constellations, Greek names are presented in Latinized form; except in this context, the original Greek forms have been used in this volume, and the hero will otherwise be called Heracles, and the winged horse will be called Pegasos as in the name of the constellation.

name was rendered more definite as a result of later myth-making is the Swan, which was originally just the Bird.

Only five of the constellations that represent persons had personal names from the very beginning, namely the constellation Orion, which was known as such to Homer and Hesiod, and four that illustrate the famous myth in which Perseus rescued Andromeda from a sea-monster. The latter group is exceptional because the myth itself inspired the invention of the whole group of constellations, evidently by a single person at a relatively late period, probably in the fifth century. Otherwise the ship in the heavens was apparently identified as Jason's *Argo* from a quite early period, and the celestial river as the Eridanos, that being the semi-mythical river in the far west into which Phaethon was said to have plunged.

In these examples, one can see the beginning of the process by which the constellation-figures came to be caught up with myth. It was natural to ask what these figures in the heavens, vaguely named as they were, really represented, and since they were splendid figures set in a sacred space, to seek the answer in the world of myth; and in the course of time, even if there was no resulting change of name, all of them came to be identified with people, creatures, and things from myth and legend. Perhaps the Maiden in the sky (Virgo) is the corn-goddess Demeter, because she is holding an ear of corn, figured forth in the star of that name (Stachys, or Spica in Latin); or perhaps she is blind-eyed Fortune because her head is faintly lit. As for the Horse, that must surely be the winged horse Pegasos, who flew up to the heavens after his rider Bellerophon fell off in the attempt. And the Ram is surely the famous ram with the golden fleece, and the Lion the invulnerable Nemean lion that Heracles strangled to death with his bare hands. In most cases it was no more difficult than that to think of at least one plausible identification.

Merely to identify constellations with beings or things does not call into being anything that could specifically be called astral mythology, even if it is a precondition for the invention of constellation myths. That comes about only when myths are devised to explain how these beings or things came to be set in the sky in the first place, as the result of events that had previously taken place down below on earth. If a mythical being or thing came to be transferred to the sky, that could only have happened, one might think, because some deity had intervened to bring it about for some good reason. The Lyre in the sky, for instance, might call to mind the famous myth that told how the infant Hermes had constructed the first lyre, making use of the shell from a tortoise that he had seen by his cradle; and an astral myth of the most elementary kind could be created by suggesting that the god then commemorated his invention by setting the lyre in the heavens (thus Aratus on p. 145). As for the Crown—there was only one as yet— the idea seems to have arisen quite early that it is the crown of Ariadne, the mortal wife of Dionysos. In his Argonautic epic Apollonius refers to it in passing as 'a crown of stars which men call Ariadne's crown' (3.1004), and the very thought that it is her crown carries with it the suggestion that her divine husband would have placed it in the sky after her death, to serve as a memorial, as is stated by Aratus (see p. 140). Although these stories are as short and simple as could be, it was from such beginnings that astral mythology originated.

Since the people who are represented in the constellations were usually identified with major figures from legend, it was often possible to look to old and familiar myths to find circumstances that might explain how they came to be transferred to the heavens. The above-mentioned constellation of the Kneeler portrays a kneeling man who has one foot set on the neighbouring Dragon, and is holding one of his arms upraised as though to strike it. This inevitably called to mind the myth in which Heracles killed the huge dragon that guarded the golden apples of the Hesperides, when he had been sent out to fetch some of the apples as his penultimate labour. If Zeus had decided to commemorate the episode and his son's valour by portraying it among the stars, that could explain the origin of two constellations all at once. If there is a Crab in the zodiac, what else could that be but the crab that had attacked Heracles when he was battling against the many-headed Lernaian hydra? And in that case, his enemy Hera could be said to have placed it in the sky after the hero crushed it under his foot. Although some myths had to be altered to a lesser or greater degree if they were to be enlisted for this purpose, many astral myths follow the pattern that can be observed in these examples, in which the bringing into being of a constellation, through the action of Zeus or some other deity, is explained by appending the necessary addition to a well-known myth, as a sort of coda. Although the deed by which the constellation is actually created is quickly accomplished and can be described very briefly, the astral myth as a whole becomes more substantial than in the rudimentary myths mentioned previously.

Although it may be supposed that astral myths of this kind were first developed by attaching a new end to an old myth, wholly new myths were also invented, especially to account for the origin of constellations from abroad which called to mind nothing from Greek myth. But even where that was the case, the myths were often devised by attaching a new episode to a well-known story, as in a myth for the Asses (a pair of stars in the Crab), in which the beasts were said to have earned their place in the heavens by inducing panic fear in the Giants through their braying, during the course of the battle between the gods and the Giants. As we have seen with Heracles and the Dragon, astral myths did not necessarily refer to constellations taken in isolation. Two or more constellations or asterisms could be pictured together as forming a tableau in the sky, and joint myths could be devised to account for two or more in conjunction, as in the case of the Water-snake, Bowl, and Crow (see pp. 110 ff.). The existence of such a tableau could occasionally inspire the invention of myths that were entirely new. Since the Scorpion rises as Orion sets, it could be imagined that Orion is being pursued by it, and it was this thought that inspired the myth in which he was said to have been killed by a huge scorpion, which was sent against him by Earth or perhaps by Artemis. Indeed, this came to be the standard account of his death, although the story had formed no part of his traditional mythology. The myth of Orion's pursuit of the daughters of Atlas, as represented in the Pleiades, owed its origin to similar considerations. Since the Pleiades can be seen to be fleeing from him up in the sky, a notion already expressed as a poetic fancy in Hesiod's *Works and Days* (618–20), an astral myth could easily be developed by saying Orion really had pursued them through his native Boeotia during their earthly existence, and that Zeus had come to their rescue by transferring them to the heavens. The few myths that were inspired by such considerations are sometimes described, if not altogether happily, as true or genuine star-myths.

Catasterisms

The Greeks devised a special term to describe the process by which people or things are set in the sky, calling it a catasterism (*katasterismos*; there was also a corresponding verb, *katasterizein*, to 'catasterize'). But what exactly does it mean to set a being or thing in the sky? In their general form, these astral myths which end in a catasterism bear a close resemblance to transformation myths, and some have regarded them as forming a special category of transformation myth. According to a quite ancient transformation myth, the ill-fated Arcadian heroine Callisto was transformed into a bear, and a catasterism was subsequently attached to this story, by saying that Zeus had later transferred her to the sky to become the Great Bear. Could it be said that she was first turned into a bear and then into a constellation? That seems inappropriate; the two processes are analogous rather than identical, and the ancient narratives describe them rather differently.

If one turns to those narratives, one finds that they are in fact inconsistent in the way in which they describe catasterisms, sometimes saying the beings or things are raised up to the heavens, and sometimes that these are portrayed in the sky as images. In the case of Callisto, we are told that Zeus raised her up to the sky to save her from suffering an ignominious death, while in the case of Heracles and the Dragon, Zeus is stated to have placed an image of their confrontation in the sky by way of commemoration. It would plainly be wrong to conclude from this that the constellations, in a mythical context, were imagined as differing in nature, some being real persons or things whereas others are mere images of them. The choice of language is determined by the logic of the story and the demands of the narrative. If Zeus turned himself into a swan to father Helen, and then commemorated the episode by placing a swan in the heavens, it would hardly have been possible for him to transfer the original swan to the sky. If the celestial horse, on the other hand, is Pegasos, who can still be seen in the sky after having flown there as the old myth recounted, this must be the real Pegasos; and another flying beast, the golden-fleeced ram, could be said to have flown up in a similar way to become the Ram in the zodiac. These two stories show, incidentally, that catasterisms were not always said to have been contrived by a god; other solutions could be permitted if the story allowed it.

In connection with some myths, then, constellations could not be other than an image, while in other cases the story demands that the being or thing should have passed up to the sky, and in others again it makes no difference how the matter is viewed. The inconsistency did not matter because catasterisms were never imagined to be anything other than inventions, and they were not thought to have any real explanatory power; all that mattered was that the story should be appealing and appropriate in each particular case. That being said, the constellations, in a mythical context, were basically regarded as being images, which portray beings or things from the mythical era for the sake of the viewer down below. If deities contrive catasterisms, it is almost always to commemorate something worthy of recall, and so to add to the commemorative picture-gallery in the sky; or very occasionally, a person or creature is set in the sky as a sign of infamy. When persons are rewarded by being placed in the sky, it is for the sake of the glory that they gain by being portrayed there, and not to enable them to continue their life there in a new form. Orion may be mentioned in Homeric epic as a hunter in the sky, but the real Orion is seen by Odysseus engaging in a ghostly hunt in the Underworld. The real Heracles, on the other hand, would be imagined as having passed up to Olympos to join the company of the gods, while the Heracles in the sky is a commemorative image.

The early history of astral mythology

Although some stars and constellations acquired mythical associations at a very early period, astral mythology first began to develop into a specific genre of myth when catasterisms were introduced, in the fifth century or possibly somewhat earlier, and it was not until Hellenistic times that the genre really began to flourish. It needs to be kept in mind that the Greek picture of the sky was itself not brought to full development until the fifth century, and that only a very limited number of stars and star-groups were used for practical purposes in early times, for navigation or as indicators for the seasons or weather, and were thus widely known. Astral mythology accordingly, in so far as it set out to provide mythical accounts of the origins of a wide range of constellations, was not a popular form of myth with early roots, but was developed at a relatively late period among well-educated people. It was, furthermore, a learnedly playful form of myth; most constellations were known to have been of quite late invention, and the myths that were attached to them were never regarded as holding more than poetic value.

The early development of true astral mythology is now impossible to trace, even if one would like to know for sure when catasterisms were first devised, and when the origins of a good number of constellations first came to be explained by means of them. The early sources for such myths have not survived, and problems arise from the way in which later authors who wrote about these myths reported their sources. Since catasterisms were often appended to well-known myths from the earlier tradition, it does not follow, when a relatively early source is cited for the main narrative, that the author in question had already ended the story with a catasterism. Sophocles and Euripides are cited, for instance, as sources for the myths that were attached to the constellations of the Perseus–Andromeda group, and it was once widely believed that catasterisms were thus announced in plays written by these authors from the fifth century; but there is no indication whatever of that in any ancient writings not connected with astronomy, and the idea has rightly fallen out of favour. It would be most interesting to know if the Hesiodic *Astronomy*, a work probably dating to the sixth century, included any catasterisms, as might be inferred from the way in which 'Hesiod' is cited as the source for certain constellation myths, but that must remain doubtful for the same reason. It does seem likely, however, that Pherecydes, a mythographer of the fifth century, provided a catasterism for the star-cluster of the Hyades, and he was quite possibly the author who first put forward the suggestion that Ariadne's crown was placed in the sky by Dionysos.

It is only in the early third century that we really arrive on firm ground, as a result of the quite frequent mythical allusions in Aratus's astronomical poem, the *Phaenomena*, although it could be assumed in any case that mythical identifications had been found for almost all the beings and things represented in the constellations by that period, and that catasterisms would have been devised to account for the origin of many of them. One does not gain the impression that Aratus had any special interest in the myths of the stars, but it would not have suited his purpose anyway to include much in the way of mythical narratives, because it would have been distracting to interrupt his account of the constellations in such a way. He was clearly not attempting to record a full range of myths, and was usually quite allusive in what he did say, expecting the reader to be able to fill out the story. A list of the mythical references in his poem can be found on p. xxxix.

The poem makes explicit mention of only three catasterisms. For the Lyre, it is briefly indicated that Hermes placed it in the sky, as its inventor; and for the Crown, that Dionysos had placed it there as a memorial to his dead wife. As for the two Bears, they had been raised to the heavens by Zeus, 'if what people say is true', because they had been his nurses. This shows how allusive Aratus was able to be in his treatment of these myths, for we are now unable to tell whether Zeus had been suckled by bears in the myth that he was referring to, or whether these were human nurses who were later transformed into bears. Aratus also indicates, without being quite explicit, that it had been Zeus who had transferred Andromeda and her parents to the sky, as might also be assumed of the Goat (the star Capella in the Archer), since this is stated to have been the sacred goat that had suckled Zeus.

For three asterisms, Aratus alludes to mythical associations that were probably quite ancient, or definitely so in the case of the Pleiades, which had long been identified as the daughters of Atlas; to identify the celestial ship as Jason's *Argo* would have been a very obvious thought, and likewise to identify the celestial river as the Eridanos with its rich mythical associations.

Full narratives are developed in connection with two constellations alone. One narrative explains how Orion came to be killed by a scorpion, which can itself be seen in the sky; the story is explicitly indicated to have been an old one, and it was indeed old enough for conflicting versions already to have been in circulation. The rather unusual version recounted by Aratus is in fact of hybrid character (see p. 105). No catasterism is supplied, it is merely remarked that these events that had taken place on earth are now illustrated in the sky, where Orion can be seen to be fleeing from the Scorpion. The longest narrative, which was of Aratus's own invention (even if it incorporates material from Hesiod), is not a conventional astral myth, but an allegory which describes how Justice withdrew from human company as human injustice increased, to finally remove herself completely by flying up into the sky to become the constellation of the Maiden (Virgo).

Finally the celestial Horse is said to have been the one that created the spring of Hippocrene on Mount Helicon; since Aratus was invoking Hesiodic associations here, as quite often in this poem, and the spring had come to be associated with poetic inspiration, it may be assumed that the present idea was introduced by Aratus himself. He felt no need to explain how that horse had come to be set in the sky.

The only other mythical references are of a negative character, in connection with the constellation then known as the Kneeler (now Hercules). When first describing it, Aratus states that no one knows who this person is, or on what task he is engaged, and he makes further allusion to the mysterious character of this figure later in the poem. This is significant in itself—by that time people would have expected to be able to say who is represented in a constellation-figure, and it would be irritating to be unable to do so—but it seems likely that, in this case, an identification had actually been proposed already, and that Aratus was being deliberately mystifying, expecting his readers to be able to solve the riddle for themselves (see p. 29).

If Aratus's poem gives at least some idea of how astral mythology had developed by the time at which he was writing, and of the different approaches that could be taken to it, the crucial turning-point in the development of this genre of myth came somewhat later, when it aroused the interest of Eratosthenes, a distinguished Alexandrian polymath who was born about thirty years later than Aratus. He set to work to compile an exhaustive compendium of astral myths, recounting tales to explain the origin of every constellation, often with variants and alternative myths. Although the work in question is now lost, it established the canon, and the great majority of the astral myths translated in the present volume were ultimately derived from it.

If mythical narratives formed the core of the work, Eratosthenes also listed the stars in each constellation, to describe how the figure is constructed, and presumably indicated its position. It was important for the impact of the work, quite apart from its quality, that it was both comprehensive and specifically astronomical in its focus. Although catasterisms had been used as an element in mythical narratives for two centuries or more, it did not follow that if a catasterism was attached to a narrative, that was the central point of the story, let alone that the author's primary concern was to provide a mythical explanation for the origin of the relevant constellation. In most cases the catasterism would have been an additional and subsidiary feature, briefly recounted and almost external to the main story. By drawing together a full range of constellation myths in a single volume, specifically as aetiological myths in an astronomical context, Eratosthenes seems to have played a leading role in ensuring that the constellations would become bound up with myth in the common imagination from his time onward.

Eratosthenes and his catasterisms

Eratosthenes was born at Cyrene in North Africa in the early third century BC, and died at an advanced age in the first decade of the second. He studied at Athens and had very wide interests, embracing philosophy, literature, geography, mathematics, astronomy, and much else. He coined the term *philologos* to apply to himself, meaning by that a lover of learning in general rather than a philologist in the narrower modern sense. His polymathy earned him the nickname of 'Beta', which implied that he had spread his efforts so widely that he never came to be more than second-best at anything; but that hardly did justice to his accomplishments—as a geographer, to take one notable example. He is remembered, for instance, for the surprisingly accurate estimate that he made of the circumference of the earth. As his reputation grew, he was invited to Egypt to become tutor to the king's son, and was subsequently appointed to be the third director of the great library at Alexandria.

He also wrote poetry in such spare time as was left to him, including two poems that had some astronomical content. In one, the *Erigone*, which was based on a local legend from Attica, he told how a peasant of that land from long ago came to be transferred to the stars along with his daughter and the family dog (see pp. 37–8); and in his epic poem *Hermes*, which has been lost like the other, he not only recounted standard myths of the god, but also ascribed a cosmological role to him, describing how he was supposed to have organized the heavens. One can understand the appeal that astral mythology could have held for someone of his turn of mind, in enabling him to divert himself with a field of study in which his scholarly, scientific, and literary interests were all brought together, if in a none too earnest endeavour.

As to the title of his compendium, there are three references in ancient sources to what he said 'in his catasterisms'. Although we cannot be absolutely certain that this was the formal title of the work, since the writers could have been using the word descriptively in reference to the nature of its contents, it may be accepted as the title with due reservation for want of better evidence.

So in compiling his *Catasterisms*, how did Eratosthenes set about the task? His approach would have been determined by the distinctive nature of these myths, in which catasterisms were appended, for the most part and where the possibility presented itself, to stories from earlier myth associated with major figures. Most constellations would already have been identified with specific beings or things from myth in the existing literature. Working in this regard as a literary scholar and mythographer, Eratosthenes had to construct the founding narrative by reference to the best and most appropriate early sources, and even if a catasterism had already been attached to the myth in question, he would have had considerable latitude in this respect. Whereas Aratus merely says, for instance, that Hermes placed his newly invented lyre in the sky, Eratosthenes offered an account in which Hermes passed it on to Apollo, and Apollo to Orpheus, and it was transferred to the sky after Orpheus met his death, drawing on a lost play by Sophocles to explain why and how Orpheus came to meet an early and violent end (for there were conflicting traditions about the matter). All that was left was to explain why it was that Zeus should have wished to place the lyre in the sky, through a catasterism that may have been of Eratosthenes' own invention.

According to the circumstances, Eratosthenes would have invented catasterisms to attach to narratives of that kind, or would have adopted catasterisms that had already been devised, in altered or unaltered form. When they were available in the existing literature, they would usually have been of later invention than the myths to which they were attached. Although there would have been cases in which myths were specially invented along with the catasterism, either by Eratosthenes himself or earlier authors, the usual pattern in his book would have been to have a narrative founded on a good early source or sources, duly cited, and for it to be followed by a catasterism that had been added on, briefly recounted and without any comparable indication of its origin.

Eratosthenes was writing at a sufficiently late period for alternative astral myths to have been developed for a fair number of constellations, as we have seen with Orion and the Scorpion; but it seems likely, on the other hand, that myths had yet to be devised for some of the more awkward constellations, especially those like the Fishes or Capricorn (representing a goat-fish) which called to mind nothing from Greek myth. In some cases Eratosthenes would have had gaps to fill, while in others he would have been able to include alternative accounts, sometimes expressing a judgement about which was preferable. He seems to have criticized Aratus's account of the Horse, for instance, arguing that it was preferable to identify it as Pegasos, and rejecting the common notion that the Archer is a Centaur. This was all part of the game, appropriateness and aesthetic considerations serving as criteria rather than any strict notion of truth. His *Catasterisms* was a work of synthesis, then, in which he recorded myths from the earlier literature, altering or improving them as he thought fit, and also making innovations of his own. Remarkably few innovations were introduced thereafter; Eratosthenes established and defined the canon through this single work, in a way that was unparalleled in any other genre of myth.

We have to consider next how this canon of astral mythology, as established by Eratosthenes in this lost work, became part of the general culture. For just as educated people in later Hellenistic and Roman times would be expected to have a knowledge of the constellations and basic astronomy, they would also be expected to have a knowledge of the myths associated with those constellations. To understand why this came about, it is necessary to consider how astronomy, or at least a form of astronomy, was taught as a standard subject of the school curriculum in later Hellenistic and Roman times, and how the destiny of Eratosthenes' compendium became intertwined with that of the work that was adopted for that purpose as a textbook, Aratus's *Phaenomena*.

Aratus's Phaenomena

Aratus (or Aratos to give the proper Greek form of his name) was born in about 310 BC at Soloi in Cilicia, a southern province of Asia Minor, and subsequently spent several years in Athens, studying under the Stoic philosopher Zeno, among others. The nature of the universe is interpreted in his poem in accordance with Stoic doctrine, in which the cosmos is said to be governed from within by the divine reason that pervades it, directing everything to the good of the whole. This providential reason is invoked at the beginning under the name of Zeus, and Aratus makes it his central purpose to show how the Governor of the universe, in his paternal benevolence, has ordered the heavens and set signs in them to bring benefit to mortals. In 276

Aratus received an invitation from Antigonos II Gonatas to come to the Macedonian court, and he probably wrote the *Phaenomena*, his only surviving poem, at Pella, the capital of Macedonia, during the following years.

As to the title of the poem, the Greek term *phainomena* ('things that appear', phenomena) could be used without further specification to refer to celestial phenomena in particular, and Eudoxos of Cnidos, an astronomer of the preceding century, had already used this as the title of a major work on astronomy. It was from Eudoxos's *Phaenomena* that Aratus drew most of his astronomical information, and he used it as the source for his full account of all the constellations. Since Eudoxos's work, which established the canonic picture of the sky, has not survived, Aratus's poem is a historical document of the highest importance, and would be worth including in the present volume for its description of the constellations alone; but it is not a mere versification of Eudoxos's work, as is sometimes misleadingly suggested, but was composed as a didactic poem with its own distinctive structure and aims.

It falls into two main parts, the first part (1–757) being devoted to astronomical matters, while the second part (757–1141) is concerned with weather-signs. The signs in the latter are not only provided by heavenly bodies and certain asterisms, but also by a whole variety of natural phenomena, including the behaviour of animals and birds; and the information was drawn not from Eudoxos, but from a lost work on weather-signs, a fuller version of the surviving compendium that is ascribed to Theophrastos, a follower of Aristotle. Although not relevant to our main subject, this second part of the poem is perhaps the most enjoyable part of it, and contains a large amount of interesting if not altogether reliable weather-lore.

The astronomical section falls in turn into two separate parts, giving the poem a tripartite structure overall. After the initial account of the heavens, with its successive descriptions of all the constellations (1–459), Aratus goes on to explain how time can be measured, through the night and year, by observation of the heavens (460–757). This latter part forms a bridge to the final section of the poem, because one needs to be able to estimate the time of year, month, or night if one is to make proper use of weather-signs. Now time-measurement is a big subject, and Aratus is very selective in his treatment of it, concentrating on one specific aspect in particular, namely on how the zodiac can be used as a clock to tell how much of the night has passed. For since six signs of the zodiac rise each night, and six set, irrespective of the time of year, this enables the observer to form an accurate estimate of the stages of the night. Aratus thus begins this part of the poem by discussing the circles on the celestial sphere in so far as they are relevant to an understanding of the zodiac (465–558; the polar circles are not even mentioned). Although the zodiac can also be used to estimate the time of year, Aratus then passes straight on to his main subject, its use as a night-clock. One might think that this could be explained and passed over in a few lines, but since the relevant sign of the zodiac may be obscured at the time of its rising or setting, one needs to know what other constellations rise and set at the same time, to be able to gain the required knowledge indirectly, and most of the following lines (559–732) are thus devoted to an inventory of these simultaneous risings and settings. The subject is then concluded with a very brief discussion of the days of the month and times of the year (733–57).

Astronomy in education and in the general culture

As in modern times, people who had a special interest in astronomy could seek out their own books and teachers, and adopt a proper scientific approach; some mathematical knowledge and interest would naturally be required for this. But astronomy of a certain kind also formed part of the more general culture, it was taught in schools as part of the curriculum from the Hellenistic period onwards, and any cultivated person would be expected to have some knowledge of it; and by the second century BC at least, Aratus's *Phaenomena* established itself as the standard school textbook. It may strike us as surprising that a poem should have been chosen for this purpose, when elementary handbooks were available, written by authors with some specialist knowledge; but the poem provided an attractive literary account of all the constellations, which could be used in conjunction with a globe to teach the pupils about the ordering of the heavens. It is worth noting in this connection that people relied almost entirely on globes and charts for their knowledge of the stars, few would have attempted much in the way of direct observation of the night sky. Little would have been taught of the more scientific side of the subject, beyond an explanation of the nature of the celestial sphere and of its main circles and zones; and Aratus does say something about the zodiac, ecliptic, and tropics. The poem's adoption as a textbook helped to advance it on a glorious career that could hardly have been predicted for it at the time of its writing. Any educated person would have been familiar with it. After having been introduced to it at school, where only the first part of it was read, people would also refer to it in later life as a main source of astronomical knowledge.

As an astronomical textbook, especially when used as a work of reference in later life, the poem did have distinct limitations. It contains no mathematics, no enumeration of the stars in each constellation, and only a very brief and incomplete account of the celestial sphere. A certain amount of prior knowledge was originally assumed on the part of the reader, and if the poem was to fulfil the role that was later assigned to it, readers would have to gain additional knowledge from elsewhere. This encouraged the production of commentaries and supplemented editions, which would almost always have been the work of grammarians (men of letters) rather than of people who had any specialist knowledge. As can be seen from the surviving Aratean literature, the astronomical information which they provided, and which the general reader could be expected to know, rarely rose above a very basic level, and a gulf thus grew up between scientific astronomy and what one might call poetic astronomy, the astronomy that centred primarily around the study of Aratus and formed part of the wider culture. This gulf was broadened by the fact that the grammarians who worked on Aratus tended to be more interested in—and more expert in—the mythology of the stars than in the technicalities of astronomy.

Conditions had thus arisen under which, among the general educated public, astral mythology could come to be associated on virtually equal terms with study of the constellations and celestial sphere, and astronomy could be approached in a primarily aesthetic spirit. After Eratosthenes had provided the initial impulse to this development, by bringing astronomy and mythology into conjunction in his compendium, his book came to be used, in effect, as a mythological commentary to Aratus's *Phaenomena*, which had now come to be seen as sadly deficient in this regard. It has even been suggested that he wrote the work with that in mind, although that must be regarded as more than a little doubtful; but it is undoubtedly the case that, as regards the propagation of knowledge in this area, the Aratean and

Eratosthenian traditions became indissolubly intertwined. As has been noted, mythology would have been an attractive subject to the grammarians who devoted attention to Aratus, and they would have relied on Eratosthenes' handbook as their main source of information; and in the course of time many readers, or even most, came to draw their information about astral mythology not directly from the handbook itself, but from supplemented editions of Aratus, which conveniently gathered together everything that they needed to know, astronomical and mythological, within a single source. This helps to explain why Eratosthenes' *Catasterisms* has failed to survive, unlike Aratus's poem; for it was assuredly not as a result of any lack of interest in constellation myths in later antiquity.

Aratus's *Phaenomena* can still be of help in approaching our main subject of astral mythology. Although astral mythology was not one of the author's primary concerns, the poem does make a wider range of allusions to it than any other surviving work from Aratus's period or earlier, and perhaps more importantly, it contains a full and readable account of that Greek picture of the sky as presented by Eudoxos, describing in their due position all the constellations to which myths were attached in Eratosthenes' handbook. This is the more valuable because Eratosthenes' own descriptions have survived only in very imperfect summaries, too imperfect to be worth translating for this volume. And thirdly, there is the factor that has just been discussed, that the fates of these two very different books became interconnected.

It is as a result of that interconnection that we possess one of the main sources for the myths that were recounted by Eratosthenes in his lost work. For we have summaries, short and selective though they may be, of myths from that work for every constellation, ultimately derived from a supplemented edition of Aratus's poem. The constellations are thus covered in the same order as they are described in the *Phaenomena*, rather than in the order originally adopted in Eratosthenes' handbook (which is known from two surviving lists of its contents). The edition of Aratus for which these summaries were originally prepared, known in the scholarly literature as 'Phi', is believed to have been of fairly late origin, dating from the second to the third century AD. Although it was of miscellaneous content and low scholarly standard, it evidently answered to the needs of its readers, because it was popular and successful. As usual, it contained added astronomical and mythological material, and the aforesaid summaries themselves included both, because the mythical narratives for each constellation are followed by an enumeration of its stars. The latter information would have been useful to the edition's readers because Aratus merely described the constellations without setting out to provide a catalogue of stars, which would have been out of place in a poem.

This précis or epitome of the *Catasterisms* did not originally form a continuous work, since its contents would have been interspersed through the first part of Aratus's poem, which was interrupted at regular intervals for this additional material to be inserted. At a later period, probably in Constantinople around the tenth century AD, this Eratosthenian material was extracted and brought together to create a little handbook of astral mythology. Its contents have been transmitted to us, rather imperfectly, along two separate lines. The edition known as the Epitome contains myths for all the constellations, while the so-called Fragmenta Vaticana, or Vatican Fragments, contain nineteen fewer chapters but sometimes offer fuller accounts than can be found in the Epitome, and include a few myths that are omitted from it. Even in its original form, this collection of summaries would not have included all the myths that were recounted by Eratosthenes, as is confirmed by other witnesses; and the summaries were not even made directly from Eratosthenes' text, but were summaries of summaries.

The edition of Aratus from which they came also served as the source for other surviving material, the most important from our point of view being the so-called Germanicus scholia. Rather than being a collection of short comments on lines or passages from Germanicus' Latin adaptation of Aratus's poem, as that title would suggest, these are in fact free Latin adaptations of the Eratosthenian material from 'Phi', arranged to recount the myths for each successive constellation as in the Greek summaries. Although of lower quality than those summaries, the Germanicus scholia includes some material that is missing from them, as well as some of wholly separate origin, and we will thus have occasion to refer to it in the editorial commentaries in the present volume. There is also a Latin Aratus that is based on this edition, but that need not concern us.

Another source connected with Aratus should also be mentioned, the ancient scholia to Aratus. Of varied origin and date, these make regular reference to myths connected with the constellations, recording identifications for some of them which are not mentioned in our main sources. Where that is the case, these will be mentioned in the commentaries, but useful though the scholia are, they do not contain narratives that are worth translating for the present volume.[2]

Hyginus's Astronomy *as a source for constellation myths*

If we had to rely solely on these sources connected with Aratus for our knowledge of the Eratosthenian tradition of astral mythology, that knowledge would be sadly deficient, at least as far as narratives are concerned; but fortunately there is a separate witness to that tradition which stands apart from all the others, a Latin manual of astronomy ascribed to Hyginus. It has been disputed whether this work and another which was definitely from the same pen, the *Fabulae* or *Mythical Tales*, were really written by Gaius Julius Hyginus (died AD 17), who was appointed by Augustus to be director of the Palatine Library and was a prolific author who wrote on a wide variety of subjects. The argument has turned mainly on the errors and scholarly deficiencies that are to be observed in these works. In recent times the consensus has shifted, with fewer scholars taking a resolutely negative line, and more admitting the possibility that Hyginus, who seems to have been more notable for the breadth of his learning than for its depth, may have been the true author. For our present purposes the matter is of no great importance, except in so far as it affects the dating of the *Astronomy*.

The *Astronomy* makes no pretence to be of any scientific depth; the author was merely setting out to provide his Latin-speaking readers with the same kind of knowledge as was conveyed in supplemented editions of Aratus, and the work thus gives a very good idea of the kind of astronomical knowledge that the average educated person would aspire to have. Hyginus refers several times to errors and obscurities in Aratus, and it is clear that he was intending this to serve as a convenient alternative source for the knowledge that could be attained through the study of Aratus and of his commentators.

It is significant that the second of the four books that make up the *Astronomy*, which is devoted to astral mythology, should be by far the longest and also the best. The sections that describe how the constellations are constructed, and their position in the sky, are separated out

---

[2] In the preceding discussion, I have followed the standard work on these matters, Jean Martin's *Histoire du texte des Phénomènes d'Aratos* (Paris, 1956).

into a separate book, the third, instead of being set after the mythical narratives for each constellation as in the Greek summaries, and also in the work of Eratosthenes on which they were based. The first and fourth books, which set out to introduce the reader to the celestial sphere and the fundamentals of astronomy, never rise above a basic level and make painful reading; they show all too clearly the disadvantages that people would suffer if they relied on literary men like Hyginus, and Aratus's commentators, for their knowledge of astronomy, instead of authors who had made a proper study of the subject and, above all, had some real feeling for it. Because of their poor quality, these two chapters have not been translated for the present volume. Some brief extracts have been included instead from an introductory work written by a Greek astronomer of the first century AD, the *Introduction to the Phaenomena* of Geminos of Rhodes (see Appendix).

When the mythical narratives in Hyginus's *Astronomy* correspond with those in the Greek Epitome, it is immediately apparent that they are closely similar, even if Hyginus's narratives tend to be fuller. It was once commonly believed that if there is no corresponding narrative in the Epitome (or Vatican Fragments), Hyginus must have derived it from another source than Eratosthenes' compendium; but as has been noted, it is clear from other references in the Aratean literature that Eratosthenes recounted myths that are not recorded in the Epitome, which is hardly of sufficient comprehensiveness and quality in any case to be regarded as a touchstone in that regard. It is striking that Hyginus should cite only a single author (Parmeniscos, second century BC) who definitely lived later than Eratosthenes, and only three authors (Euhemeros, Asclepiades, and Istros) who were apparently not cited as sources in the *Catasterisms*. It is generally believed nowadays that Hyginus drew almost all of his mythological material from a single source, Eratosthenes' compendium or something closely derived from it, and that the *Astronomy* is accordingly the best and most direct witness to that work. As well as often offering fuller accounts of the myths included in the Epitome, it recounts many that are not to be found in the Greek summaries, not infrequently several for the same constellation.

The constellations of the Greek canon

The astral mythology of the ancient world has retained its interest because it relates to constellations that are familiar and still in use.

The list of ancient constellations that came to be accepted as canonic in modern times is that compiled by Ptolemy (Claudius Ptolemaeus) in the second century AD. In his work the *Mathematical Syntaxis*, more familiar under its Arabic name, the *Almagest*, which summarized all the astronomical achievements of the Greeks, Ptolemy included a catalogue of 1,022 stars. To indicate their position, he explained how they are placed in—or in relation to—forty-eight constellation figures, and also made use of a system of coordinates to give their latitude and longitude. Along with Berenice's Hair, which is mentioned by Ptolemy but not accepted as a standard constellation, the forty-eight came to form the base from which the modern picture of the sky was built up, serving the same function in enabling stars to be placed and in marking out areas of the sky. For a table of the Ptolemaic constellations, see p. xxxvi.

These ancient constellations were supplemented in the course of time by almost as many new ones, to produce the eighty-eight constellations of the modern canon. This was achieved in three main stages. In the first place, the Dutch geographer Petrus Plancius devised constellations to cover areas of the southern sky unknown to the Greeks and Romans, using information collected by Dutch navigators in the 1590s. To achieve a fuller and more even spread of constellations in the northern sky, the Polish astronomer Johannes Hevelius added new constellations in a star catalogue published in 1687, taking two over from Plancius and devising the others himself. And finally the French astronomer Nicolas Lacaille performed the same service for the southern sky in a work published in 1763, on the basis of observations that he had made during a stay in Cape Town. None of these new constellations was devised to refer to ancient mythology, and none can be said to have any associated myths, if one puts aside one or two biblical allusions.

If Ptolemy established the canon of Greek constellations for modern astronomers, the mathematician and astronomer Eudoxos of Cnidos (born *c.*400 BC, one of Aratus's main sources; see p. xxi) could be said to have done the same for the ancient Greeks. His *Phaenomena* provided an account of the celestial sphere and a catalogue of stars, explaining their position by how they stood in relation to the constellation-figures (for a system of coordinates had yet to be invented). Although the book itself has not survived, we are well informed about how the constellations were described in it, mainly because, as we have seen, Aratus used it as his source when drawing up his own account of them; and that shows quite clearly that the Greek picture of the sky had almost achieved its definitive form by the first half of the fourth century in Eudoxos's treatise, even if that work was by no means free of inaccuracies. Only two of the Ptolemaic constellations had yet to be devised, one in the northern sky, Equuleus (the Foal) between the Horse and the Dolphin, and one in the southern sky, Corona Australis (the Southern Crown) next to the Centaur. Eudoxos was making use of recently acquired knowledge when he set out to create his synthesis, because the Greeks had only a limited knowledge of the stars in the sixth century BC—very limited by comparison to their neighbours in the Near East—and it was only in the course of the fifth century that Greek astronomers set to work to map out the sky in a methodical manner, partly by devising new constellations of their own, but often by taking over old constellations from the East. The importation of foreign knowledge was evidently crucial to the process. Eratosthenes provided myths for all the Eudoxian constellations in his compendium, although he treated the Serpent-holder and his Serpent as a single unit, and did not provide a separate myth for the Beast (our Lupus), which was treated as an attribute of the Centaur who is holding it. Aratus had noted that the Bowl is set on the coils of the Hydra and that the Crow seems to be pecking at its back, and it may well have been with these remarks in mind that Eratosthenes developed a joint myth to account for the origin of all three constellations, which explains why they are positioned in that way. Although he referred to all forty-six of the constellations in Aratus's poem, he thus recounted their myths in forty-two chapters, adding two further chapters on the planets and Milky Way (or Milky Circle as the Greeks liked to call it). Of the two later constellations, Equuleus never acquired any myths, and the Southern Crown only a myth of a very rudimentary character, in which it is treated as an attribute of the Centaur.

There were also some smaller groups of stars that needed to be discussed. The two ancient star-clusters in the Bull, the Pleiades and Hyades, had had mythical associations from an early period, and two smaller groups, the Asses and the Goat and Kids, demanded attention too. Eratosthenes developed a myth for the dog-star, furthermore, in its specific nature as a bringer of heat (see p. 117). In his compendium and in later works that were based on it, these were all discussed in

connection with the constellations with which they are associated
(except that the Epitome has a separate chapter on the Pleiades).

The celestial sphere and its circles

Eratosthenes discussed the constellations in a rational order, in relation to the zones of the sky in which they are set, by contrast to Aratus,
who passed from area to neighbouring area, as was most practical for
his purpose. To understand this order and the ordering of the heavens
in general, it was necessary for the reader to know how the celestial
sphere is divided into different zones by the circles that can be drawn
round it, and Eratosthenes would probably have explained this in
an introductory chapter, as Hyginus does before proceeding to the
myths. For readers who are unacquainted with these matters, it may
be helpful to say something about the circles on the sphere, because
knowledge of this is assumed in the texts translated in this volume.

The stars must be imagined as being set on a sphere which rotates
around the earth from east to west. The axis of the celestial sphere
runs from north to south, passing through the earth by way of its
poles, and the celestial equator is set at ninety degrees to its axis, in
alignment with the earth's equator. Since it has the same circumference as the celestial sphere, it must necessarily form the largest possible circle on it, while circles set parallel to it to the north and south
will be smaller.

The polar circles are naturally the smallest. These came to be
identified by ancient astronomers because, at their latitudes, some
stars could be observed never to set, while others near the opposite
pole of the sky remained permanently invisible. The way in which
the sphere is seen to rotate is bound to vary according to the latitude
of the viewer. At the equator a viewer would be able to see all the
stars rising and setting perpendicular to the horizon, while a viewer
at the pole would see the stars of that hemisphere circling around
overhead parallel to the horizon, with no star at all being seen to set
or rise. Proceeding southward from the north pole, the celestial pole
will be viewed at an ever more oblique angle, and decreasing numbers of stars near the pole will be seen never to set, while a decreasing
number of stars near the opposite pole will remain permanently invisible. The latitude at which stars never set thus varies according to the
latitude on earth from which they are viewed, and in ancient times

the latitude of the polar circles was determined by the appearances, the arctic circle being defined as marking the latitude within which stars are never seen to set, while the antarctic circle marks the latitude within which stars remain forever invisible. Nowadays the polar circles are fixed by convention at about 24 degrees, irrespective of the latitude of the viewer, and the concept has thus become detached from the appearances.

The other main circles, the ecliptic (which lies at the centre of the zodiac) and the tropics, were defined in relation to the annual course of the sun. If the axis of the earth were perpendicular to the plane of its orbit, the sun would always rise and set at the equator, and the days and nights would always be of equal length in all parts of the world; but its axis is in fact tilted at a considerable angle, and the sun can be seen to rise at different points, north and south of the equator, at different times of the year. Mesopotamian astronomers worked out that its annual course could be mapped by looking to see, at regular intervals throughout the year, which constellation rises at the same point on the horizon as the sun; the observations had to be made, of course, just before sunrise or just after sunset, as one cannot see directly which constellation the sun is lying in. When this course was mapped out on the celestial sphere, it could be seen to pass through the band of constellations known as the zodiac, those constellations being defined and fixed at twelve in number in accordance with a scheme of Babylonian origin.

Starting at the equator at the spring equinox, the sun passes north until it reaches its northernmost point at the summer solstice, on the longest day of the year for those who live in the northern hemisphere. It then passes south, crossing the equator at the autumn equinox, until it reaches its southernmost point at the winter solstice, on the shortest day of the year. The tropic circles, i.e. the circles relating to the turn (tropē meaning 'turn' in Greek), are marked out by drawing circles round the sphere, parallel to the equator, at the latitudes at which the sun turns south and north. The Greeks usually referred to the two tropics as the summer and winter tropic, for obvious reasons, although they are more familiar to us as the tropics of Cancer and Capricorn, those being the signs in which the sun lies when it makes its turns.

The constellations of the zodiac must necessarily project above and below the exact course of the sun; the zodiac is thus a band, and the course of the sun is represented by a line marked out at its centre. That makes up a circle which was named the ecliptic because that is where eclipses always take place. It follows from all of this that the ecliptic is set obliquely to the equator, and is gripped between the two tropics which run parallel to the equator.

According to the resulting scheme, there are thus five parallel circles on the sphere, these being, from north to south, the arctic circle, the summer tropic, the equator, the winter tropic, and the antarctic circle; and there is a single oblique circle, the ecliptic, set between the two tropics. Since the ecliptic passes to the same latitude north and south of the equator, it is of equal length to the equator, having the same circumference as the sphere. Set at different angles, both circles divide the sphere accordingly into two hemispheres. This can be summarized in the diagram.

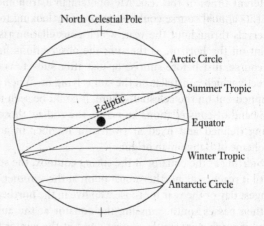

A clear ancient account of these circles, by the astronomer Geminos, can be seen in the Appendix. Ancient authors sometimes referred to the Milky Way as being the only visible circle, and two circles running north to south, called the colures, were created by drawing lines through the poles and the solsticial and equinoctial points, although those are of less interest in the present context.

The positions of the constellations could be defined and visualized in accordance with the position that they occupy in relation to these circles. The descriptions of them by Hyginus which are translated below illustrate the common procedure, by which it was described how constellations are set in relation to relevant circles and to the neighbouring constellations; the reader could then turn to a globe or chart to form a clearer picture. The same considerations determine in which order Hyginus discusses the constellations, passing through successive zones defined by the circles, and proceeding clockwise around the sphere within each zone from constellation to constellation. If his order seems to differ quite considerably from that adopted by Eratosthenes, which is followed in this volume, it is mainly because Eratosthenes chose to proceed anti-clockwise at each level rather than clockwise.

Because it was preferable to separate out the constellations of the zodiac, as forming a group with a distinct identity, such authors did not follow the simplest possible course, by passing from north to south through the zones defined by the parallel circles. As a consequence, Eratosthenes divided the observable parts of the sky (for he had no knowledge of the stars within the antarctic circle) into six zones, rather than five as would otherwise have been the case. Starting with the constellations within the arctic circle, he passed on to those between the arctic circle and the summer tropic, and then to those between that tropic and the equator in so far as they do not belong to the zodiac. Then came the zodiac, and then the constellations between the equator and the winter tropic in so far as they do not belong to the zodiac, and finally those between that tropic and the antarctic circle. Eratosthenes' book thus fell into six main parts, as does the present volume with regard to the mythical narratives, and the constellations can be seen in due relation and easily located on a map if that ordering is kept in mind.

To conclude, Greek astral mythology was a relatively late form of myth which was developed within educated circles. It first came to flourish in the Hellenistic period when a general enthusiasm prevailed for aetiological myths, in which mythical accounts were put forward, as a sort of learned game, to explain the origin of just about everything, whether of local customs, institutions and cults, or of cities and colonies, or features of the natural world and landscape. Transformation myths also belong to the same general category. Myths of that kind can seem rather inaccessible nowadays, at least to those who have no special knowledge of the ancient world, partly because of the often unfamiliar nature of the things that were to be explained, but above all because the myths that were devised to explain them tended to be artificial and recondite. But astral mythology presents no such problems, because the Greek constellations have continued to be familiar ornaments of the sky, and the myths that were put forward to explain what they represent, and how they came to be placed in the sky, were usually based on myths from the earlier tradition involving well-known figures; and even where constellation myths were arbitrarily invented for the purpose, they tend to be picturesque and appealing.

GREEK AND LATIN FORMS OF NAMES

SINCE Hyginus was writing in Latin, his narratives naturally differ from the Epitome in presenting the names of mythical characters in Latinized form. The differences are often minimal, the Latinized forms departing from the Greek original most frequently in the use of -us rather than -os at the end of male names, and having ae instead of ai and oe instead of oi. But since the Romans liked to identify Greek deities with deities of their own, completely different names could sometimes be used, Jupiter instead of Zeus, Diana instead of Artemis, and so forth.

It would obviously be confusing to have different forms of the same names within the same set of narratives; and although it is customary to use Latinized forms in translations from Hyginus, I think it preferable to use Greek forms in any case in a volume of this kind, because Hyginus was recounting Greek myths drawn from Greek sources. If he rendered the names of the mythical figures in Latinized form for Latin-speakers, there is no reason why the same should be done for English-speakers who want to read about Greek myths. It makes little sense to refer to Diana or Hercules in a Greek myth about Artemis or Heracles. Greek forms have thus been used throughout, except in a very few cases where it would be pedantic not to use Latinized or Anglicized forms. Where the Latinized forms are completely different, cross-references have been given in the index, and there is a table showing Roman identifications for Greek deities in the introduction to the index. Some indication is also given there about the pronunciation of Greek names and related matters.

Latin names are used, however, as the formal titles of constellations in modern usage. When translating from the ancient sources, I have naturally always translated the names of the constellations into English, as would be necessary in any case because the original Greek names do not always accord with the Latin names.

TABLE OF PTOLEMAIC CONSTELLATIONS

THE following table shows the 48 Ptolemaic constellations, with the Latin names in brackets, showing any deviations from the Greek originals.

Northern Constellations	Constellations of the Zodiac	Southern Constellations
Little Bear (Ursa Minor)	Ram (Aries)	Sea-monster (Cetus)
Great Bear (Ursa Major)	Bull (Taurus)	Orion
Dragon (Draco)	Twins (Gemini)	River (Eridanus)
Cepheus	Crab (Cancer)	Hare (Lepus)
Bootes	Lion (Leo)	Dog (Canis Major)
Northern Crown (Corona Borealis)	Maiden (Virgo)	Little Dog (Canis Minor)
Kneeler (now Hercules)	Scales (Libra)	Argo
Lyre (Lyra)	Scorpion (Scorpius)	Water-snake (Hydra)
Bird (now Cygnus, the Swan)	Archer (Sagittarius)	Bowl (Crater)
	Capricorn (Capricornus)	Crow (Corvus)
Cassiepeia (now Cassiopeia)	Water-pourer (Aquarius)	Centaur (Centaurus)
	Fishes (Pisces)	Beast (now Lupus, the Wolf)
Perseus		
Charioteer (Auriga)		Altar (Ara)
Serpent-bearer (Serpentarius)		Southern Crown (Corona Australis)
Serpent (Serpens)		
Arrow (Sagitta)		Southern Fish (Piscis Austrinus)
Eagle (Aquila)		
Dolphin (Delphinus)		
Foreparts of Horse (now Equuleus, the Foal)		
Horse (now Pegasus)		
Andromeda		
Triangle (Triangulum)		

NOTE ON ORGANIZATION

The two main sources for astral mythology

As has been explained in the Introduction, the canon of Greek astral mythology was established by Eratosthenes of Cyrene in the third century BC, in a comprehensive work probably entitled the *Catasterisms*; but since the original work has not survived, we have to rely on two later sources for narratives of the myths that were recounted in it. In the first place, we possess a series of later summaries of at least part of its contents, containing myths for every constellation. These summaries have been transmitted to us in two editions, the fullest being that known as the Epitome, which covers every constellation. There is also another edition, known as the Vatican Fragments, which is less complete than the Epitome but sometimes includes myths or details omitted from it. All the material in these summaries was derived from Eratosthenes' *Catasterisms*, although they appear not to have been made directly from the original text.

Our other main source is Hyginus's *Astronomy*, an introductory work on astronomy for readers of Latin which contains a large collection of mythical narratives. Most of the material in these was derived from Eratosthenes' *Catasterisms*, directly or almost directly, although a certain number of constellation myths (though probably not many) were also drawn from other sources. Since the *Astronomy* contains many more myths than are included in the Greek summaries, it is our best single source for ancient astral mythology, and also the best witness to Eratosthenes' *Catasterisms*.

If Eratosthenes is named as an author in connection with the present volume, it is not because anything has survived from his compendium to be translated, but because one of our main sources consists of summaries of part of its contents, and the narratives in the other were largely derived from it. In neither case did the author make any attempt at originality, but was merely trying to make material from the Eratosthenian tradition conveniently available. The author of the Epitome is sometimes called the pseudo-Eratosthenes, not altogether happily, because he was summarizing material that was derived from Eratosthenes, not trying to pass off foreign material under his name;

when reference is made to Eratosthenes in this volume, it is always to Eratosthenes himself rather than the author of the Epitome.

Organization of the present volume

The mythical narratives from our two main sources are brought together in connection with each constellation, and the constellations are considered in the same order as in Eratosthenes' *Catasterisms*. As explained in the Introduction, Eratosthenes adopted a rational order, in which he passed from constellation to constellation within each zone of the sphere before proceeding to the next zone, starting at the north pole and ending at the Antarctic circle; the general principles should be apparent from the table of contents.

When Eratosthenes provided a joint myth for two or more constellations within the same chapter, the same procedure has been followed here, although the individual constellations have been numbered separately. When there are myths for smaller groups of stars, such as the Pleiades, they are recounted in connection with the constellation in which they lie or to which they are closest. The myths of the forty-six early constellations, as found in Aratus, are thus presented in the above-mentioned order, and there are then two further chapters on the planets and Milky Way. The two Ptolemaic constellations that were devised after the time of Eratosthenes, the Foal and the Southern Crown, are considered separately at the end.

The mythical narratives from the Greek Epitome are placed first in each case, sometimes with supplementary material from the Vatican Fragments when they contain anything of interest that is not to be found in the Epitome. The narratives from Hyginus are placed next, preceded by his description of the constellation in question. The translated material is followed in each case by a brief commentary, in which the myths for each constellation are examined, and explanations are offered for any points of difficulty in the narratives. In these commentaries, all the various myths or identifications that are recorded in the astronomical tradition are distinguished, under separate numbers (i, ii, iii, etc.), making reference where necessary to those not mentioned in our main sources. The relevant sources, most often the Aratus or Germanicus scholia, are cited in each case.

The accounts of the astral myths in the Epitome are usually very brief, and they can thus be obscure or misleading. For that reason, they need to be read in conjunction with the corresponding narratives offered by Hyginus, which tend to be fuller, and often provide clarification as a consequence. Such difficulties as remain will be explained, as far as possible, in the commentaries. To avoid excessive repetition, the Explanatory Notes concentrate on matters that are not elucidated within the narratives themselves or discussed in the commentaries.

Additional material

Aratus's astronomical poem the *Phaenomena*, which has also been translated for the present volume in a prose version, contains a full account of the Greek picture of the sky, describing all the constellations and indicating their relative positions. Its title effectively means 'phenomena of the heavens'. The latter part of the poem, from line 733 onward, which is devoted to weather-signs, is less relevant to the main subject of the present volume, but makes interesting reading in its own right. Further explanation is offered in the Introduction about the content and structure of the poem, which falls into three main parts (see pp. xxi–xxii ff.). Because there are so few references to astral mythology in surviving Greek literature from an earlier date, the mythical references in this poem, which was written in the early third century BC, are of real value, even if one might wish that they were more frequent; they have been discussed in the Introduction (see p. xv ff.). There are two mythical narratives, for Orion and the Maiden (Virgo), and there are mythical allusions in relation to the following constellations:

The Bear, 30–5

The Kneeler (Hercules), 64–6

The Crown, 71–2

The Maiden, 98–136

The Goat (the star Capella), 163

The Perseus–Andromeda group, 179–80, 656–8

The Horse (Pegasus), 216–24

The Pleiades, 257–63

The Lyre, 268–71

The River (Eridanus), 360

Orion, 637–46

Some extracts from Geminos's *Introduction to the Phaenomena*, an elementary textbook on astronomy dating from the first century AD, are included in the Appendix. They explain the nature of the signs of the zodiac, provide an inventory of the constellations and their most important stars, and offer a brief but clear account of the circles on the celestial sphere that mark out its different zones. The constellations are much the same as the Eudoxian constellations in Aratus's *Phaenomena*, except that the standard constellations of later origin have been added (Equuleus, here called the Forepart of the Horse, and the Southern Crown), and the Centaur's lance is described as a separate constellation. Geminos otherwise makes the only surviving reference to a constellation called the Caduceus, which was not accepted into the canon.

References to other sources in the commentaries

For ancient accounts of notable stories from earlier myth on which constellation myths came to be based, or which are relevant astral mythology in some other way, I have referred in particular to Apollodorus's *Library* (or *Library of Greek Mythology* as it is called in the companion volume in the present series); although the narratives in it are quite short, they are usually based on good early sources, and the stories are placed in their proper context within the mythical history of Greece. In the general discussions, I have referred wherever possible to ancient works which are easily accessible in English translations, but the sources that are cited for astral myths (or identifications for constellations) not mentioned by Epitome or Hyginus will inevitably be more obscure in many cases, and inaccessible in translation. For reasons that are explained in the Introduction, most of these latter sources belong to the ancient literature connected with Aratus, and the Aratus scholia (schol. Arat.) and the so-called Germanicus scholia (schol. Germ.) are those most frequently cited.

Very few abbreviations have been used for sources that are likely to be of interest to the general reader, above all 'Ap.' for Apollodorus, 'Hes. *Theog.*' for Hesiod's *Theogony*, and 'A.R.' for the Argonautic epic of Apollonius of Rhodes. Other abbreviations are explained at the start of the notes.

All dates are BC unless otherwise indicated.

NOTE ON THE TEXTS AND TRANSLATION

THE best text of the Greek summaries of Eratosthenes' *Catasterisms* is that established by Jordi Pàmias i Massana; he first published an edition with an introduction and translation in Catalan, Eratòstenes de Cirene, *Catasterismes* (Barcelona, 2004), and has worked more recently with Arnaud Zucker to prepare the Budé edition, Eratosthène de Cyrène, *Catastérismes* (Paris, 2013), which contains a valuable introduction and very extensive notes. When preparing the translation, I followed the Greek text in the latter, and have consulted the translations, introductions, and notes in both volumes. I have also consulted the Italian edition (without Greek text) by Anna Santoni, Eratostene, *Epitome dei Catasterismi* (Pisa, 2009).

For Hyginus's *Astronomy*, I followed the Latin text in the Budé edition prepared by André Le Boeuffle, Hygin, *L'Astronomie* (Paris, 1983), which also contains an excellent translation. I have also consulted the Italian edition (without Latin text) of Gioachino Chiarini and Giulio Guiodorizzi, Igino, *Mitologia Astrale* (Milan, 2009).

A translation of the second book of Hyginus's *Astronomy*, which is devoted to the myths, is included in Mary Grant's *The Myths of Hyginus* (Kansas, 1960); it is faithful but rather stilted. An attractive recent volume by Theony Condos, *Star Myths of the Greeks and Romans: A Sourcebook* (Grand Rapids, 1997), concentrates more specifically on astral mythology, and is the only book to have been published in English on the subject by a classicist in recent years, although there have been a few popular books by non-specialists. It contains translations of both main sources translated in the present volume.

When preparing the translation of Aratus's *Phaenomena*, I followed in the main the Greek text in Douglas Kidd's edition, Aratos, *Phaenomena* (Cambridge, 1987), although I also consulted the Budé edition prepared by Jean Martin, Aratos, *Phénomènes* (Paris, 1998). Both editions contain fine translations and very full notes, which have proved invaluable. There is an older English translation in the Loeb series by G. R. Mair (1921), which I have also consulted. There is a recent verse translation by Aaron Poochigan (Baltimore, 2010), which is enjoyable to read, but is often very free.

For the translations from Geminos in the Appendix, I followed
the Greek text in the edition by Karl Manitius, Geminus, *Elementa
Astronomiae* (Leipzig, 1898). For a modern English of the entire work,
with good notes, see James Evans and J. Lennart Berggren, *Geminos's
Introduction to the Phenomena* (Princeton, 2006).

MAPS OF THE NORTHERN AND SOUTHERN SKIES

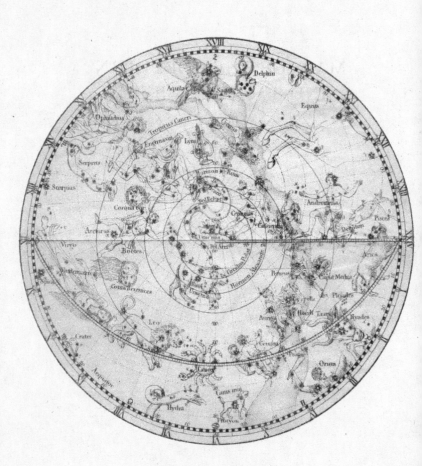

NORTHERN HEMISPHERE

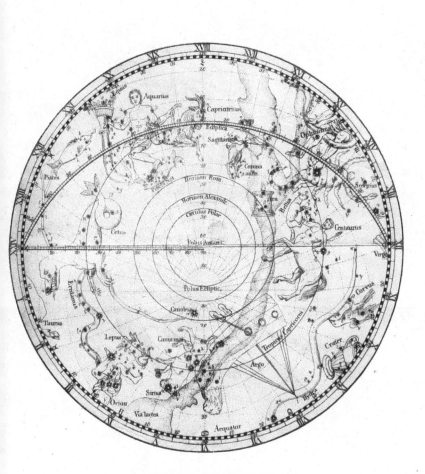

SOUTHERN HEMISPHERE

THE MYTHOLOGICAL
NARRATIVES

1–4. CONSTELLATIONS OF THE ARCTIC CIRCLE

1. URSA MAJOR, THE GREAT BEAR

EPITOME I. LARGE BEAR

HESIOD says* that this is the daughter of Lycaon,* who lived in Arcadia, and chose to spend her life with Artemis, hunting wild beasts in the mountains; after being raped by Zeus, she remained with the goddess, who did not realize what had happened, but her condition was later betrayed when, shortly before she was due to give birth, Artemis saw her while she was bathing. In her fury, the goddess then turned her into a wild beast, and after she had thus become a bear, she gave birth to a son called Arcas.

While out in the mountains, she was captured by some goatherds, who handed her over to Lycaon along with her little child. Some time later, she took it into her mind to enter the inviolable sanctuary of Zeus,* having no knowledge of the law that forbade it. Her own son and the Arcadians chased after her,* and when they were about to put her to death in accordance with the aforementioned law, Zeus snatched her away because of the bond that united them, and placed her among the constellations, calling her the Bear because of her misadventure.

After describing the events leading to the transformation of Callisto, the Vatican Fragments add this alternative account:

Amphis,* the author of comedies, says that Zeus assumed the appearance of Artemis and raped her while they were hunting together. As time passed, her belly began to swell, but when questioned about the matter, she said that no one other than Artemis was to blame for her misfortune; whereupon the goddess, in a rage, turned her into a wild beast.

At the end, it is indicated that Arcas too was placed in the sky:

Her own son chased after her, and when the two of them were about to be put to death by the Arcadians, in accordance with the aforementioned law, Zeus snatched them away, because of the bond that united him to them, and placed them among the constellations, calling her the Bear because of her misadventure.

HYGINUS

The Constellation

We will begin our account by starting out from the north pole, where the two Bears are fixed as they rotate, enclosed within the arctic circle; they are set such that, lying back to back, each seems to hide the head of the other, in such a way, however, that the head of the one that stands higher* faces toward the tail of that which is lower. The large Bear has its feet fixed on the uppermost circle.* Furthermore, it has seven stars on its head, all of them faint, and two on each ear, a bright one on its shoulders, two on its hind part, one at the top of its back, one on the first of its back thighs, two on its front paw, and three on its tail. The whole constellation thus has twenty-one stars in all.

As for the small Bear, it has a bright star at each corner of the trunk of its body, and three stars on its tail, making seven in all. Now among the stars at the bottom of its tail, there is a very faint one known as the pole star,* according to Eratosthenes, which marks the point around which the whole world is supposed to revolve; the two other stars are called the Choreutes* because they rotate around the pole. (*Astronomy* 3.1)

The Mythology

We will begin, then, as we said above, with the large Bear. According to Hesiod, she is Callisto by name, the daughter of Lycaon, who ruled in Arcadia. Her passion for hunting led her to become a devotee of Artemis, who had no slight love for her because they were so alike in character. Later she was raped by Zeus and did not dare to tell Artemis what had happened, but she could not conceal the matter for long because her body began to swell, and one day, when she was bathing her body in a river near the time for her delivery, so as to refresh herself from the fatigue of the hunt, Artemis noticed that she had failed to preserve her virginity. The goddess inflicted a punishment on her that fell in no way short of the gravity of her suspicion, by stripping her of her maidenly form to give her the appearance of a bear, which is called *arktos* in Greek; and in that form, she gave birth to Arcas.*

But Amphis, the author of comedies, says that Zeus assumed the appearance of Artemis and pursued the girl while she was out hunting, under the pretext of coming to her assistance, and once she was out of sight of her companions, proceeded to rape her. When Artemis asked how it had come about that her belly was so swollen, she replied that the goddess herself was to blame; and it was in reaction to this reply that Artemis turned her into the above-mentioned form.

While she was wandering around in the forest in animal form, she was captured by two Aetolians,* who took her to Arcadia along with her son to offer her to Lycaon as a gift. And there, so it is said, being ignorant of the law, she rushed into the sanctuary of Lycaean Zeus* with her son chasing after her. When the Arcadians pursued them and tried to kill them, Zeus, calling to mind the fault that he had committed, snatched her away along with her son and placed them among the constellations, making her Arctos* (the Bear) and her son Arctophylax (the Bear-guard); about him we will have more to say below.

It is said by others again that after Callisto was raped by Zeus, Hera in her anger* transformed her into a bear, and Artemis came across the bear while out hunting and killed it, but later, on discovering who it was, placed it among the stars.

But others say that when Zeus was pursuing Callisto in the woods, Hera gained wind of what was happening, and very much wanted to be able to say that she had caught him in the act; but Zeus, to have a better chance of concealing his misbehaviour, transformed Callisto into a bear and abandoned her. On finding the bear in that vicinity instead of a girl, Hera pointed the animal out to Artemis, who was out hunting, for her to kill. Zeus, to make it known that he was greatly upset by this event, placed an image of the bear in the sky figured forth in stars.

This constellation, as is commonly remarked, never sets, and those who want to find an explanation for this say that Tethys, the wife of Ocean, refuses to receive it when the other stars come to their setting because she had been the nurse of Hera, whose place Callisto had usurped as a mistress.

According to the mythographer Araithos of Tegea,* the girl in question was called Megisto rather than Callisto, and she was the daughter of Ceteus rather than of Lycaon; and Ceteus, furthermore, is the figure known as the Kneeler.* The rest of the story corresponds to what has been recounted above. It is indicated that these events came about on Nonacris, a mountain in Arcadia. (*Astronomy* 2.1)

Alternative account

Callisto, the daughter of Lycaon, was changed into a bear, so it is said, as a result of the anger of Hera, because she had slept with Zeus. Afterwards Zeus placed her among the number of the stars, as the constellation that is called Septentrio,* which neither moves nor sets. For Tethys, the wife of Ocean and foster-mother of Hera, prohibited it from setting into the ocean. It is the great Septentrio (Bear), about whom it is written in the Cretan verses:

> And thou, born of the transformed Lycaean nymph,
> Who, snatched from the frozen heights of Arcadia,
> Was forbidden by Tethys from ever bathing in the ocean,
> For daring to consort with the husband of her foster-child.

This Bear is called Helike, then, by the Greeks. She has two rather faint stars on her head, two on each ear, one on her shoulder, one bright star on her chest, one on her forefoot, one bright star at the end of her hips, two at the back of her thigh, two at the end of her foot, and three on her tail, making twenty in all. (*Mythical Tales* 177, Callisto)

COMMENTARY

(i) The most notable myth involving a bear was that of the Arcadian heroine Callisto, who was a virgin huntress and companion of Artemis, but came to be transformed into a bear after she was seduced by Zeus; she was the mother of Arcas, the primordial king of Arcadia who gave his name to the land. Although there were many conflicting versions of her story, and the tradition was extremely complex, her myth follows two basic patterns in so far as it was recounted to explain the origin of the Great Bear.

(*a*) In the *shorter* version, Callisto is said to have been killed and transferred to the heavens at the time at which she was due to give birth to Arcas, the child whom she had conceived to Zeus, and the motif of the jealousy of Hera is invoked. Hyginus provides a brief account of this version as an alternative tradition, saying that Zeus turned Callisto into a bear to conceal his misconduct from Hera, and that Hera, gaining wind of what had happened, pointed the bear out to Artemis, who shot it. In Apollodorus's account of the tale, which quite possibly follows Pherecydes, the important detail is added that Zeus gathered up her unborn son, Arcas, and gave him to Maia, one of the Pleiades, to rear (Ap. 3.8.2). Or else Hera herself transformed Callisto, and Artemis then killed her to gratify Hera (Pausanias 8.3.6, cf. Hyginus, *Mythical Tales* 177). In any case, the transformed Callisto is killed before giving birth, and is transferred to the sky at that point, while her unborn son is recovered and grows up in the wilds of Arcadia.

(*b*) Eratosthenes developed a *longer* version of Callisto's story, perhaps citing the former as an alternative. Here Artemis notices that she has become pregnant and inflicts drastic punishment on her, as she is accustomed to do in such circumstances, by transforming her into a bear; and Callisto then gives birth to Arcas in the wilds, while in bear form, and does not meet her death until much later, when her son has grown up. Hera for her part does not become involved in any way.

Callisto is described here as the daughter of Lycaon, king of Arcadia (as she frequently was, although the two figures were originally unconnected, and there were differing accounts of her birth), and her infant son is found by some goatherds, who gather him up and take him to Lycaon. In the surviving summaries, his bear-mother is taken to Lycaon along with him, but this seems neither necessary nor sensible, and one may doubt that Eratosthenes really said that in the original narrative. There is then an intervening episode, not immediately relevant to the astral myth, in which the infant is killed by Lycaon to be served as a meal to Zeus, but is then resuscitated by Zeus. After he has grown up, Arcas comes across his bear-mother, and tries to hunt her down, without realizing who she is. He pursues her into the sanctuary of Lycaean Zeus, which no human being was allowed to enter on pain of death, and when the local people are about to put him to death along with the bear, Zeus snatches both of them away to place them in the heavens, Callisto becoming this Bear, while Arcas becomes Bootes (or Arctophylax, the Bear-guard, as he may be more fittingly called in this connection: see pp. 37 and 40).

The summaries of this tale in both of our main sources are far from satisfactory; it seems to have become garbled at an early stage in the transmission. In the original narrative, it would surely have been Arcas who was stated to have been ignorant of the law forbidding entry to the sanctuary, rather than his bear-mother, and the local people would have pursued him as he was chasing the bear on to the forbidden ground; and on catching the pair of them, they would have been primarily concerned to put him to death, in accordance with the law, even if they set out to kill the bear at the same time. There was naturally no law to prevent animals from straying into the sanctuary, although they were said to lose their shadow if they did (Pausanias 8.38.6).

(ii) In a joint myth that set out to explain the origin of the other Bear too, and of the Dragon that lies between them, the young Zeus is said to have transformed himself and his two nurses when he came under threat from his father Cronos, turning his nurses into bears; see further on p. 11.

(iii) In addition, a mythical explanation was put forward to explain why the Bear, as a polar constellation, never sets below the horizon, or into the ocean as the Greeks often expressed the matter. Tethys, wife of Ocean, will not allow this former mistress of Zeus to be admitted into the ocean out of consideration for Hera, because she had formerly been Hera's foster-mother (as is stated by Homer, *Il.* 14.200–4). According to Ovid (*Metamorphoses* 2.527 ff.), Hera actually visited Tethys to ask her not to allow it.

(iv) If it is supposed that this constellation represents a wagon rather than a bear, it forms a joint picture in the sky with neighbouring Bootes, the Oxherd, who can be pictured as driving an oxwagon through the heavens. Although it was never suggested that this constellation was set in the sky as a result of that connection, this consideration did affect the mythology of Bootes (see p. 40).

2. URSA MINOR, THE LITTLE BEAR

EPITOME 2. SMALL BEAR

THIS is that which is known as the small Bear, but most people call her Phoenike.* Artemis held her in high regard,* but since she was unaware that Zeus had raped her, she turned her into a wild beast; but later, when the girl had been saved, Artemis added to her glory by placing a second image of her among the constellations, so that she should be honoured twice over.

Aglaosthenes* says, however, in his *Naxian Tales*, that this is Cynosura, nurse of Zeus, who was one of the nymphs of Ida. In a city called Histoi, which was founded by Nicostratos* and his followers, the port and the land around is named Cynosura after her.

Aratus for his part calls her Helike and says that she was from Crete; she was Zeus's nurse, and was thus thought worthy of being honoured in the sky.

HYGINUS

The Mythology

According to Aglaosthenes, author of the *Naxian Tales*, this is Cynosura, one of the Idaean nymphs who were nurses of Zeus; it was after her that at the city of Histoi, found by Nicostratos and his companions, the port there and most of the land around came to be named Cynosura. She lived with the Curetes, who were attendants of Zeus. According to some authors, however, the nymphs Helike and Cynosura were the nurses of Zeus, and the two were thus placed in the sky as a reward for their services, both being called Bears. Our people* have named them the Septentriones (Seven Plough-oxen).

But many have said that the great Bear resembles a wagon, and the Greeks have called it Hamaxa* accordingly. The following explanation has been handed down for this; those who first observed the heavens and marked out the various stars in each constellation called this one, not the Bear, but the Wagon, because two of its seven stars, being much alike and closest together, could be pictured as oxen, while the five others resembled the outline of a wagon. As a result, they chose to call the neighbouring constellation Bootes (the Oxherd), about which we will have more to say later.

Aratus says* for his part that neither Bootes nor the Wagon acquired their name for this reason, but rather because the [great] Bear seemed to turn around the north pole like a wagon, while Bootes was said to be driving it. In this Aratus seems to commit no small error. For later, as Parmeniscos* states, the seven stars were brought into a group of twenty-five established by certain astronomers, in such a way that the figure of the Bear was no longer made up of seven stars. And so accordingly, the figure that previously followed the Wagon under the name of Bootes* (the Oxherd) came to be called Arctophylax (the Bear-guard), and in Homer's time the first figure was named the Bear. For Homer says of the Septentriones that this constellation was called both the Bear and the Wagon;* and as for Bootes, nowhere does he mention that it was called Arctophylax.*

Many people also fall into error as to why the small Bear is called Phoenike, and why those who sail by it are said to navigate with greater precision and accuracy, and why, if this constellation is more reliable than the great Bear, all do not sail by it. People do not seem to realize why it was that this constellation came to be called Phoenike. Thales, who carried out careful research into the matter and was the first to call it Bear, was of Phoenician descent, as Herodotus of Miletos states,* and the Phoenicians sail by the constellation that was revealed to them by its discoverer, and through careful observation of it, they are thought to be able to navigate more accurately, and in fact, they call it Phoenike after the race of its discoverer. (*Astronomy* 2.2)

COMMENTARY

(i) According to the main tradition, which provided an explanation for the origin of both Bears, these had been the two nurses who had looked after the infant Zeus when he was hidden away from his father Cronos in Crete. Aratus (30 ff.) already reports that Zeus set his Cretan nurses in the sky as the Bears, but fails to explain why they are represented in that form; since he makes clear at the beginning that he is referring to an older tradition, he would presumably have expected his readers to be able to fill out the details for themselves. It is possible that there may have been a Cretan tale in which Zeus was said to have been suckled by bears, but it seems more likely that Aratus was referring to a transformation myth like those that will be considered below. Helike and Cynosura are mentioned by him as names for the constellations at least (36–7), without there being any definite indication as to whether the nurses already had those names during their earthly existence. They undoubtedly originated as names for the constellations, only being transferred to the nurses at a secondary stage; Cynosura means 'Dog's tail', an apt name for the group of stars that make up the present constellation, while the name Helike apparently refers to the way in which the other Bear can be seen 'turning' around the pole.

We cannot tell for sure how Eratosthenes recounted the tale of these nurses because the Epitome and Hyginus do not provide any coherent account of the myth. They cite the Naxian author Aglaosthenes as saying that Cynosura had been one of the

Idaean nymphs who were nurses of Zeus, the other plainly being Helike, who is mentioned together with her by Hyginus, though not in connection with this author. Neither offers a summary of his narrative (as Eratosthenes would surely have done), which must have explained why the nymphs came to be represented as Bears, presumably as the result of a transformation on earth. By a fortunate chance a myth of that kind is recorded elsewhere (schol. *Od.* 5.272), but without mention of its source, or indeed of the names of the nurses. The possibility remains, however, that this is the missing narrative from Aglaosthenes. When Cronos came searching for the young Zeus in Crete, so we are told, Zeus deceived him by turning his nurses into bears, and himself into a dragon; and later, after he rose to power, he commemorated the episode by placing images of all three of them within the arctic circle. There is thus a triple catasterism, accounting for the origin of the two Bears along with the Dragon in between, as an interconnected group.

(ii) It seems that Eratosthenes also included an alternative story in which the lesser Bear too was wound into the myth of Callisto. The Epitome presents it in somewhat garbled form, giving the misleading impression that the transformed companion of Artemis was called Phoenike (which was a name applied to this constellation in so far as the Phoenicians used it for navigational purposes). But the narrative plainly refers to the myth of Callisto, in the long version (see p. 7) as recounted by Eratosthenes in connection with the Great Bear; but an additional catasterism is now added, which must presumably have been explained as follows. Artemis transformed Callisto into a bear after discovering that she was pregnant, but later realized that she had acted unjustly when she discovered that the girl had been raped by Zeus; so after Callisto was rescued by Zeus (i.e. saved from being put to death along with Arcas after they entered the sanctuary of Lycaean Zeus) and transferred to the sky, Artemis contrived that she should be honoured twice over by placing a second image of a bear in the sky.

(iii) This constellation was also attached to Callisto in another way (schol. Arat. 26–7), through the suggestion that it represents her hunting-dog, which died at the same time as she did; the constellation owes its name accordingly to the fact that it has a dog's tail (that being the meaning of its name Cynosura).

3. DRACO, THE DRAGON

EPITOME 3. SERPENT

THIS is the large Serpent, the one that lies between the two Bears. They say that it is the one that guarded the golden apples and was killed by Heracles; it was placed among the constellations by Hera, who had appointed it to guard the apples in the land of the Hesperides.* For according to Pherecydes, when Hera married Zeus, the gods brought gifts for her, and Earth came with golden apples; on seeing them, Hera was filled with admiration, and asked that they should be planted in the garden of the gods, which lies near Atlas; and because the daughters of Atlas constantly stole the fruit, she stationed this enormous snake there as a guard.

HYGINUS

The Constellation

The Dragon is located between the two Bears, and it seems to enclose the small Bear in a coil of its body in such a way that it can be seen almost to touch its feet, while it reaches the head of the large Bear with its curved tail; it draws in its head, as it were, to touch the arctic circle, and its body is coiled as though in a spiral. And if one looks a little more closely, one can distinguish the head of the Dragon in the region of the tail of the large Bear. It has a star on each temple, a star on each eye, one on its chin, and ten distributed over the whole of the rest of its body. So there are fifteen stars in all. (*Astronomy* 3.2)

The Mythology

With its huge body, it [the Dragon] is shown as lying between the two Bears. It is said to be the serpent that guarded the golden apples of the Hesperides; it was killed by Heracles, and was placed among the constellations by Hera because it was at her bidding* that Heracles had set out to confront it. This is the snake, so it is believed, that watched over the gardens of Hera. For according to Pherecydes,* when Zeus took Hera as his wife, Earth arrived bringing branches with golden apples on them, and Hera so admired them that she asked Earth to plant them in her garden, which stretched out toward the Atlas; and because the daughters of Atlas were constantly plucking the apples from the trees, Hera is said to have stationed the snake there as a guard. Further indication of this is provided by the fact that the figure of Heracles is shown in the heavens as looming over the Dragon, as Eratosthenes points out; so anyone can understand from this that the name of dragon belongs to this figure above all.

According to some accounts, however, this is the dragon that was hurled at Athena by the Giants when she was fighting against them; but she seized the writhing serpent and hurled it into the sky, fixing it to the very pole of the heavens. And so it can be seen there to this day with its twisted body, as though it had only just been transferred to the sky. (*Astronomy* 2.3)

COMMENTARY

(i) This was generally identified as the dragon that guarded the golden apples of the Hesperides, which was killed by Heracles when he was sent to fetch some of the apples as his last or penultimate labour (Diodorus 4.26.2–4); since the Kneeler, now known as Hercules, has his front foot set above the head of the Dragon and seems to be confronting it, this provided an obvious way of accounting for the origin of both constellations (see also pp. 26 ff.).

(ii) Hyginus mentions an alternative story from the early history of the gods, in which a huge snake was hurled at Athena during the battle between the gods and the Giants, and she projected it up into the sky. Although serpents sometimes appear at Athena's side in early depictions of the Gigantomachy, either striking out from her aegis or acting separately in assistance, there is no previous or independent record of the present tale, which was probably invented by Eratosthenes himself for the specific purpose of explaining the origin of the constellation. By hurling the serpent up to the axis of the sky, where it would never set, the goddess could create a permanently visible memorial of the incident and the battle.

(iii) Or in a joint myth (schol. *Od.* 5.272) already discussed in connection with the Bears, set at an even earlier period of mythical history, the young Zeus transformed himself into a dragon when he came under threat from his father while hiding in Crete (see further on pp. 10–11). In that case, this constellation is an image of Zeus himself in his transformed state.

(iv) This constellation was otherwise identified with two famous dragons from myth. Perhaps it is the dragon Python (schol. Arat. 45), which guarded the Delphic oracle in the earliest times, and was shot by Apollo when he took possession of the oracle (*Homeric Hymn* 4, to Apollo, 281 ff., Ap. 1.4.1).

(v) Or according to another account recorded by the same source, it is the dragon that once guarded the spring of Ares at the site of Thebes. Cadmos killed it before founding the city, and sowed its teeth, from which armed men sprang up; although most of the men killed one another in a fight that immediately ensued, five survived to become the ancestors of notable families at Thebes (Ap. 3.4.1).

4. CEPHEUS

EPITOME 15. CEPHEUS

HE is set in fourth place* in the order of the constellations; from his feet to his chest he lies within the arctic circle, while the rest of his body up to the top of his head falls between the arctic circle and the summer tropic. He was king of the Ethiopians, according to Euripides,* and the father of Andromeda; he is supposed to have exposed his own daughter as prey to the sea-monster, but Perseus, son of Zeus, came to her rescue, and because of her Cepheus too was placed among the constellations at the will of Athena.

HYGINUS

The Constellation

Cepheus is located behind the small Bear, and is enclosed within the arctic circle from his feet to his chest, so that no part of his body can be seen to set except for his shoulders and head. He lies no great distance from the curve that the Dragon seems to form with its head. Cepheus is depicted with both hands stretched out in front of him, and he is separated from the feet of the small Bear by the same distance* as that which lies between his own feet. His body can be seen to set with the rising of the Scorpion, and to rise with the Archer.

He has two stars on his head, one on his right hand, one faint star on his elbow, a star on his left hand and left shoulder, one on his right shoulder, three bright stars can be seen on the belt that divides his body in the middle, while he has a faint star on his right side, two stars on his left elbow, one on each foot, and four above his feet. That makes nineteen stars in all. (*Astronomy* 3.8)

The Mythology

Euripides and the rest have shown him [Cepheus] to be the son of Phoenix, king of the Ethiopians, and the father of Andromeda, who was exposed to a sea-monster according to the very familiar legends. She was rescued from danger by Perseus, who took her as his wife. So that the whole family should remain united forever, Cepheus too was included among the constellations by the ancients. (*Astronomy* 2.9)

COMMENTARY

This constellation and the three that follow immediately afterwards form the Perseus–Andromeda group, along with the Sea-monster (see p. 105), which lies somewhat apart from the others south of the equator. As in the case of Orion, these constellations were always known by the name of a specific figure from myth, but they differed from Orion and his companions in the hunting-scene in having all been invented together, at a relatively late period (see p. x), to illustrate a famous story from myth. Their inventor may well have been inspired by Attic tragedy, and specifically by plays (now lost) that Sophocles and Euripides had written about Andromeda. In any case, the constellation group illustrates the story of Perseus and Andromeda as presented in those plays, as is indicated in our sources. Only one detail of any note is missing from the summaries offered in our sources (cf. Ap. 2.4.2–3), that it had been revealed by an oracle that Andromeda would have to be exposed to the monster if the land was ever to be delivered from it; for the fault that had provoked Poseidon to send it had been committed within her own family, when her mother Cassiepeia had claimed to rival the Nereids—divine sea-nymphs—in beauty.

5–13. CONSTELLATIONS BETWEEN THE ARCTIC CIRCLE AND THE SUMMER TROPIC

5. PERSEUS

EPITOME 22. PERSEUS

IT is recounted that he was placed among the constellations because of his renown. Zeus fathered him by having intercourse with Danae in the form of a shower of gold. When he was sent out by Polydectes* to confront the Gorgons, he received his helmet from Hermes, and the sandals that enabled him to fly through the air; he is also supposed to have received an adamantine* sickle from Hephaistos. As Aeschylus, the author of tragedies, recounts in his *Phorcides*, the Gorgons had the Graiai* as guards, and these had only a single eye, which they passed in turn from one to another to keep guard. Perseus lay in wait until the time came for it to be passed on, and seized hold of the eye and threw it into Lake Tritonis;* in that way, he advanced against the Gorgons while they were asleep, and cut off Medusa's head, which Athena placed on her chest; but she also set an image of it among the stars for Perseus, who can thus be seen likewise carrying the Gorgon's head.

HYGINUS

The Constellation

The summer tropic divides his left leg and left shoulder from the rest of his body. With his right hand he touches the arctic circle, and he seems to trample the head of the Centaur with his right foot as he passes. He sets at the rising of the Archer and of Capricorn, leaning down in the direction of his head, and he rises vertically with the Ram and Bull.

He has a star on each shoulder, and one that shines brightly on his right hand, with which he is said to hold the sickle, the weapon that he employed to kill the Gorgon; and he has another star on his left hand, with which he is supposed to hold the Gorgon's head. He has a star, furthermore, on his belly, another on his loins, and one on his right thigh, one near his knee, one on his leg, and a faint one on his foot, and one on his left thigh, another on his knee, two on his leg, and four on his left hand, these being called the Gorgon's head. That makes nineteen stars in all. No stars can be seen in his head and sickle.* (*Astronomy* 3.11)

The Mythology

It was because of his [Perseus's] noble spirit, and because he was conceived in a most unusual manner,* so it is said, that he came to be transferred to the stars. When he was sent out against the Gorgons by Polydectes, son of Magnes, he received winged sandals and a cap from Hermes, who is supposed to have been very fond of him, and also a helmet which rendered its wearer invisible to any enemy. According to the Greeks, this helmet was thus called *Aidos* (the Invisible), though not because Perseus wore the helmet of Hades* himself, as some highly ignorant people have interpreted the matter; that is something that no serious scholar could accept. He is also said to have received an adamantine sickle from Hephaistos, which he put to use when killing the Gorgon Medusa, a deed that is not described in any writings.*

As Aeschylus, the author of tragedies, says in his *Phorcides*, the Graiai kept watch over the Gorgons; that is something that we have written about in the first book of our *Genealogies*.* The Graiai are supposed to have had only a single eye between them, and each of them would thus take it in turn when keeping watch. While one of them was passing it to another, Perseus snatched it away and threw it into Lake Tritonis. And so after he had rendered the guards blind in this way, he was able to kill the Gorgon with ease while she was asleep. Athena is said to have placed the Gorgon's head on her breast. Euhemerus claims, to be sure, that it was Athena who killed the Gorgon;* we will speak further about that on another occasion. (*Astronomy* 2.12)

COMMENTARY

This constellation forms part of the Perseus–Andromeda group. Since Perseus rescued Andromeda while returning from fetching the Gorgon's head, which he can still be seen to be holding in the sky, our sources offer a summary of that tale (cf. Ap. 2.4.2–3).

6. ANDROMEDA

EPITOME 17. ANDROMEDA

SHE is set among the constellations at the will of Athena to commemorate the feats of Perseus, with her arms outstretched as when she was exposed to the sea-monster. In exchange for what Perseus had done for her, she chose not to remain with her father and mother, but went away with him to Argos by her own choice, in accordance with her noble spirit. This too is clearly described by Euripides in the play that he wrote about her.

HYGINUS

The Constellation

Andromeda can be seen very close to Cassiepeia, a short distance above the head of Perseus. She is enchained with her arms spread out, as recounted in the old tales that have been handed down to us. Her head comes together with the belly of the horse Pegasos, and the same star* is indeed identified both as the navel of Pegasos and head of Andromeda. The summer tropic cuts through the middle of her chest and left hand. She sets with the second of the two Fishes—the one that is located below Andromeda's arm, as stated above—at the rising of the Scales and Scorpion; her head reaches the horizon before the rest of her body. She rises with the Fishes and the Ram.

On her head she has one star, as we mentioned above, which shines very brightly, and she has one star on each shoulder, one on her right elbow, one on her arm, another on her hand, three on her girdle, four above her girdle, one on each knee, and two on each foot. There are thus twenty stars in all. (*Astronomy* 3.10)

The Mythology

She [Andromeda] is said to have been placed among the constellations by favour of Athena, because of the bravery of Perseus, who rescued her from danger when she was exposed to the sea-monster. Nor did she respond in a less generous spirit to the good deed that he had performed for her; for neither her father Cepheus nor her mother Cassiepeia could dissuade her from abandoning her parents and homeland to follow Perseus. Euripides has written about her in a most admirable fashion in the play that bears her name. (*Astronomy* 2.11)

COMMENTARY

Another constellation in the Perseus–Andromeda group, Andromeda is represented in the sky as she was when she was chained up
to become prey to the monster; after she was rescued by Perseus,
she married him and accompanied him to the Argolid, where he
became king of Tiryns.

7. CASSIOPEIA, known in the ancient world as CASSIEPEIA

EPITOME 16. CASSIEPEIA

THE tragic poet Sophocles recounts of her in his *Andromeda* that
she fell into misfortune because she claimed to rival the Nereids in
beauty,* and Poseidon sent a sea-monster to ravage her country; it
was because of her that her daughter was exposed to the monster. She
is represented near her daughter, seated on a chair.

HYGINUS

The Constellation

Cassiepeia is seated on a throne. The front of this seat and of
Cassiepeia herself are set directly on the circle that is known as the
arctic circle; the image of her body extends, however, to the summer tropic which she touches with her head and her right hand. She
is cut almost through the middle by the milky circle, and is located
very close to the constellation Cepheus. She sets at the rising of the
Scorpion and can be seen to be revolving with her head and seat
upside down; she rises with the Archer.

On her head one star can be seen, and one on each shoulder,
a bright one on her right breast, a large one on her loins, two on
her left thigh, one on her knee, one at the tip of her right foot, and
one on each corner of the square that makes up her chair, these being
brighter than the rest. So she thus has thirteen stars in all. (*Astronomy*
3.9)

The Mythology

According to Euripides, Sophocles, and many other authors, she
[Cassiepeia] boasted that she surpassed the Nereids in beauty. Because
of that, she came to be placed among the constellations, seated on

a throne; but because of her impiety, she seems to be carried along head downwards as the sky revolves. (*Astronomy* 2.10)

COMMENTARY

The final northern constellation in the Perseus–Andromeda group; it was Cassiepeia who provoked Poseidon to send the sea-monster.

8. CYGNUS, THE SWAN, originally known as THE BIRD

EPITOME 25. BIRD

THIS is what they call the large Bird, and it is represented as a swan. Zeus is said to have assumed the form of that creature when he conceived a passion for Nemesis, because she constantly transformed herself to preserve her virginity and then became a swan. So Zeus in turn assumed the form of that bird and flew off to Rhamnous in Attica, where he seduced her. She laid an egg from which Helen hatched and was born, as the poet Cratinos reports.* And because Zeus had flown up to the heavens just as he was, without changing form, he set an image of the swan among the constellations; it is in full flight, just as it was at that time.

HYGINUS

The Constellation

One of its wings reaches the circumference of the circle that is known as the arctic, while the tip of its left foot touches the figure which is known as the Kneeler. Its left wing stretches a little beyond the summer tropic, almost coming into contact with the feet of Pegasos. The summer tropic divides its beak from the rest of its body. The Swan sets at the rising of the Maiden and the Claws, its head preceding the rest of its body as it descends toward the horizon; it rises with Capricorn.

It has one brightly shining star on its head, another of the same brightness on its neck, five on each of its wings, and one on its tail. In all, it has thirteen stars. (*Astronomy* 3.7)

The Mythology

The Greeks call this constellation Kyknos (the Swan), but many people, through ignorance of its legend, have called it Ornis, using the name that is applied to birds in general. The following explanation has been handed down to us with regard to it. When Zeus fell in love with Nemesis and could not persuade her to sleep with him, he satisfied his desire by means of this ruse. At his bidding, Aphrodite assumed the appearance of an eagle, while he turned into a swan; and as though in flight from the eagle, he took refuge with Nemesis, settling on her lap; she for her part did not reject him, but held him in her arms and fell asleep, and while she was asleep, Zeus raped her. He then flew away, and because people saw him flying high into the sky, they said that the swan had been set among the constellations. So as to prevent a falsehood from being spread, Zeus really did place it in flight there, along with the eagle in pursuit. As for Nemesis, in consequence of her union with the feathered bird, she brought forth an egg in due time, and Hermes carried it off and took it to Sparta, where he threw it into Leda's lap.* From it was born Helen, who surpassed all other women in beauty, and Leda passed her off as her daughter. According to other accounts, however, Leda was the woman who slept with Zeus after he had turned into a swan; but we will leave that point unresolved. (*Astronomy* 2.8)

COMMENTARY

(i) Although this constellation is usually called the Bird in ancient sources, it also came to be called the Swan because Eratosthenes explained its origin by appealing to the famous myth in which Zeus changed himself into a swan to father Helen, either by Nemesis or by Leda.

(*a*) According to the *Cypria*, an early epic in the Trojan cycle, Helen's mother was Nemesis, the goddess who personified the retribution that is invoked by infringements of the moral and natural order; in view of the boundless suffering that would be provoked by Helen's abduction and adulterous relationship with Paris, the poem was making a symbolic point when it presented Nemesis as having been her mother.

Nemesis constantly changed shape as she vainly attempted to escape the advances of Zeus, but he followed her example and finally mated with her in animal form. In the original story the two of them mated as geese (*Cypria* fr. 10 PEG), but in Eratosthenes' account, Zeus was said to have mated with her as a swan, as was generally assumed in the later tradition.

Our sources above refer to two versions of the story. In one, Zeus mated with her as a swan after she had turned herself into a swan; in the other, as recounted by Hyginus, he had intercourse with her as a swan while she lay asleep in her *normal form*. In the latter case, he fulfilled his desire through a ruse, contriving that he should appear to be a swan that was in flight from an eagle, so that Nemesis should take him on to her lap out of pity, and so provide him with his opportunity when she fell asleep.

For part of the story at least, Eratosthenes cited Cratinos, an Athenian author of comedies from the fifth century, as his source. Cratinos set the tale in Rhamnous on the east coast of Attica, where Nemesis had an important cult and impressive sanctuary, which had just been rebuilt when Cratinos wrote his play, the lost *Nemesis*. To know how Eratosthenes originally recounted the astral myth, we would have to know whether, in that play, Nemesis was said to have been in her normal form or in swan form when Zeus had intercourse with her; and unfortunately, neither our present sources nor the surviving fragments from the play allow that question to be answered with any certainty. Since Hyginus recounts the story of the ruse without providing any separate account of Cratinos's portrayal of the episode, as presented by Eratosthenes, one might be tempted to suppose that this was Cratinos's version; but the Epitome mentions only the traditional version in which Zeus turned into a bird because Nemesis had previously done so. Nor is there any mention of the ruse in the Germanicus scholia, a related source. It is quite possible, nonetheless, that Eratosthenes may have referred to the earlier version before passing on to that of Cratinos, if it was indeed the latter who invented the story of the ruse.

Whatever the truth of the matter, it had the advantage of enabling a joint explanation to be provided for the origin of the two neighbouring bird constellations, the Swan (or Bird) and the Eagle. It was certainly of no late origin, because Euripides alludes to it in his *Helen* (16 ff.), first produced in 412 about twenty years after Cratinos's *Nemesis*, although in that play it is Leda rather than Nemesis who is said to have fallen victim to the wiles of Zeus.

(*b*) In the more familiar tradition derived from Homer (*Il.* 236–8, *Od.* 11.298–300), Helen was the daughter of Leda, the wife of Tyndareos, king of Sparta. By the time of Euripides, as has been indicated, it had come to be suggested that Zeus had approached Leda herself in the form of a swan; since she was a mortal woman rather than a goddess, she naturally remained untransformed for her own part. This alternative tradition came to be cited in connection with the origin of the constellation. Hyginus mentioned both alternatives, declining to make a judgement, while Germanicus (275–7) for his part opted for Leda; but Eratosthenes' account apparently remained dominant in writings on astral mythology (schol. Arat. 275).

(ii) Some said that a swan was placed in the heavens in honour of Apollo, because it is a musical bird (schol. Arat. 273). It would have been a significant consideration in this regard that the Swan lies next to the Lyre. The supposed musicality of swans, revealed most notably in the way in which they sing before they die, was a theme derived from folklore.

(iii) There was a transformation myth in which Cycnos ('Swan'), king of the Ligurians, a friend or relation of Phaethon, was said to have mourned so grievously for Phaethon after his premature death (see p. 127) that the gods took pity on him and turned him into a swan (hence the origin of swan-songs). Although Claudian (28, 170 ff.), a Latin poet of the fourth century AD, is the first author to state that Cycnos was transferred to the sky in his new form to become this constellation, an apparent allusion by Virgil (*Aeneid* 10.189) suggests that the idea was familiar at a much earlier period.

9. LYRA, THE LYRE

EPITOME 24. LYRE

IT holds ninth place among the constellations, and it belongs to the Muses. It was first fashioned by Hermes from a tortoise and the cattle of Apollo;* it had seven strings in accordance with the number of the daughters of Atlas.* Apollo acquired it from Hermes, and after having composed a song on it, passed it on to Orpheus, who, being a son of Calliope, one of the Muses, gave it nine strings to accord with the number of the Muses. He made great advances in the playing of it, and won such renown among men that it came to be supposed that he could charm even rocks and wild beasts through his singing. Ceasing to honour Dionysos, he regarded Helios, whom he also called Apollo,* as the greatest of the gods. He used to wake up at night, and as dawn approached, would climb up the mountain known as

Pangaion* and await the sunrise, so as to be the first to catch sight of Helios. Dionysos in his anger sent the Bassarids against him, as the poet Aeschylus recounts.* They tore him apart and scattered his limbs in every direction. The Muses gathered them together again and buried them at the place known as Leibethroe.* Having no one to whom they could give the lyre, they asked Zeus to place it among the constellations in memory of Orpheus and of themselves; and Zeus granted their wish and placed it there. It indicates the misfortune of Orpheus, setting at due season.

HYGINUS

The Constellation

This is located opposite the region of the sky that lies between the knee and left hand of the figure known as the Kneeler. Its shell faces toward the arctic circle, while the top of it seems to be directed toward the south pole. This Lyre can be seen to set at the rising of the Maiden, and its rising coincides with that of the Archer. It has one star on each side of the shell, one at the top of each of the points that are connected to the shell like arms,* one in the middle of these, in the part that Eratosthenes pictures as their shoulders, one on the back of the shell itself, and one at the bottom of the Lyre which seems to form the base of the whole. (*Astronomy* 3.6)

The Mythology

The Lyre was placed among the constellations for the following reason, according to Eratosthenes. It was originally made by Hermes from a tortoise-shell, and he passed it on to Orpheus, son of Calliope and Oiagros, who was extremely fond of the instrument. Through his musical skill he was thus supposedly able to charm the wild beasts which came to listen to him. In his grief at the death of his wife Eurydice, he made his way down to the Underworld,* so it is thought, where he sang in praise of the whole race of the gods, with the sole exception of Dionysos; for he overlooked him through a failure of memory, just as Oineus forgot Artemis* when offering sacrifices. So later, while Orpheus was taking pleasure in song while seated on Mount Olympos so many say, which separates Macedonia from Thrace, or on Mount Pangaion according to Eratosthenes, Dionysos sent the Bacchants against him, so the story goes, and they killed him and tore his body apart. Others say, however, that he suffered this fate because he had spied on the secret rites of Dionysos. The Muses gathered up his remains to bury them, and as the greatest favour that they could confer, they placed his lyre in the heavens, figured forth in stars, to honour his memory. Apollo and Zeus agreed to this, because Orpheus had praised Apollo in the very highest terms, or, in the case of Zeus, as a favour to his daughters.*

Others say that when Hermes invented the lyre on Mount Cyllene in Arcadia, he inserted seven strings to correspond with the number of the daughters of Atlas, because his mother Maia had belonged among them. Later, after having driven away the cattle of Apollo, he was caught by that god, and to gain pardon the more easily, he agreed to Apollo's request to be accorded the credit for having invented the lyre, and received a wand* from him by way of compensation. While he was travelling to Arcadia with this wand in his hand, he saw two snakes which were gripping one another with their bodies intertwined, as though in a fight; and when he placed his wand between them, they drew apart. As a consequence, he declared that the wand was an instrument of peace. Some people, when they make caducei, make them with two snakes intertwined around the rod, because this had been an instrument of peace for Hermes. Following his example, a wand is used at athletic contests and other competitions of that kind.

But to return to the matter in hand, Apollo was given the lyre, so it is said, and he taught Orpheus to play it; and later, after he himself had invented the cithara,* he handed the lyre over to Orpheus.

Some also say that when Aphrodite and Persephone came to Zeus to seek his judgement as to which of them should be entrusted with Adonis,* he assigned the Muse Calliope, the mother of Orpheus, to them as a judge; and her verdict was that each of them should have Adonis for half of the year. But Aphrodite was so angry that he had not been granted to her exclusively that she inspired all the women of Thrace to fall in love with Orpheus, and each of them to try to take him for herself, so it came about that they tore him limb from limb. His head, which fell down the mountain into the sea, was washed ashore by the waves on the island of Lesbos,* where it was gathered up and buried by the local people. As a result of this good deed, they are thought to be exceptionally gifted in the art of music. The lyre for its part was placed among the constellations by the Muses, as we have already mentioned. Some say that because Orpheus was the first to have turned to the love of boys,* he gave the appearance of having insulted women, and it was for that reason that they killed him. (*Astronomy* 2.7)

COMMENTARY

(i) It might naturally be supposed that this is the first lyre, invented by the infant Hermes, who hollowed out a tortoise-shell to make the body of the instrument (*Homeric Hymn* 4, to Hermes, 24 ff., Ap. 3.10.2), and Aratus (268–71) remarks accordingly that Hermes placed it in the sky after creating it. Now Hermes was no musician, and in the Homeric Hymn he is said to have handed the lyre over to Apollo, the god of music, who developed the art of singing to the lyre; and in the astral myth developed by Eratosthenes, Apollo is said to have passed it on in turn to Orpheus, the greatest of mortal musicians. There were conflicting traditions about the death of Orpheus, but the version presented by Aeschylus in a lost play, the *Bassarids*, was selected for present purposes. 'Bassarids' was another name for Maenads or bacchants, devotees of Dionysos who entered into a state of ecstatic frenzy; after Orpheus was torn apart by them in the circumstances recounted above, the Muses asked Zeus to place his lyre in the sky, having no other suitable person to pass it on to. Or else they handed it on to Mousaios (schol. Arat. 269, schol. Germ.), another mythical musician, and Zeus set a mere image of it in the sky.

(ii) Although there are no other astral myths for the Lyre, it was sometimes associated with figures represented in neighbouring constellations, as an attribute. If the Kneeler (later known as Hercules) could be identified with Theseus, this could be seen as his lyre (see p. 28).

(iii) Or if the Dolphin is identified as that which came to the rescue of the poet and musician Arion, this could be seen as his lyre (Serv. Ecl. 8.56); see pp. 107–8.

10. HERCULES, originally known as ENGONASIN, THE KNEELER

EPITOME 4. THE KNEELER

THIS is Heracles, so they say, standing on the Serpent. He can clearly be seen to be standing there with his club upraised, and wrapped in the lion's skin. It is recounted that when he went to fetch the golden apples, he killed the serpent that had been stationed as a guard;* Hera had placed it there for the very purpose of confronting Heracles. That is why, after he had accomplished this perilous deed, Zeus judged the contest to be worthy of commemoration and set the image among the constellations. The serpent is there with its head upraised, while Heracles tramples on it, holding it down with one knee as he treads on its head with his other foot, and he is brandishing his club with his right hand, as though about to strike it, his left arm being wrapped in the lion's skin.

The Vatican Fragments add further details to explain why it was so dangerous to confront the snake:

Because it had many voices and was of exceptional size and wondrous strength, and sleep never laid hold of it.

HYGINUS

The Constellation

Situated between two circles, the arctic circle and the summer tropic, he [Engonasin] marks out the arctic circle with both feet and his right knee, as we mentioned above, in such a way that he touches the circle with the toes of his right foot, while with his entire left foot he tries to crush the head of the Dragon. With his shoulders he seems to be holding up the summer tropic, which he touches with his outstretched right hand, while his left hand is extended toward his left knee, halfway between the summer tropic and that knee. At his setting, his head precedes the rest of his body in descending toward the horizon. When he is fully set, he seems to hang by his feet from the arctic circle, and at his rising, his feet proceed ahead of his other limbs.

He has one star on his head, one on his left arm, one brightly shining star on each shoulder, one star on his left hand, another on his right elbow, one on each flank, that on the left being the brighter, two on his left thigh, one on his knee, one on his shin, two on his leg, one on his foot with is said to be bright, and four on his left hand, which make up the lion's skin in some accounts. [That makes nineteen in all.] (*Astronomy* 3.5)

The Mythology

According to Eratosthenes, this is Heracles, set above the Dragon, which we have already discussed, and as though prepared for the fight, holding a lion's skin in his left hand and a club in his right hand, as he strives to kill the dragon that guarded the Hesperides, which was supposed never to close its eyes to sleep, a sure proof that it was stationed there as a guard. Panyasis* talks about this too in his *Heracleia*. So Zeus, in admiration of their fight, placed them among the constellations. For the Dragon has its head upraised, while Heracles, kneeling on his right knee, tries to crush the right side of its head with his left foot; with his right arm raised as if to strike, and his left stretched out holding the lion's skin, he appears to be very much in the posture of a combatant. Even though Aratus claims* that no one can prove who he is, we will try to show nonetheless that we can say something plausible.

But Araithos, as we remarked above,* says that this is Ceteus, son of Lycaon and father of Megisto. He seems to be lamenting his daughter's transformation into a bear; kneeling down on one knee, he is raising his hands to the heavens to ask that she may be returned to him.

According to Hegesianax, however, this is Theseus, who seems to be raising up the rock at Troezen; for Aigeus is supposed to have placed an Ellopian sword* beneath it, and to have instructed Aithra, the mother of Theseus, not to send him to Athens until he was strong enough to lift the rock, and could bring the sword to his father. He can thus be seen striving to raise the rock as high as possible. For this reason too, some have claimed that the Lyre, which lies very close to this constellation, is the lyre of Theseus, for being accomplished in all the arts, he seems to have learned to play the lyre. And this is what Anacreon* has to say,

'Near Theseus, son of Aigeus, lies the Lyre.'

Others say that this is Thamyris, who, after being blinded by the Muses, is kneeling down as a suppliant; or others that this is Orpheus, who was killed by the Thracian women for having spied on the rites of Dionysos. Aeschylus says in his play *Prometheus Unbound* that this is Heracles, fighting not with the dragon, but with the Ligurians; for he says that while Heracles was driving away the cattle of Geryon, he passed through the territory of the Ligurians, and when they tried to seize the cattle from him, a fight broke out and he shot many of them with his arrows; but when he ran out of arrows, Heracles, overwhelmed by the hosts of barbarians and his lack of weapons, sank down on to his knees, having already suffered many wounds; Zeus took pity on his son, however, and brought it about that there should be a large number of stones all around him, by use of which Heracles was able to defend himself and put the enemy to flight.

There are some too who say that this is Ixion, with his arms bound for having tried to rape Hera; or according to others, this is Prometheus enchained on Mount Caucasus. (*Astronomy* 2.6)

COMMENTARY

(i) Since the Kneeler has one foot set on the head of the Dragon, and holds one hand raised as though to strike it, the idea inevitably arose that this is Heracles engaged in his celebrated feat as a dragon-slayer, confronting the dragon that guarded the golden apples of Hesperides. The dragon had been stationed there, in the farthermost west, by Hera, who owned the trees that bore the apples (see further on pp. 12–13). When Heracles was sent to fetch some of the apples as his last or penultimate labour, he was thus obliged to kill the dragon, and can be seen up in the sky raising his club to do so. For an account of this labour, see Diodorus 4.26.2–4 (Apollodorus offers a different account in which Prometheus fetched the apples on Heracles' behalf). This provided occasion for a joint catasterism with the Dragon (see p. 12). Aratus repeatedly stresses the mysteriousness of this figure, placing such emphasis on the matter that one is tempted to think that he may have been playing a game with his readers, describing the constellation in such a way that they would be bound to protest in their own minds that this is surely Heracles confronting the dragon; for the idea was such an obvious one that one may doubt that Eratosthenes was the first to propose it.

(ii) Hyginus also records an alternative account, suggested once again by the posture of the figure, in which Heracles is confronting, not the dragon, but the Ligurians, people who attacked him in what is now southern France as he was returning from the far west with the cattle of Geryon (as his tenth labour: see Ap. 2.5.10). He can be seen kneeling down to throw stones at them, because Zeus had provided him with a supply of stones for that purpose after he ran out of more conventional weapons. The myth was devised to explain how the Plaine de Crau, between Marseille and the Rhone, came to be thickly strewn with stones of corresponding size; it was recounted in a lost play by Aeschylus, *Prometheus Unbound* (Dionysius, *Roman Antiquities* 1.41.3, with a brief quotation).

(iii) Again in relation to the posture of the figure, this could be seen as Theseus, shown as he was when he knelt to raise the rock at Troezen under which the tokens of his paternity had been placed; he needed to recover them to be able to prove that he was the son and heir of Aigeus, king of Athens, who had fathered him by a Troezenian princess, Aithra, during a brief visit to the city (for the story of how this came about, and his subsequent journey to Athens, see Plutarch, *Life of Theseus* 3 ff.). If this is Theseus, the neighbouring Crown could be regarded as an attribute of his (see p. 33), and likewise the neighbouring Lyre; the lyre was a symbol of aristocratic education, and thus of nobility and cultivation, and Theseus is quite often represented with one in vase-painting. It has indeed been suggested that these three constellations may originally have been invented together as a group.

(iv) As the first of two other identifications suggested by the proximity of the Lyre, this is Thamyris, a legendary musician of Thrace who was blinded by the Muses for claiming to be able to compete with them in musical skill. The story goes back to Homer (*Il.* 2.594–600, cf. Ap. 1.3.3). In the present context he could be seen as kneeling in supplication after being defeated in the contest.

(v) Or it is Orpheus cowering as he comes under attack from the Bacchants; for the story, see pp. 24–5.

(vi) In connection with the large Bear, which also lies quite close, this constellation could be drawn into the myth of the Arcadian heroine, usually named as Callisto, who was transformed into a bear (see further on p. 37). In this version of her story, however, she is called Megisto instead (meaning 'Very Great' as against 'Very Beautiful', both names having originated as cultic titles of Artemis), and she is now said to be Lycaon's granddaughter rather than daughter, her father being named as Ceteus, who is shown sinking down on to his knees as he laments his daughter's fate.

(vii) The idea that this is Prometheus, shown as he had been when he was bound to the Caucasus, was suggested by the proximity of the Eagle, which could be seen as the eagle that gnawed at his liver, and of the Arrow, which was sometimes explicitly identified as the arrow that Heracles had used to shoot the eagle (see further on pp. 53–6).

(viii) Or this is Ixion, tied to his wheel for having tried to rape Hera (a story that goes back to the *Iliad*, 14.317–18, cf. Pindar, *Pythian Ode* 2.21 ff.).

(ix) In addition to these alternatives cited by Hyginus, the scholia to Aratus (269) mention that the Kneeler was identified with three other figures from myth, two of them men of pain like Ixion, who suffered in the world below for having offended the gods, either Sisyphos (see *Od.* 11.593 ff. and Ap. 1.9.3 for the nature of his offence),

(x) or Tantalos, who killed his son Pelops and served him up to the gods as a meal (*Od.* 11.582 ff., Pindar, *Olympian Ode* 1.59 ff.).

(xi) Or this is Salmoneus, who had the temerity to put himself on a level with Zeus (see Ap. 1.9.7).

11. CORONA BOREALIS, THE NORTHERN CROWN,
originally known as THE CROWN

EPITOME 5. CROWN

THIS is said to be the crown of Ariadne. Dionysos placed it among the constellations when the gods were celebrating her wedding on the island known as Dia.* She was the first bride to be crowned in this way, having received it as a gift from the Seasons and Aphrodite. It was a work of Hephaistos, so they say, made from fiery gold and Indian jewels. It is also reported that it was by use of this crown that Theseus managed to escape from the labyrinth, because of the light that it emitted. They also say that the lock of hair that can be seen below the Lion's tail is that of Ariadne.*

The fuller account in the Vatican Fragments makes clear that the Epitome has run two separate stories together:

This is said to be the crown of Ariadne. Dionysos placed it among the constellations when the gods were celebrating her wedding on the island known as Dia, because he wanted to make it visible to all. She was the first bride to be crowned in this way, having received it as a gift from the Seasons and Aphrodite. The author of the *Cretan Tales** says that when Dionysos visited Minos with the intention of seducing Ariadne, he gave it to her as a gift, and that is how he won her over. It was a work of Hephaistos, so they say, made from fiery gold and Indian jewels; it is reported that it was by use of it that Theseus managed to escape from the labyrinth, because of the light that it emitted. It was later placed among the constellations, as a sign of their love when the two of them arrived on Naxos, with the common agreement of the gods. They also say that the lock of hair that can be seen below the Lion's tail is that of Ariadne.

HYGINUS

The Constellation

With his right shoulder Arctophylax seems almost to touch the Crown, while the figure known as the Kneeler is connected to it by the back of his right foot. It can be seen to set at the rising of the Crab and the Lion, and it rises with the Scorpion. It is made up of nine stars arranged in a circle, but three of them shine more brightly than all the rest. (*Astronomy* 3.4)

The Mythology

This is supposed to be Ariadne's crown, which was placed among the constellations by Dionysos. For it is said that when Ariadne married Dionysos on the island of Dia and all the gods brought wedding presents, she received this crown as her first gift, from Aphrodite and the Seasons.

But according to the author of the *Cretan Tales*, when Dionysos visited Minos with the intention of seducing Ariadne, he gave her this crown as a gift; and she was delighted with it and did not reject the terms. It is said, furthermore, that it had been made by Hephaistos from gold and Indian jewels, and that it is supposed to have enabled Theseus to escape from the darkness of the labyrinth into the light of day, because the gold and jewels produced a glow of light in the darkness.

But the authors of the *Argolica** offer the following explanation. When Dionysos had obtained permission from his father to bring his mother Semele back up from the Underworld,* and was seeking a way down, he arrived in the land of the Argives and met someone there called Polymnos, a man worthy of our own age, who showed him how to get down to the Underworld when asked to do so. For on seeing this youth whose physical beauty was beyond compare, Polymnos asked* to be granted in return what that young man could give him without suffering any loss; and Dionysos, being eager to recover his mother, swore to satisfy his wish if he managed to bring her back (though only as a god would swear to a shameless man); in return for which, Polymnos showed him the way down.* When Dionysos arrived at the place in question and was about to make his descent, he deposited his crown, a gift from Aphrodite, at a place that would be known thenceforth as Stephanos (Crown), because he did not want to take it with him, for fear that a gift from an immortal would get polluted by contact with the dead. After having brought his mother back unharmed, he is said to have placed the crown among the constellations so that her name would be commemorated for ever.

According to others, this is the crown of Theseus, and it was placed next to him for that reason—for the constellation known as the Kneeler is supposed to be Theseus.* We will have more to say about him later. The story goes that when Theseus came to Minos in Crete with seven maidens and seven boys,* Minos was so captivated by the radiant beauty of one of the girls, named Eriboia, that he wanted to force himself on her. Theseus declared that he would not allow it, but said that it would be unfitting for him, as a son of Poseidon,* to fight with a tyrant over a girl's safety. And so the argument centred no longer on the girl, but on the parentage of Theseus, as to whether or not he was a son of Poseidon. Minos pulled a gold ring from his finger, so the story goes, and threw it into the sea, telling Theseus to recover it if he wanted it to be believed that he was a son of Poseidon; while for his own part, he could easily prove that he was a son of Zeus. So praying to his father, Minos asked him to send a sign to show that he was indeed born from him, and a clap of thunder and flash of lightning provided immediate confirmation. With the same end in view, Theseus, without invoking his father in prayer or oath, hurled himself into the sea. And at once a huge throng of dolphins leapt through the sea in front of him, and conducted him through the gentlest of billows to the Nereids; from them he obtained the ring of Minos, and from Thetis* a crown that she had received from Aphrodite as a wedding present, one that glittered with a mass of jewels. Or according to others it was the wife of Poseidon who gave him the crown; he is said to have presented it to Ariadne as a gift when, because of his valour and his greatness of heart, she was granted to him in marriage. And after Ariadne's death, Dionysos placed it among the stars. (*Astronomy* 2.5)

COMMENTARY

(i) This was usually identified as being the crown of Ariadne, daughter of Minos, who helped Theseus to escape from the labyrinth; he took her with him as he fled from Crete, but abandoned her on the way back to Athens, on the island of Dia or Naxos, either of his own accord or at the will of the gods, and Dionysos then arrived on the island and took her as his wife (Ap. Epit. 1.7–9, Plutarch, *Life of Theseus* 19–20).

(*a*) Aratus states (71–3) that Dionysos placed her crown in the sky as a memorial to her after her death; or else he placed his own ivy-leaf crown there for that purpose (schol. Arat. 71).

(*b*) Or according to what would become the dominant tradition, the crown was a gift that she received at her wedding to Dionysos, and it was placed in the sky at that time. In that case, it could be seen as the first bridal crown. The early mythographer Pherecydes (3F148) recounted that Athena appeared to Dionysos to tell him to sail on his way without Ariadne, and Dionysos then arrived to take her as his wife, and gave her a golden crown, which was set in the heavens by the gods as a favour to him. Eratosthenes' main account follows the same pattern except that the crown is a wedding-present from Aphrodite and the Horai (Seasons), and it is Dionysos himself who places it in the sky.

(*c*) Or else the crown had been owned by Theseus originally, who had received it from Thetis or Amphitrite in circumstances that are explained by Hyginus. Bacchylides, a lyric poet of the fifth century, offers the classic account of this tale, in which it was given to him by Amphitrite, the wife of his father Poseidon (for some said that his true father was that sea-god rather than Aigeus: see p. 180). Hyginus provides little detail about the subsequent events that are more directly relevant to the catasterism, merely indicating that Theseus gave the crown to Ariadne, and that Dionysos placed it in the sky after her death, which would imply that she became the wife of Dionysos as in the usual tradition.

(*d*) In yet another account ascribed to Epimenides of Crete, which was already mentioned by Eratosthenes, this was a crown that Dionysos presented to her on Crete, before the arrival of Theseus, when he came there for the purpose of seducing her. It was a wondrous crown made by Hephaistos, and Theseus later used it to light his way through the labyrinth (rather than relying on Ariadne's thread as in the usual story), before it was placed in the heavens as a sign of the love that united Theseus and Ariadne. It seems clear that Theseus did not abandon her in this version, but we do not know what became of her afterwards.

(ii) In a wholly different story, also involving Dionysos, the crown was a gift that he had received from Aphrodite, and he placed it in the sky in honour of his mother Semele after bringing her up from the Underworld. As in the case of his wife Ariadne, his mother was of mortal birth, a daughter of Cadmos, king of Thebes, but he contrived to rescue her from death, as Hyginus describes, and she then became a goddess under the name of Thyone.

12. BOOTES, THE OXHERD, also known as ARCTOPHYLAX, THE BEAR-GUARD

EPITOME 8. BEAR-GUARD

THIS is said to be Arcas, the son of Callisto and Zeus; Lycaon cut him up and served him to Zeus* at table while the god was staying with him as a guest. So Zeus overturned the table—that is why the city of Trapezous* is called by that name—and struck Lycaon's house with a thunderbolt in disgust at his cruelty. He then reassembled Arcas, making him whole again, and raised him up to be set among the constellations.*

The Vatican Fragments provide a fuller account, explaining how Arcas came to be transferred to the heavens:

This is said to be Arcas, the son of Callisto and Zeus; he lived near the sanctuary of Lycaean Zeus, where Zeus had raped his mother. Pretending to have no knowledge of the matter, Lycaon invited Zeus to visit him, as Hesiod recounts,* and cut up the baby [Arcas] and served him at table;* whereupon Zeus overturned the table—that is why the city of Trapezous is called by that name—and struck the house with a thunderbolt, and transformed Lycaon into a wild beast, turning him into a wolf. He then reassembled Arcas, making him whole again, and the boy was reared by a goatherd. When he had grown up to become a young man, it would seem that he rushed into the sanctuary of Lycaean Zeus and, without realizing who she was, had intercourse with his mother.* When the local people were about to sacrifice the two of them in accordance with the law, Zeus snatched them away because of the bond that united him to them, and raised them up to be set among the constellations.

HYGINUS

The Constellation

His left hand is enclosed within the arctic circle, so that it can be seen neither to set nor to rise. He himself is located between the arctic circle and the summer tropic, inclined longitudinally, and with his right foot set on the summer tropic. His shoulders and chest are divided from the rest of his body by the circle that passes through the two poles and touches the Ram and the Claws (i.e. the equinoctial colure). Because he sets with the rising of the Bull, Twins, Crab, and Lion, he is said to be late in his setting. He arrives at the horizon well upright on his feet, but can be seen rising obliquely at greater speed along with the Claws.

On his left foot he has four stars which are said never to set, and he has one star on his head, one on each shoulder, one on each nipple, that on the right being brighter and standing above the other, which is faint, and a bright star on his right elbow, and one on his belt* which is brighter than all the others, and is known as Arcturus, and a star on each foot. In all, fourteen. (*Astronomy* 3.3)

The Mythology

This is said to be Arcas, son of Callisto and Zeus, whom Lycaon is supposed to have served up at table, chopped up along with some other meat, when Zeus was visiting him as a guest. For Lycaon wanted to know whether the person who had sought his hospitality really was a god.* Through this deed he brought no slight punishment on himself, because Zeus immediately overturned the table and burned his house down with a thunderbolt, turning Lycaon himself into a wolf. As for the boy, he gathered up his limbs and reassembled them, and then entrusted him to the care of an Aetolian.* While Arcas was hunting in the forest after he had grown up to become a young man, he caught sight of his mother who had been changed into a bear, without knowing who she was. Intent on killing her, he pursued her into the temple of Lycaean Zeus, even though anyone who enters it is subject to the penalty of death under Arcadian law. It thus came about that, since both of them would have to be killed, Zeus took pity on them and snatched them away to place them among the constellations, as we have already stated.* So Arcas can be seen following the bear, and as guardian of the Bear he has been given the name of Arctophylax (Bear-guard).

Or according to some authors, this is Icarios, the father of Erigone. Because of his righteousness and piety, Dionysos is supposed to have entrusted the gift of wine to him, and the vine and the grape, so that he could show people how to cultivate the vine, and what use to make of its fruit once it had grown. When he had planted the vine and tended it with great care, easily causing it to flourish, a goat broke into the vineyard, so the story goes, and nibbled away the most tender leaves that it could see there. In his anger at this, Icarios killed the goat and made a bag from its hide, which he inflated and tied up; and he then threw it among his companions, telling them to dance around it. Eratosthenes says accordingly:

'At the feet of Icarios they first danced around a goat.'*

Others say that Icarios, after receiving the vine from Dionysos, immediately set to work to load up a cart with wine-skins; because of that, he is also called Bootes (the Ox-driver). Passing through Attica, he introduced wine to the shepherds, and some of them, full of greed and much attracted by this new form of drink, sank to the ground in a stupor, one in one place and one in another. As though half-dead, they threw their limbs around and babbled away in an unseemly fashion, and the other shepherds, thinking that Icarios had administered poison to them to drive their flocks away to his own land, killed him and threw his body into a well, or, according to other accounts, buried him at the foot of a tree. Those who had fallen asleep, however, declared on awakening that they had never enjoyed better rest, and enquired after Icarios, wanting to reward him for his gift; troubled by their conscience, his murderers immediately took flight, and made their way to the island of Ceos. And receiving a friendly welcome there, they decided to make it their home.

But when Erigone, the daughter of Icarios, who had been overcome by longing for her father when she did not see him return, was about to set off in search of him, the dog of Icarios, Maira by name,* returned to her, howling as if it was lamenting the death of its master. This gave her no small reason to suspect that he had met his death, for the timid girl could only suppose that he had been killed, now that he had been away for so many days and months. The dog for its part grasped her dress with its teeth and led her to his body. At the sight of it, his daughter was filled with despair, and overcome by the thought of her loneliness and destitution, she shed many tears of sorrow and took her own life, hanging herself on the very tree that marked her father's grave. And the dog appeased the spirit of the dead girl through its own death. According to some accounts, it threw itself into a well called Anigros, with the result that no one has drunk from that well ever since that time, so tradition reports. Taking pity on the three of them for their misfortune, Zeus represented their bodies among the stars, and many have thus identified Icarios as Bootes, and Erigone as the Maiden (about whom we will speak later); as for the dog, on account of its name and form it has come to be called Canicula (the Little Dog). Because it rises before the larger Dog, the Greeks call it Procyon* (the Foredog). According to other accounts, it was Dionysos who represented them among the stars.

In the mean time, many girls on Athenian territory took their own lives for no apparent reason by hanging themselves, because Erigone had prayed at her death that the daughters of the Athenians should meet the same death as the one that she was to suffer, if the Athenians did not investigate and avenge the death of Icarios. And so, when the events just described came about, the Athenians consulted Apollo, and were told that, if they wanted to be delivered from their predicament, they would have to appease Erigone. Since she had hanged herself, they established the custom of suspending themselves on ropes with a plank attached at the bottom, so as to be moved about like a hanged person agitated by the wind. They established this as an annual rite,* which they celebrate both in private and in public, calling it the Aletides, because when Erigone had been searching for her father with his dog, as one who was necessarily unknown and solitary, she had been called a mendicant, *aletides* being the Greek name for such people.

Canicula, furthermore, when rising with its heat,* robbed the territory and fields of the Ceans of their crops, and struck the Ceans themselves with disease, causing them to expiate through their own sufferings for the death of Icarios, as punishment for having harboured the criminals. Their king Aristaios, son of Apollo and Cyrene, and father of Actaion, asked his father what needed to be done to deliver his land from this affliction; and the god told him to expiate for the death of Icarios through many sacrifices, and to pray to Zeus that when Canicula rises, he should cause a wind to blow for forty days to temper its heat. Aristaios fulfilled these orders, and obtained as a favour from Zeus that the Etesian winds should blow. Some have called them etesian because they blow up at a fixed time each year, since *etos* is the Greek word for a year; although some have said that they are called by that name because they were 'requested'* from Zeus and came to be granted accordingly. But we will leave the matter unresolved, lest we should be thought to be claiming to have an answer prepared for every question.

But to return to our main subject, Hermippos,* the author of astronomical works, says that Demeter slept with Iasion, son of Theseus, and was struck with a thunderbolt as a consequence, as is reported by many authors, including Homer.* According to Petellides of Cnossos,* the author of histories, two sons were born from that liaison, Philomelos and Ploutos (Wealth), who are said to have been on bad terms with one another; for Ploutos, who was the richer, was unwilling to share any of his wealth with his brother. Under force of necessity, Philomelos scraped together all that he possessed to buy two oxen, and became the first man to construct a wagon. And he was thus able to support himself by ploughing and cultivating the fields. In admiration for his invention, his mother Demeter placed him among the constellations in the form of a ploughman, and called him Bootes (the Oxherd). It is said that he had a son called Parios, and that it was after him that the Parians and the town of Parion* were named. (*Astronomy* 2.4)

Alternative account

When Dionysos went to visit human beings to show them the sweet and agreeable nature of his fruits, he enjoyed generous hospitality from Icarios and Erigone. He gave them a skin filled with wine as a gift, and told them to spread knowledge of it to all other lands. Icarios loaded up a wagon, and, accompanied by his daughter Erigone* and dog Maira, went to see the shepherds of Attica, and showed them what pleasure can be found in wine. After having drunk to excess, the shepherds fell down intoxicated, and thinking that Icarios had given them poison to drink, they clubbed him to death. By howling in front of the corpse of Icarios, the dog Maira showed Erigone where her father was lying unburied. On arriving there, she took her own life by hanging herself on a tree above her father's body. Angered by what had happened, Dionysos inflicted a corresponding penalty on the daughters of the Athenians. When the Athenians consulted the oracle of Apollo about the matter, they were told that they had failed to pay any heed to the deaths of Icarios and Erigone. On receiving this response, they inflicted punishment on the shepherds, and founded the festival of swinging in honour of Erigone as a result of that affliction, resolving that, at the grape-harvest, the first fruits should be dedicated to Icarios and Erigone. By will of the gods, these latter were placed among the stars, Erigone becoming the constellation of the Maiden, whom we call Justice,* while Icarios received among the stars the name of Arcturus,* and the dog Maira that of Canicula. (*Mythical Tales* 130, Icarios and Erigone)

COMMENTARY

(i) In so far as the constellation-figure was named as Arctophylax, the Bear-guard, it could be associated with the neighbouring large Bear, and a joint myth was put forward to explain the origin of both constellations, in which the Arcadian hero Arcas was said to have been transferred to the sky together with his mother Callisto, who had been transformed into a bear (see pp. 5–7).

(ii) The other two myths that were proposed with regard to this constellation are founded on the notion that this is Bootes, the Oxherd or Ox-driver. One is the myth of Icarios, who received the gift of wine from Dionysos, and loaded wine-skins on to an ox-drawn cart to spread knowledge of wine through Attica. Icarios, who is presented as a humble farmer, was the eponym of the village of Icaria, near Athens. There were two myths in which both bread and wine, as basic features of civilized life, were said to have been revealed to the human race in Attica, bread by Demeter at Eleusis, to be spread by Triptolemos (see p. 60 ff.), and wine by Dionysos at Icaria, to be spread by Icarios. The myth turns on the ambiguous character of wine, as a source both of delight and of frenzy; Icarios, who sets out as a benefactor, meets his death because its effects are misinterpreted, and his daughter Erigone commits suicide as a consequence. Eratosthenes, who lived in Athens for a while, wrote a lost poem, the *Erigone*, in which the tale of Icarios was developed into an astral myth; although there is no reference to Icarios and Erigone in the Epitome, it is hard to believe that

Eratosthenes would have omitted this story from his compendium of constellation myths. The story gave occasion for three catasterisms: Icarios could be identified with Bootes for the reason already indicated—Hyginus mentions specifically that he was driving an ox-cart (cf. schol. *Od.* 5.272); while Erigone could be said to have been placed in the sky as the neighbouring constellation of the Maiden, which lies under Bootes; and finally there was the family dog, which could be said to have become the scorching dog-star, so enabling a remarkable coda to be added to the myth: see further on p. 117.

(iii) Or this is Philomelos, the inventor of the wagon and the plough. There was an ancient myth (Hes. *Theog.* 969 ff., Homer, *Od.* 5.125 ff.) in which the corn-goddess Demeter was said to have slept with Iasion in a thrice-ploughed field, to conceive a child Ploutos (Wealth), who symbolized the wealth of the earth and the riches of the grain-harvest. This inspired a certain Petellides, who is otherwise unknown, to develop a little tale on the basis of the folk-motif of the rich and poor sons, in which, as customary, the rich brother refuses to help the poor brother, who comes out best in the end nonetheless. In this case, the poor Philomelos makes his two agricultural inventions under force of necessity, and is raised to the sky as a consequence by his divine mother. Both the wagon and the plough could be drawn by oxen, but Hyginus's narrative places more emphasis on the plough.

13. AURIGA, THE CHARIOTEER; with the associated star-group of THE GOAT AND KIDS

EPITOME 13. CHARIOTEER

THIS, so they say, is the man whom Zeus first saw to harness horses to a chariot, namely Erichthonios, son of Hephaistos and Earth. Impressed by the way in which Erichthonios had yoked white horses, and had driven the chariot in imitation of Helios,* and by the fact that he was the first to have conducted a procession on the Acropolis in honour of Athena, and had moreover brought splendour to the sacrifice with which she is honoured, Zeus [placed him among the constellations].

Euripides reports* as follows about the manner of his birth.

Hephaistos conceived a passion for Athena and wanted to make love with her, but she rejected him because she preferred to remain a virgin, and hid herself away in a place in Attica which, so they say, is named the Hephaisteion* after that god. He thought that he could take her by force, but when he tried to do so, he received a blow from her spear, so that his desire was cut short and his semen fell on to the ground; and from it, so they say, a child was born, who was named Erichthonios as a result of this course of events. When he grew up, he made the aforementioned invention, and won renown as a competitor in the games. He organized the Panathenaia* with great care, and drove his chariot with a companion at his side who carried a small shield and wore a three-crested helmet on his head; it was after the example of that passenger that the so-called dismounter* was introduced.

Within this constellation are depicted the Goat and the Kids.* Musaeus* recounts that after Zeus was born, Rhea entrusted him to Themis,* who passed the infant on in turn to Amaltheia;* and the latter placed him with a she-goat that she owned, so that it became the nurse of Zeus. This goat was a child of Helios, and it was so terrifying to behold that the gods of the age of Cronos, struck with horror at its appearance, had asked Earth to hide it away in one of the caves in Crete; so she hid it there, placing it under the care of Amaltheia, who fed Zeus with its milk. When the boy came of age and was preparing to make war against the Titans, an oracle advised him, since he had no weapons, to make use of the goat's hide as a weapon,* because it was impenetrable and terrifying, and because it had a Gorgon's head set on the middle of its back. Zeus acted accordingly, and appeared twice as strong as a result of this stratagem. He covered the bones of the goat with another hide, and brought it back to life again and rendered it immortal. It is said that he [raised it to the sky to become] a heavenly star.

Others say that this is Myrtilos, the charioteer of Oinomaos, who was a son of Hermes.

HYGINUS

The Constellation

The Charioteer is crossed by the summer tropic at the level of his knees,* while also being crossed from his left shoulder to his waist by the milky circle that we mentioned above. His right foot is joined to the left horn of the Bull by a single star.* He is portrayed as though holding reins in his hands. On his left shoulder the Goat is supposed to be represented, and on his arm two Kids in the form of two stars. He is located wholly at the feet of Perseus, and has his head facing toward the large Bear. He can be seen to set at the rising of the Archer and of Capricorn, and to rise at the setting of the Serpent-holder and Kneeler.

He has one star on his head, and one on each shoulder, that on the left, which is known as the Goat, being the brighter, and he has a star on each elbow, and two on his arm, known as the Kids, formed from stars which are almost fading out. (*Astronomy* 3.12)

The Mythology

In Latin we call him Auriga, and his name is Erichthonios, as Eratosthenes shows. When Zeus saw him yoking horses to a four-horse chariot, as the first man to do so, he marvelled that a human mind could match the invention of Helios, who had been the first of the gods to make use of a four-horse chariot. Erichthonios first introduced such chariots, as we have just said, and the cult of Athena, and he raised the first temple on the Acropolis at Athens. As regards his birth, this is what Euripides reports. Hephaistos was so captivated by the beauty of Athena that he begged her to marry him, but without success; and she hid herself away at the place that would be known as the Hephaisteion because of his love for her. Hephaistos followed her there, so the story goes, and tried to take her by force. In a high state of arousal, he went up to her and tried to embrace her, but he was pushed away and shed his semen on to the ground. Overcome by shame, Athena spread some dust over it with her foot; and from it there was born the serpent Erichthonios, who owed his name to the earth (*chthon*) and to their struggle (*eris*). Athena is said to have hidden him in a small casket like those used at the Mysteries,* and she took it to the daughters of Erechtheus and entrusted it to their care, ordering them not to open it. But since human beings are inquisitive by nature, and the more eager to find out about something the more often they are told not to, the girls opened the casket and caught sight of the snake. As a result, they were driven mad by Athena, and hurled themselves down from the Acropolis. The serpent for its part fled to Athena's shield, and was brought up by her.

Others have said, however, that Erichthonios merely had legs in snake-form, and that during his earlier years he founded the Panathenaic Games in honour of Athena, competing in person in the four-horse chariot-race; and it was by way of reward for that, so it is said, that he was placed among the constellations. Or according to some authors who have written about astronomical matters, it was a man of Argos called Orsilochos* who first introduced the four-horse chariot, and won a place among the constellations because of his invention. Others have said that it is the son of Hermes and Clytia, Myrtilos by name, who was the charioteer of Oinomaos; after he met his death in circumstances that are well-known to everyone, his father is said to have placed his body in the sky.

On his left shoulder there stands the Goat, and on his left arm the Kids seem to be set. Some report as follows about them. There was a son of Hephaistos called Olenos, and he had two daughters, the nymphs Aix and Helike, who were nurses of Zeus. Others say too that some cities are named after them, Olenos in Elis, Helike in the Peloponnese, and Aiga in Haimonia; Homer talks about this in the second book of the *Iliad*. According to Parmeniscos, however, there was a certain Melisseus,* king of Crete, and it was to his daughters that Zeus was entrusted to be nursed. But because they had no milk, they brought him to a she-goat called Amaltheia, and this goat is said to have reared him. It always used to give birth to a pair of kids, and had just given birth when Zeus was brought to it to be suckled; and so, in reward for the services rendered by their mother, Zeus is said to have placed the kids too among the stars. Cleostratos of Tenedos* is said to have been the first to have pointed them out in the sky.

But according to Musaeus, Zeus was nursed by Themis and the nymph Amaltheia, having been entrusted to them by his mother Rhea; and Amaltheia had a goat as a pet, which is said to have suckled Zeus. Some say, however, that Aix was a daughter of Helios who was almost unmatched for the brilliant whiteness of her body, but had a face that was terrible to behold and was out of keeping with her beauty. The Titans were so terrified that they asked Earth to hide her body away, and Earth is said to have hidden her in a cave on the island of Crete. Aix subsequently became the nurse of Zeus, as we have already indicated. And when Zeus, placing confidence in his youth, was preparing to make war against the Titans, he received an oracle saying that, if he wanted to win, he should wage war wearing the skin of a goat (*aigos*) and the Gorgon's head; the Greeks have named this the aegis. So after he had acted as we have explained above, Zeus defeated the Titans and attained supreme power. He then covered the remaining bones of the goat with a goat's skin, brought it back to life again, and made an image of it in the stars to preserve its memory; and later he made a gift to Athena of the aegis that he had worn when achieving his victory.

According to Euhemerus,* there was a certain Aix who was the wife of Pan; after being raped by Zeus, she gave birth to a son whom she passed off as being the child of her husband Pan. So the child was called Aigipan, while Zeus was called the title of Aigiochos (Aegis-bearing). Because he loved her very greatly, he placed an image of a goat among the stars to recall her memory. (*Astronomy* 2.13)

COMMENTARY

The Charioteer

(i) This Charioteer could be identified either as the inventor of the chariot or as a famous charioteer. Erichthonios, a primordial king of Athens (Ap. 3.14.4), was an appropriate candidate on both accounts, because he was said not only to have invented the four-horse chariot, but also to have competed in it after founding the Panathenaic Games. Chariots of such a kind were used for that purpose alone in historical times. The founding of the games was an aspect of his activity as the founder of the principal cult at Athens, that of Athena, since athletic contests were attached to religious festivals rather than being purely secular events as in modern times.

(ii) Or this is an alternative candidate for the honour of having invented the four-horse chariot. For it was claimed at Argos that its inventor had not been an Athenian, but an Argive, whose name, which appears in garbled form in the present text of Hyginus, was Trochilos (*trochos* meaning a wheel in Greek). He is described as a grandson of Peiras, the founder of the cult of Argive Hera, the principal cult which was comparable to that of Athena at Athens, and the son of Callithuia, the first priestess of Hera at Argos (schol. Arat. 161); his 'talking name' suggests that he was invented specifically to be the inventor of the chariot, which he is said to have dedicated to Hera.

(iii) The most famous chariot-race in myth was that in which Pelops was said to have defeated Oinomaos, king of Pisa, to establish himself in the Peloponnese (Ap. Epit. 2.3–8). Oinomaos forced his daughter's suitors to set out ahead of him in a chariot, and killed them when he caught up with them, until Pelops managed to escape that fate; it was often said that Pelops bribed Myrtilos, the charioteer of Oinomaos, to ensure that the king would be thrown from his chariot, which he achieved by sabotaging the wheel-pins. In connection with this myth, it was suggested that the Charioteer in the heavens is (a) Myrtilos, who was soon killed in his turn by Pelops; since he was a son of Hermes, it could easily be explained why he came to be placed in the sky. Or (b), he is Cillos (schol. Arat. 161), this being the name of the charioteer of Pelops according to the Olympian tradition (Pausanias 5.9.7). Or (c), he is Oinomaos himself (schol. Arat. 161); Germanicus (159 ff.) argues that this interpretation accords better with the appearance of the constellation than that in which it is said to portray Erichthonios, because the figure has no chariot, and can be pictured as grieving, with broken reins, for the daughter who had been robbed from him through the treachery of Pelops.

(iv) Pausanias (2.32) reports a local tradition from Troezen, a coastal town in the north-eastern Peloponnese, which claimed that the Charioteer is Hippolytos, son of Theseus. After Phaidra, the wife of Theseus, falsely accused her stepson of raping her, Theseus prayed to Poseidon to cause his death, and the god responded by sending a bull up from the sea as he was driving his chariot by the shore at Troezen, causing him to be thrown off (Ap. Epit. 1.18–19). The Troezenians claimed, however, that he had not been killed as the usual story suggested, and thus had no grave there, but had been transferred to the heavens to become this constellation.

(v) In late poetic sources alone (Claudian, 28.168 ff., Nonnus, *Dionysiaca* 38.242 ff.), this is sometimes said to be Phaethon, who met his death when trying to ride the chariot of his father Helios (see p. 127).

The Goat and Kids

(i) There were traditions that claimed that the infant Zeus had been suckled by a goat when he was hidden away from his father Cronos, and these provided the starting-point for the myths that were developed to explain the origin of this star-group of the Goat and Kids. Aratus (162–4) merely states that the Goat is the one that suckled Zeus without any further detail. He calls it the Olenian goat, apparently in reference to a tradition in which Zeus was said to have been suckled by a goat at Aigion, near Olenos in Achaea (Strabo 8.7.5); there may also be a punning allusion to the fact that the Goat lies on the elbow (*olene*) of the Charioteer, as a scholiast noted. In any case, 'Olenian' came to be a purely conventional title for the Goat in the heavens. In standard myth, the goat was often said to have been owned by a Cretan nymph called Amaltheia, or else, secondarily, the goat itself was said to bear that name, and authors who recounted the astral myth sometimes filled out the story accordingly. Ovid thus writes (*Fasti* 5.115 ff.) that the Goat was that of Amaltheia, who lived on Mount Ida in Crete, and that it had had two kids of its own when it was put to work to suckle Zeus, hence the origin of the two Kids in the sky; and Hyginus refers to a version in which the infant Zeus was entrusted to the daughters of Melisseus, king of Crete, who had a goat called Amaltheia, again with two kids.

(ii) Eratosthenes offered a remarkable account in which the goat was a wondrous beast which was the offspring of Helios, and became the source of Zeus's strange weapon and attribute, the aegis ('goat-skin'), a fringed hide or the like, which caused terror when he shook it (*Il.* 15.307–10 etc.). This became the goat of Amaltheia after it was hidden away in Crete because the Titans were terrified by its appearance, and Zeus subsequently used its hide as a weapon when waging war against the Titans to seize supreme power, providing additional reason for him to represent the goat among the stars.

(iii) The goat was also brought into connection with Aigipan (Goat-Pan) to develop a joint myth in which the goat suckled him along with Zeus, and both he and the goat were later transferred to the heavens (see p. 79). Hyginus records a rationalized version of this myth, no less facile than most of its kind, at the end of his summary of the myths of the Charioteer.

14–20. CONSTELLATIONS BETWEEN
THE SUMMER TROPIC AND THE EQUATOR

14. TRIANGULUM, THE TRIANGLE, also known
in the ancient world as DELTOTON

EPITOME 20. TRIANGLE

THIS constellation is set above the head of the Ram; since the latter is said to be somewhat faint, this letter is set above it as a conspicuous sign, as the first letter of the name of Zeus, having been placed there by Hermes, who arranged the placement of the constellations in the sky.

Some say, however, that Egypt derives its shape from the Triangle that lies among the stars, and that the Nile, by giving this conformation to the land, both ensures its safety, and makes the land easier to sow and brings a climate that is favourable to the harvesting of the crops.

HYGINUS

The Constellation

Deltoton is shaped like a triangle, with two equal sides, and one that is shorter, although it is almost as long as the others. This constellation lies between the summer tropic and the equator, above the head of the Ram and not far from the right leg of Andromeda and left hand of Perseus. It sets with the whole of the Ram, but rises with the front half of it. It has a star at each corner. (*Astronomy* 3.18)

This constellation is triangular in shape like the Greek letter and owes its name to that fact. Hermes is supposed to have placed it above the head of the Ram so that it might indicate, owing to its brightness, the position of that faint constellation, and represent the first letter of the name of Zeus. Some see in it the outline of Egypt, or others the region where the Nile separates Ethiopia from Egypt; while others think that it represents Sicily, or others that it owes its triangular shape to the fact that the gods divided the world into three parts. (*Astronomy* 2.19)

COMMENTARY

(i) The Triangle differs from other constellations in being exactly what it represents, a geometrical figure. Eratosthenes suggested accordingly that it was placed in the sky by Hermes as a marker, to indicate the position of the Ram, as the first constellation of the zodiac. In the literature of poetic astronomy, emphasis is always laid on the faintness of the Ram from Aratus (228) onward, at the expense of some exaggeration. The Triangle or Delta-shaped figure was especially suitable as a marker, being easy to distinguish, as simple geometrical figures naturally are, and because it was the first letter of the name of Zeus (which begins with a delta—Greek d—in its conjugated forms, the genitive being Dios).

(ii) Or it could be appropriately thought to represent Egypt or specifically the Nile delta, because, as a land of exceptional fertility, it could be seen as divinely blessed in so far as its form imitates this divine archetype. The same considerations would apply if it represents the three-cornered island of Sicily, a corn-rich land which was associated with Demeter, goddess of the harvest.

(iii) According to another geographical conception, it symbolizes the tripartite division of the world, that is to say into Europe, Africa, and Asia, the three great continents of which the world was thought to be composed.

15. PEGASUS, originally known as THE HORSE

EPITOME 18. HORSE

ONLY the front half of it is visible, down to its navel. According to Aratus,* this is the horse that created, with a blow of its hoof on Mount Helicon, the spring that is known accordingly as Hippocrene (the Horse's Spring).

Others say, however, that this is Pegasos, which flew up to heaven after Bellerophon's fall; but some regard this account as implausible because the Horse has no wings.

Euripides for his part says in his *Melanippe* that this is Hippe, the daughter of Cheiron, who was deceived and seduced by Aiolos, and had to flee into the mountains because her belly swelled up. As she was about to give birth there, her father came in search of her, and when she was on the point of being discovered, she prayed to be transformed and become a horse to save her from being recognized. And so, because of her piety and that of her father, she was placed among the constellations by Artemis, in a position in which she is out of sight of the Centaur (for that constellation is said to be Cheiron*). The hind part of her body is invisible, so that no one should know that she is female.

The Vatican Fragments give a slightly more detailed account of the Hippe story:

It is recorded that she was brought up on Mount Pelion, was fond of hunting, and devoted herself to the study of nature. After she was tricked and seduced by Aiolos, she managed to conceal the matter for a certain length of time, but when it became evident through the swelling of her belly, she fled into the mountains; and as she was about to give birth there, her father came in search of her, but when she was on the point of being discovered, she prayed to be transformed so as not to be recognized, and she was thus turned into a horse and gave birth to her child.

HYGINUS

The Constellation

The Horse, which looks toward the arctic circle, can be seen to be resting its hooves on the summer tropic, and to be touching the head of the Dolphin with the end of its muzzle. The right hand of the Water-pourer touches the back of its neck, and it is hemmed in by the two Fishes, which belong among the twelve signs, as we will show later. Its body can be seen to be depicted among the stars only as far as its navel. It sets with the first of the two Fishes, that which is above its back; and it rises with the Water-pourer as a whole, with the Fish with which its sets, and with the right hand of the Water-pourer.

It has two faint stars on its muzzle, one on its head, one on its jaw, and one on each ear, and four faint stars on its neck, the brightest being that which is closest to its head, and one bright star on its shoulder, one star on its chest, one on its back, a star on its navel, as the hindmost, which is also called the head of Andromeda, and one on each knee, and one on each shin. There are thus eighteen stars in all. (*Astronomy* 3.17)

The Mythology

According to Aratus and many other authors, this is Pegasos, offspring of Poseidon and the Gorgon Medusa, who kicked the ground with his hoof on Mount Helicon in Boeotia to open up a spring, which is named Hippocrene (the Horse's Spring) after him.

Others say that when Bellerophon* came to visit Proitos, the king of the Argives, the king's wife, Anteia, fell in love with the guest, and begged him to satisfy her desires, promising him her husband's throne. When she failed to achieve her wish, she feared that he would denounce her to the king, and so forestalled him by telling her husband that he had tried to rape her. Having taken a liking to Bellerophon, Proitos was unwilling to inflict punishment on him directly, but knowing that he had the horse Pegasos, sent him over to Iobates,* the father of Anteia (who is sometimes called Stheneboia),* to allow Iobates to defend his daughter's honour by sending him out against the Chimaira,* which was devastating the land of the Lycians at that time with the flame that it breathed out. Bellerophon escaped victorious, however, and after the spring was created, tried to fly up to the heavens,* but when he was not far short of his goal, he looked down toward the earth and was so overcome by fear (so the story goes) that he fell off and was killed. The horse for his part flew up on his way, and Zeus established him among the constellations. According to other accounts, he fled from Argos not because of Anteia's accusations, but so as not to have to listen any longer to what he had no wish to hear, and so as not to allow himself to be moved by her pleas.

Euripides for his part says in his *Melanippe* that Hippe, daughter of Cheiron, was previously called Thetis; she was brought up on Mount Pelion, and was extremely fond of hunting, but was seduced one day by Aiolos, son of Hellen, a grandson of Zeus, and found herself pregnant. When the time was approaching for the birth of her child, she fled into the forest to prevent her father, who still supposed her to be a virgin, from seeing her give birth to a grandson. When her father set out in search of her, she thus appealed to the power of the gods, so it is said, not to allow her to be seen by her father in childbirth. The gods granted her wish, and after she had given birth to her child, she was changed into a mare and placed among the constellations. Or according to some accounts, she was a prophetess, but was turned into a horse because she was in the habit of divulging the plans of the gods* to mortals; while Callimachus says for his part that because she stopped hunting and ceased to worship Artemis, the goddess changed her into the aforementioned form. This is also why she is out of sight of the Centaur, so they say, who is sometimes said to be Cheiron, and indeed why only half of her is visible, because she did not want it to be known that she was a woman. (*Astronomy* 2.18)

COMMENTARY

(i) Three identifications were suggested for the Horse, as this constellation was originally known, all of them mentioned by Eratosthenes. On Mount Helicon in Boeotia there was a spring known as Hippocrene (the Horse's Spring); Hesiod refers to it when invoking the aid of the Heliconian Muses at the beginning of his *Theogony*, as the place where the Muses washed before dancing, and it came to be associated with poetic inspiration. Aratus (216 ff.) suggests that the Horse in the heavens is the one that created this spring, without explaining how it came to be placed there. He does not name it as Pegasos, and it would seem that Eratosthenes explicitly contrasted Aratus's interpretation with that in which it is presented as being Pegasos. In the subsequent tradition, however, the two horses came to be identified with one another (e.g. Pausanias 9.31.3), and the two originally separate astral myths came to be combined accordingly, as can be seen in Hyginus.

(ii) This is the winged horse Pegasos, on which Bellerophon rode out to confront and kill the monstrous Chimaira; Hyginus offers a full account of that hero's life (cf. Ap. 2.3.1; Pegasos is already mentioned in connection with the Chimaira in Hesiod, *Theogony* 319–25). According to a tale first recounted by Pindar (*Isthmian Ode* 7.43–8), Bellerophon came to a bad end after his moment of glory, falling from the back of Pegasos, or being forced off, when he tried to transcend human bounds by riding up to heaven on him. For present purposes, it could be said that Pegasos continued his way after his master fell off, and can still be seen flying through the heavens.

(iii) It is stated in the Epitome that 'some think' that the Horse in the sky cannot be Pegasos because it has no wings. Since it had no wings in Eratosthenes' description, and this third story also explains why only the front part of it is represented, it may well have been presented by Eratosthenes himself as being the most plausible. This is the tale in which Hippe ('Mare'), daughter of Cheiron, prayed to the gods to be transformed to prevent her father from seeing her give birth to a child outside wedlock. The catasterism was added to a version of her story that had been presented in one of Euripides' two lost plays about Melanippe (that being the name of the daughter who was brought to birth by her in the circumstances that led to her transformation).

16. SAGITTA, THE ARROW

EPITOME 29. ARROW

THIS is an arrow for a bow, and it is said to have belonged to Apollo, who, to avenge Asclepios, used it to kill the Cyclopes who had forged the thunderbolt of Zeus. Apollo hid it in the land of the Hyperboreans,* at the place where the temple made from feathers* was also located. It is said that he retrieved it as soon as Zeus pardoned him for the murder and released him from his servitude to Admetos, which Euripides talks about in his *Alcestis*. The arrow is supposed to have been transported back through the air on this occasion together with Demeter the Fruit-Bringer. It was of an enormous size, as Heracleides of Pontos* reports in his treatise *On Justice*. And so Apollo set the arrow among the stars as a constellation to commemorate the fight that he had engaged in.

HYGINUS

The Constellation

The Arrow, which lies between the two circles of the summer tropic and the equator, is set above the constellation of the Eagle, and is crossed by the circle which, fixed to the two poles, passes through the Crab and Capricorn [i.e. the solsticial colure]. One point is directed toward the region of the Horse's hooves, while the other end points toward the shoulders of the Serpent-bearer. It sets at the rising of the Maiden and rises with the Scorpion. In all it has four stars, one at the beginning of the shaft, another in the middle, and the two last at the place where the arrow-head is normally fixed, these lying visibly apart from one another. (*Astronomy* 3.14)

The Mythology

This is identified as being one of the arrows of Heracles, the one with which he killed, so the story goes, the eagle that gnawed at the liver of Prometheus; this is a matter about which it would seem not unprofitable to talk at greater length. The ancients used to offer up sacrifices to the immortal gods with the greatest reverence, and it was their custom to allow the victims to be wholly consumed by the flames. And so because the poor were being prevented from offering sacrifices because of the high expense, Prometheus, who was supposed to have created men* by use of his extraordinary mental powers, is said to have won permission from Zeus, through his appeals, for them to throw only part of the victim into the fire, and to keep part for their own consumption. This would subsequently become a practice that was hallowed by custom. Having won this permission with ease from a god, rather than as from a covetous man, Prometheus himself offered up two bulls in sacrifice. After having first placed the entrails on the altar, he collected together the rest of the meat from the two bulls and wrapped it in the hide of one of the bulls, and wrapping all the bones, for their part, in the other oxhide, he laid them out, and allowed Zeus to choose the share that he preferred. Zeus showed no sign of divine wisdom, however, nor did he act as a god should be able to, as one who can foresee all things, but rather—since we have decided to put our faith in legends—allowed himself to be deceived by Prometheus, and supposing that both shares consisted of meat from the bull, selected the bones for his half. And so ever since that time, in solemn rites and sacrifices, the meat from the sacrifices has been eaten, while the rest, which is the gods' portion, is burned in the same fire.*

But to return to the matter in hand, when Zeus discovered what had happened, he was enraged and snatched fire away from the possession of mortals, to prevent the favour of Prometheus from seeming to outweigh the power of the gods, and to prevent meat from having any value for mortals now that it could not be cooked. But Prometheus, being an inveterate schemer, thought up a way to restore to mortals the fire that had been taken away from them because of him. And so, while all the other gods were away, he went up to the fire of Zeus, removed a small amount, and enclosed it in a fennel stalk;* and in such a state of joy that he seemed to be flying rather than running, he shook the stalk to prevent the smoke from extinguishing the flame as it collected in the narrow space. Thus to this day, men come with all speed for the most part when they have good news to report. In contests at the games, moreover, custom dictates that runners should run in the manner of Prometheus, shaking a torch* as they go.

In response, Zeus wanted to bestow a comparable favour on mortals, and he gave them a woman* who had been fashioned by Hephaistos, and was endowed with all manner of gifts by favour of the gods; for that reason she was called Pandora ('All-Gifts'). As for Prometheus, Zeus tied him down with a chain of iron on a mountain in Scythia called Caucasos; according to the tragic poet Aeschylus,* he was chained there for thirty thousand years. Zeus sent an eagle, furthermore, to gnaw constantly at his liver, which grew back again each night. This eagle had been born to Typhon and Echidna according to some accounts, or to Earth and Tartaros according to others; but most say that it was fashioned by Hephaistos and brought to life by Zeus.

As to why Prometheus came to be set free, the following tale has been handed down to us. When Zeus sought to win Thetis as his wife, being captivated by her beauty, he failed to gain the consent of the timorous girl, but wanted to achieve his wish nevertheless. Now in those days the Fates used to prophesy, so it is said, what would come about in accordance with nature's will, and they declared that whoever married Thetis would father a son whose renown would outshine that of his father;* and Prometheus, who remained awake by necessity rather than through any wish of his own, heard this prophecy and reported it to Zeus.* So Zeus, fearing that he would suffer the very fate that he had inflicted on his father Cronos in the same circumstances, by being forced to surrender his father's throne, gave up all thought of marrying Thetis; and to show due gratitude to Prometheus for his good deed, he set him free from his chains. But because he had sworn an oath about the matter, Zeus did not release him thenceforth from every bond, but told him to wear, by way of commemoration, a ring made of two materials [associated with his enchainment], that is to say, stone and iron. Men have adopted this practice to make reparation to Prometheus, and have thus come to wear rings made of stone and iron. Some say that Prometheus also wore a crown, so as to proclaim his victory in escaping punishment for his crime. And so in times of great joy and in victory, men have established the custom of wearing crowns, as can be seen at athletic contests and banquets.

But I should now return, I think, to my explanation [of the freeing of Prometheus] and to the death of the eagle. Heracles was sent by Eurystheus to fetch the apples of the Hesperides,* but having no idea how to get there, he arrived in front of Prometheus, who was chained on Mount Caucasos as has already been stated. He learned the way from Prometheus, and when he was returning victorious, he was eager to tell him about the killing of the dragon, which we have already discussed, and to thank him for the good turn. For he hastened to pay him, to the best of his ability, the honour that he deserved. [So he shot the eagle, and ever since it was] put out of the way, men have followed the practice, when offering sacrifices, of burning the livers of the victims on the altars of the gods, so as to satisfy them with that in compensation for the liver of Prometheus.

According to Eratosthenes' account of the Arrow, it was with this arrow that Apollo killed the Cyclopes, who had made the thunderbolt that Zeus had used to kill Asclepios, as many authors have stated. Apollo buried the arrow on the Hyperborean mountain; when Zeus pardoned his son, however, it was carried back to him by the wind, together with the fruits of the season. So that is why it can be seen among the constellations. (*Astronomy* 2.15)

COMMENTARY

(i) This is the arrow with which Apollo shot the Cyclopes. When his son Asclepios was struck with a thunderbolt by Zeus for resuscitating the dead (see pp. 59 and 62), Apollo was enraged, but he could hardly take action against Zeus himself, so he quenched his anger by killing the Cyclopes (see pp. 118–19) who had made the thunderbolt.

(ii) Or it is the arrow that Heracles used to kill the eagle that gnawed at the liver of Prometheus (Hyginus recounts the story of Prometheus at length; for the present aspect of it, cf. Ap. 1.7. and 2.5.1, and the early account by Hesiod (*Theogony* 5.21–31). This idea that this might be that arrow was evidently suggested by the proximity of the Eagle, which is set immediately above the Arrow, although it should be noted that this myth is never invoked to explain how the Eagle came to be set in the sky. The constellation of the Kneeler, moreover, which also lies nearby, was commonly thought to show Heracles in confrontation with the dragon of the Hesperides (see pp. 26–8), and he was said to have killed this eagle while travelling back from that labour. There was also an alternative tradition in which the Kneeler was identified as Prometheus himself.

17. AQUILA, THE EAGLE

EPITOME 30. EAGLE

THIS is the eagle that carried Ganymedes through the sky to Zeus, so that he might have a cup-bearer; it is also among the constellations because, at an earlier time, when the gods were dividing the birds between them, this bird fell to Zeus. It alone of all creatures flies directly toward the sun without yielding to its rays, and it holds dominion over all the other birds. It is represented with its wings outstretched, as though gliding.

Aglaosthenes says in his *Naxian Tales* that when Zeus, after his birth in Crete, was being ruthlessly hunted down, he was stolen away from Crete and taken to Naxos; and when he grew up and came of age, he assumed sovereignty over the gods. As he was setting off from Naxos to attack the Titans, an eagle appeared and accompanied him on his way; seeing this as a good omen, Zeus appointed the eagle to be his sacred bird, and that is why it was adjudged worthy of the honour of being represented in the sky.

HYGINUS

The Constellation

With its right wing the Eagle stretches across the equator, while its left wing can be seen to be depicted not far from the head of the Serpent-bearer. Its beak is separated, furthermore, from the rest of its body by the circle which, as we have said above, runs from the Crab to Capricorn. The central part of it is marked by the milky circle as we have pointed out above. It sets at the rising of the Lion, and rises with Capricorn. It has one star on its head, one on each wing, and one on its tail. (*Astronomy* 3.15)

The Mythology

This is the eagle that is said to have snatched away Ganymedes to deliver him to Zeus, who had taken a fancy to him; Zeus is also said to have chosen the eagle above all other birds. It alone, so the story goes, strives to fly straight into the rays of the rising sun. And thus it can be seen flying above the Water-pourer, for that is commonly imagined to be Ganymedes.

Or according to some accounts, there was a certain Merops, who reigned over the island of Cos, which he named after his daughter, while naming its inhabitants the Meropians after himself. He had a wife called Ethemeia, who was born from the race of the nymphs; when she stopped worshipping Artemis, the goddess began to transfix her with her arrows, but she was finally carried off to the Underworld by Persephone while still alive. Merops for his part yearned so desperately for his wife that he wanted to kill himself; but Hera took pity on him and turned him into an eagle and placed him among the stars, so that he would not retain his memory and long for his wife, as he would have done if she had placed him there in human form.

Aglaosthenes, the author of the *Naxian Tales*, recounts that Zeus was secretly removed from Crete and taken to Naxos, where he was reared. When he grew up to become a man and wanted to make war against the Titans, an eagle appeared to him as an omen while he was offering a sacrifice; he paid due heed to the omen and placed the eagle among the stars.

Some say that Hermes, or according to others, Anaplades,* was captivated by the beauty of Aphrodite and fell in love with her; but when he failed to win his way with her, he became disheartened, as though he had suffered an insult. But Zeus took pity on him, and while Aphrodite was bathing in the river Acheloos,* he sent an eagle to carry her slipper off to Amythaonia in Egypt* and entrust it to Hermes. So Aphrodite set off in search of it and arrived in the presence of her admirer; and on achieving his desire, Hermes rewarded the eagle by placing it in the heavens. (*Astronomy* 2.16)

COMMENTARY

(i) This is the eagle that abducted Ganymedes, as represented in the constellation of Water-pourer, which lies nearby, south of the equator; he was taken up to Olympos to become cup-bearer to Zeus (see pp. 81–2). Although the myth of Ganymedes was very ancient, appearing in the *Iliad* (20.298 ff.), there is no mention of the eagle in early sources; the fifth Homeric Hymn, to Apollo, talks merely of a heaven-sent whirlwind, and the eagle is not attested even in the visual arts before the fourth century. As with Europa's bull, there was disagreement as to whether Zeus sent it or assumed its form, but the former alternative is chosen here, as would be expected. We are also told that the eagle deserved its place in the heavens because it was the bird of Zeus, possessing certain remarkable qualities, but Eratosthenes seems to have put this forward as additional justification, rather than an alternative explanation for why it was placed there as in the case of the Lion (see pp. 69–71).

(ii) Or in another account, relating to the early life of Zeus, the eagle was thought worthy of being placed in the sky because it had provided a favourable omen to Zeus before he set out against the Titans; this explains at the same time why it became the bird of Zeus.

(iii) Merops, a primordial king of Cos, so grieved for his dead wife that Hera, as goddess of marriage, transformed him into an eagle and set him in the heavens. The idea that the transformation would save him from being tormented by painful memories seems reasonable enough, but that does not explain why he was turned into an eagle specifically. Since *merops* means bee-eater in Greek, it is possible that he was turned into that bird in the original story, and was later said to have been turned into an eagle instead for the specific purpose of explaining the origin of this constellation.

(iv) Zeus sent his eagle to help Hermes to seduce Aphrodite, and it was Hermes who placed it in the sky. Hermes says in the *Odyssey* (8.335–42) how much he would like to sleep with Aphrodite, but the stolen slipper, rather like Cinderella's shoe, is a motif from folklore, and the story as a whole follows the pattern of a folktale. A very similar tale is recorded, in which an eagle took the slipper of the courtesan Rhodopis and dropped it into the lap of the king of Egypt, who arranged for the owner to be tracked down, and then took her as his wife (Strabo 17.1.33, Aelian, *Historical Miscellany*, 13.37).

(v) Since the Eagle lies close to the Swan, the main myth associated with that constellation, in which Zeus changed into a swan to father Helen, was adapted to provide a joint explanation of the origin of the two neighbouring bird constellations (see pp. 20–2).

(vi) According to the early Hellenistic poet Moiro, this is an eagle that had brought nectar to the infant Zeus; see further on p. 92.

18–19. OPHIUCHUS, THE SERPENT-BEARER, and THE SERPENT

EPITOME 6. SERPENT-BEARER

THIS is the figure who is set above the Scorpion, holding a serpent in both hands. It is said that this is Asclepios, and that Zeus raised him to the stars as a favour to Apollo. Asclepios practised the art of medicine with such skill that he even brought those who were already dead back to life, including Hippolytos* last of all, and because the gods grew angry at this, fearing that the honours that they received from human beings would be brought to an end if Asclepios accomplished such extraordinary deeds, it is said that Zeus, in anger, struck his house with a thunderbolt; afterwards, however, out of regard for Apollo, he raised Asclepios up to the stars. He can be distinguished with no great difficulty, being set above the largest constellation, I mean the Scorpion, and his image is easily recognizable.

HYGINUS

The Constellation

Ophiuchus has his head in the position of a man who is leaning backwards, and he is represented as holding a serpent in his hands. His shoulders are divided from the rest of his body by the summer tropic, and the tip of his knee reaches up to the equator;* with his left foot, he is trampling on the eyes of the Scorpion, and he is resting his right foot on its carapace. As for the Serpent that he is holding, it almost touches the Crown with the tip of its mouth, while it seems to entwine itself around Ophiuchus with the middle of its body; the hind part of its body is shorter than the front part, where the left hand of Ophiuchus himself is portrayed. The end of its tail comes together with the tail of the Eagle at the equator. At his setting, he reaches the horizon at the rising of the twins, Crab and Lion; at his rising he appears at the same time as the Scorpion and Archer.

He has one star on his head, one on each shoulder, three on his left arm, four on his right arm, two on his loins, one on each knee, one on his right leg, and one on each foot, the brighter being on his right foot. So that makes thirteen stars in all.

The Serpent has two stars on the top of its head, four under its head, all in one place, two on the left hand of Ophiuchus, of which the one nearest to his body is the brightest, and five on the back of the Serpent where it comes together with the body of Ophiuchus, four on the first bend of its tail, and six on the second in the direction of its head. So that makes twenty-three stars in all. (*Astronomy* 3.15)

The Mythology

Called Anguitenens* by our authors, he is set above the Scorpion, holding in his hands a snake which is coiled around his body. This is commonly said to be a man called Charnabon, who was king of the Getai who live in Thrace. He held power at the very time when the grain of cereal crops is first thought to have been entrusted to mortals. For when Demeter was bestowing her benefits on the human race, she placed Triptolemos, whose nurse she had been, in a chariot drawn by dragons—he is said to have been the first man to make use of wheels so as not to be delayed in his progress—and she instructed him to travel around the territories of all peoples distributing grain, to enable them and their descendants to advance more easily beyond a primitive way of life. When he came to the king of the Getai whom we have just mentioned, he initially received a hospitable welcome from him; but he was then subjected to a treacherous attack, as though he were the cruellest of enemies rather than a generous stranger who had come with no bad intent, and this man who had come to prolong the lives of others thus came close to losing his own life. For at the order of Charnabon, one of his dragons was killed, to prevent Triptolemos—who had suspected that an ambush was being prepared—from hoping to find safety in his chariot. But Demeter arrived, and returned the chariot to the young man from whom it had been stolen, attaching another dragon to it; and she inflicted no slight punishment on the king to avenge his malevolent plot. For according to Hegesianax, Demeter portrayed Charnabon as an image among the stars as a reminder to the human race, holding a dragon in his hands as if he were about to be killed by it. He had lived such a cruel life that he was only too happy to bring death upon himself.

Others indicate that this is Heracles, killing a snake in Libya beside the river Sagaris, after it had slaughtered a great many people and robbed the river-banks of their grain. As a reward for this deed, Omphale, the queen of the land, sent him back to Argos loaded with gifts, and Zeus placed him among the constellations because of his valour.

Some have said, however, that this is Triopas, king of the Thessalians. Seeking to roof his palace, he pulled down the temple of Demeter which had been built by the men of old; and in response, Demeter afflicted him with such hunger that, ever afterwards, he is supposed never to have been able to find enough food to satisfy it. Finally, when his life was drawing to its close, a dragon was sent against him, and he underwent many sufferings, and when he finally met his death, he was placed among the constellations at the will of Demeter. And so he can be seen to this day with a dragon coiled around him, as it inflicts well-deserved punishment on him for all eternity.

Polyzelos* of Rhodes indicates, however, that this is a man called Phorbas, who had performed very valuable services for the Rhodians. For when that island had been infested with large numbers of snakes, such that the inhabitants called it Ophioussa (Snake Island), and among this host of wild beasts there was a dragon of enormous size which had killed a huge number of people, so that the island was coming close to being deserted, it is said that Phorbas, son of Triopas and Hiscilla, daughter of Myrmidon, was carried there by a storm and killed every one of these beasts, including the dragon. Since he was a particular favourite of Apollo, he was placed among the constellations in the guise of dragon-slayer by way of praise and commemoration. And so the Rhodians, whenever they set off any distance from the shore in their fleet, begin by offering a sacrifice to honour Phorbas for his arrival, so that their compatriots might find, through unexpected valour, glorious success such as that which brought Phorbas to the heavens, little realizing what awaited him.

Many astronomers have supposed that this is Asclepios, who was placed among the stars by Zeus as a favour for Apollo. For Asclepios, when he was living among mortals, surpassed all others in the art of medicine to such a degree that he was not satisfied merely to alleviate human sufferings, but even brought the dead back to life. Last of all, so it is said, he revived Hippolytos after he had been killed as a result of the malice of his stepmother and the ignorance of his father, as Eratosthenes recounts. Some have said that Glaucos, son of Minos, was brought back to life through his skills. As punishment for this transgression, Zeus burnt his house down by striking it with a thunderbolt, but placed Asclepios himself in the sky with a snake in his hands, out of regard for his skill and for the sake of his father Apollo.

This, according to some accounts, is the reason why he is holding a snake. When he was forced to revive Glaucos and was imprisoned in a secret place, and was thinking about what he should do, staff in hand, a snake is said to have crept toward his staff. In his alarm, he killed it, hitting it repeatedly with his staff as he drew away. Later, so the story goes, another snake arrived there, carrying a herb in its mouth, and placed the herb on the head of the first snake; and after that, both snakes took to flight. Whereupon Asclepios made use of that same herb to bring Glaucos back to life. As a result, so it is said, the snake was placed both under the protection of Asclepios and among the stars. His successors followed his example and passed down the knowledge by which physicians make use of snakes. (*Astronomy* 2.14)

COMMENTARY

(i) Since snakes were emblematic of the cult and person of the healing-god Asclepios, who was often represented holding a staff with a snake coiled around it, Eratosthenes chose to identify him primarily as the Serpent-bearer in the sky. In myth, he was described as a son of Apollo by Coronis, a mortal woman, and he thus resembled Heracles in having been a mortal hero who attained divine status only after his death. He became the finest of healers, but met his death when he proceeded to subvert the natural and divine order by raising men from the dead (see Ap. 3.10.4, with a catalogue of those who benefited). It could be claimed in the present context that Zeus, after striking him dead in punishment, had set him in the sky as a favour to his father Apollo. The revival of the Cretan prince Glaucos, son of Minos, which Hyginus ascribes to Asclepios, was usually ascribed to the Theban seer Polyidos (e.g. Ap. 3.3.1, Hyginus, *Mythical Tales* 136), and more appropriately too, because Asclepios was supposed to have learned how to revive people through further development of his own medical skills.

(ii) There was a well-known myth in which Demeter was said to have transmitted her gift of grain to mortals at Eleusis, near Athens, using a man of that town, Triptolemos, to spread it through the world in a chariot drawn by winged dragons. Various tales were developed in which people were said to have tried to interfere with his mission, among them a certain Charnabon, king of the Getai in Thrace, who caused one of his dragons to be killed; the story was recounted in the lost *Triptolemos* of Sophocles, and a catasterism was then added by Hegesianax. Hyginus is our only source for the full story. By contrast to most astral myths in which people are represented in the sky by way of reward and commemoration, Charnabon is represented so that his fate may serve as a warning to others.

(iii) To pass on to tales in which the killing of dragons could be regarded as a useful service, some authors apparently appealed to a myth in which Heracles was said to have killed a huge snake in Lydia while serving Omphale, a queen of that land, as a slave (see Ap. 2.6.3 for the circumstances). If it had not already been used in another context, in connection with the Kneeler and the Dragon (see pp. 26–8), a more obvious choice would have been the myth in which Heracles killed the dragon of the Hesperides. This Lydian tale is relatively obscure, Hyginus is indeed our only source for it.

(iv) A certain Phorbas, who was honoured in hero-cult on Rhodes, was supposed to have delivered that island from an infestation of snakes. Of Thessalian birth, he was said to have been invited over for that purpose on the advice of the oracle at Delphi, and to have settled there with his followers (Diodorus 4.58.4–5). A Rhodian author appealed to this legend to explain the origin of the Serpent-bearer. We are told that Apollo portrayed Phorbas among the stars because he was a favourite of his, which implies some special connection with the god, even if he is now said to have arrived on the island by accident rather than on the advice of Apollo. Although it would have sufficed to say that he is represented in the sky with a snake to symbolize his services as a serpent-killer, the myth is altered to explain this through the idea that one of the snakes was of wholly exceptional size.

(v) The Thessalian king who was struck with insatiable hunger for violating a temple or grove of Demeter was usually identified as Erysichthon, son of Triopas, and this Erysichthon was said to have perished when he finally started to consume his own body; the story is first recounted by Callimachus (*Hymn* 6, 31 ff.), but some earlier allusions suggest that it was quite ancient. A tradition is also recorded, however, in which Triopas himself was said to have desecrated a grove of Demeter, though not to have suffered any divine punishment but merely to have been obliged to move abroad because his behaviour had angered the local people (Diodorus 5.61.1–3). But in the astral myth recorded by Hyginus, Demeter is said not only to have afflicted him with hunger, as in the case of Erysichthon, but also to have sent a snake against him toward the end of his life, the latter detail evidently being added to the story simply to account for the form of the constellation. As in the case of Charnabon, the catasterism is to be a source of infamy rather than of glory. This Triopas was sometimes said to have been the father of Phorbas.

20. CANIS MINOR, THE LITTLE DOG, known to the Greeks as PROCYON

EPITOME 42. PROCYON

THIS is the dog which is set in front of the large Dog; it is called Procyon (the Foredog) because it lies ahead of the Dog. It is the dog of Orion. For it is said to have been placed next to Orion because he was so fond of hunting. It can be seen, moreover, that the Hare and other beasts lie in its vicinity.

HYGINUS

The Constellation

Fixed on the milky circle, it touches the equator with its feet.* It looks toward the west, being located as it is between the Twins and the Crab. Because it rises before the large Dog, it is called Procyon (the Foredog). It sets at the rising of Capricorn, and rises with the Lion. In all it has three stars. (*Astronomy* 3.35)

The Mythology

It seems to rise before the larger Dog, but some think it to be Orion's dog. For that reason it is called Procyon (the Foredog), but all the same tales are ascribed to it as to the previous Dog. (*Astronomy* 2.36)

COMMENTARY

As a doublet of the large Dog, this constellation provided something of a problem for mythographers. Although the large Dog (or initially the dog-star within it) was the original dog of Orion, and it is better situated for that role than the lesser one, being set at the feet of Orion and in front of the Hare, Eratosthenes preferred to identify it with the dog of Procris, and reserve the role of Orion's dog for this constellation. There was another possibility, of course, namely that Orion had had more than one dog (schol. Arat. 450). Although Hyginus remarks that the other myths of the large Dog can also be ascribed to this constellation, it is not identified as the dog of Procris in any surviving source. The myths connected with the dog-star Sirius in its nature as a bringer of heat (see pp. 38–9), plainly cannot be transferred to this constellation (even if Hyginus does seem to suggest at one point that the dog of Icarios was set in the sky as this constellation—see p. 38 and relevant note).

21–32. CONSTELLATIONS OF THE ZODIAC

21. CANCER, THE CRAB; with the associated star-group of THE ASSES

EPITOME 11. CRAB

IT would seem that it was placed among the stars by Hera, because when Heracles was trying to kill the hydra* with the assistance of the others, it jumped out of the lake and bit him on the foot, as Panyasis recounts in his *Heracleia*.* They say that Heracles in a fury crushed it with his foot, and that the crab attained the great honour as a consequence of being numbered among the twelve signs of the zodiac.

Some of the stars in this constellation, known as the Asses, were raised up to the stars by Dionysos. They are marked out by a distinguishing sign, the Manger,* and the following tale is told about them. When the gods were setting out to make war against the Giants, it is said that Dionysos, Hephaistos, and the Satyrs rode out on asses; and when the Giants had not yet caught sight of them, but they were not far away, the asses began to bray, and on hearing that noise, the Giants took fright. For that reason, the asses were granted the honour of being set on the Crab, on the west side of it.

HYGINUS

The Constellation

Crab. Divided through the middle by the summer circle, it looks toward the Lion and the east. It is located a short way above the head of the Water-snake, and it rises and sets with the hind part of its body coming first. It has on its shell the two stars called the Asses, which we have already discussed.

It has one faint star on each right foot, two on its left back foot, two faint stars on the second, two on the third, one faint one on the front of the fourth, one on its mouth, three similar stars of no great size on what is known as its right claw, and two similar stars on its left claw. That makes seventeen stars in all. (*Astronomy* 3.22)

The Mythology

It is said to have been placed among the constellations by favour of

Hera, because while Heracles was confronting the Lernaian hydra, it came out of the marsh to seize him by the foot and bite him; so Heracles was moved to anger and killed it. Hera placed it among the constellations, however, to become one of the twelve signs that the sun passes through principally on its circuit.

In a certain part of this figure, there are the stars known as the Asses, which have been depicted by Dionysos on the shell of the Crab in the form of two stars in all. For Dionysos, after he was sent mad by Hera, is said to have fled through Thesprotia* in a state of frenzy, with the intention of reaching the oracle of Zeus at Dodona* to ask how he might recover his normal state of mind. On arriving at a huge swamp which he was unable to cross over, he encountered two asses, and catching one of them, he managed to get across without getting wet in the slightest degree. And so, when he reached the temple of Dodonian Zeus, he was immediately delivered from his madness, so the story goes, and expressed his gratitude to the asses by placing them among the stars. According to some accounts, he granted a human voice to the ass that had carried him, and it later entered into a contest with Priapos with regard to the size of its sexual organ, and was defeated and killed by him. Taking pity on it for this, Dionysos placed it among the stars; and to make it known that he had done so as a god, rather than as a timorous man fleeing Hera, he placed the Ass on the Crab, which had been fixed in the heavens as a favour from that goddess.

Another tale is also recounted about the Asses. According to Eratosthenes, at the time when Zeus declared war on the Giants and summoned all the gods to attack them, Dionysos, Hephaistos, and the Satyrs and Seilenoi* arrived mounted on asses; and on finding themselves at no great distance from the enemy, the asses, so the story goes, were overcome by panic and brayed very loudly one and all, letting out such a sound as the Giants had never heard, so that the enemy all took flight in response to their braying, and were thus defeated. A similar tale is told about Triton's horn;* for after hollowing out a seashell that he had found, so we are told, he brought it with him when he came to fight the Giants, and made a noise with the shell such as had never been heard before. Fearing that this was the bellowing of some monstrous beast which had been brought against them by their adversaries, the enemy took flight, and they were thus defeated and fell into the power of their opponents. (*Astronomy* 2.23)

COMMENTARY

The Crab

The only crab to appear in Greek myth is that which harassed
Heracles while he was confronting the hydra of Lerna (Ap. 2.5.2;
a very ancient story, appearing in images by about 700 BC). It was
said to have been reared as an adversary for Heracles by Hera (Hes.
Theog. 313–15), who resented him as an illegitimate son of Zeus;
and she accordingly could be thought to have placed it among the
stars. Its intervention justified Heracles in seeking the help of his
half-brother Iolaos in his battle against the many-headed hydra,
although the narrative in the Epitome seems to imply that he
was already receiving help from other people when it appeared
(the plural is surprising: the author was perhaps alluding to the
presence of Athena as a supporter of Heracles, even if she did not
intervene directly).

The Asses

(i) It might seem difficult to explain how these unassuming and
even rather comical creatures could have been judged worthy of
a place in the heavens. As in the case of Capricorn (see p. 79),
a none too serious myth was developed by invoking the notion of
panic fear, in which it was claimed that the gods' victory in their
battle against the Giants (Ap. 1.6.1–2) could be ascribed to panic
induced by the braying of donkeys, after Dionysos and his retinue,
and the lame Hephaistos, had ridden out to battle on them. In vase-
paintings from the Classical period, Satyrs, and indeed Maenads,
can sometimes be seen confronting the Giants from a safe distance,
and the theme doubtless appealed to authors of Satyr plays; but
this contribution from the asses may well have been invented by
Eratosthenes for his specific purposes.

(ii) The other story, in which an ass comes to the assistance of
Dionysos, is attributed to the Alexandrian tragic poet Philiscos
(schol. Germ.), and it was presumably derived from a Satyr play. It
need not be assumed that asses were said to have been transferred
to the stars in his version, and the story is indeed poorly suited for
that purpose, because there are two Asses in the sky and only one
ass plays any active part in assisting Dionysos to reach his destin-
ation. To develop the astral myth, it had to be suggested that the

one that carried Dionysos had a companion when he met it, and he thus placed the two of them in the sky.

In Hyginus's account of the second version, in which the catasterism takes place after the ass has entered into a contest with Priapos, no explanation is offered at all for why there is a second Ass in the sky; but it is stated in the Germanicus scholia that Priapos wanted to kill the ass after the contest, but Dionysos snatched it to safety, substituting another, and then placed both of them in the sky. So the double catasterism was contrived in a no less clumsy fashion than in the other version. Priapos was an ithyphallic fertility god whose cult had originated at Lampsacos; asses, which were regarded as exceptionally lustful creatures, were sacrificed to him in connection with his cult there. The tale of the contest is a parody of the kind of myth in which mortals enter into contests with deities, for instance with regard to musical skill, and come to a bad end when they try to demonstrate their skill; here the contestants have to demonstrate the relative size of their erections.

22. LEO, THE LION; with the neighbouring constellation of COMA BERENICES, BERENICE'S HAIR

EPITOME 12. LION

THIS is one of the more conspicuous constellations; it would seem that this sign of the zodiac was granted that honour by Zeus because the lion holds the leading position among four-footed beasts. Some say that it was placed there to commemorate the first labour of Heracles; for this was the only beast which, for love of glory, he killed without the aid of weapons, by strangling it between his arms; the tale is recounted by Peisandros of Rhodes.* This also explains why Heracles carries the lion's skin, as an emblem of the glorious deed that he had accomplished. This is the lion that was killed by him at Nemea.

Above the Lion there can also be seen seven faint stars, forming a triangle by its tail; these are called the Lock of Berenice Euergetis.*

HYGINUS

The Constellation

Looking toward the east, the Lion is set above the Water-snake, from the snake's head, which lies above the Ram, to the central part of it, and is divided through the middle by the summer tropic in such a way that its hind foot lies under that circle. It sets and rises head first.

It has three stars on its head, two on its neck, one on its chest, three on its upper back, one in the middle of its tail and another at the end, two under its chest, a bright star on its front paw, a bright one on its belly, with another large one below, one on its loins, one on its hind knee, and a bright one on its hind paw. That makes nineteen stars in all. (*Astronomy* 3.23)

The Mythology

Zeus placed it [the Lion] in the sky, so it is said, because it is reckoned to be the king of the beasts. Some authors add that Heracles fought against it as the first of his labours, and killed it without the aid of weapons. Peisandros and many others have written about this episode.

Above its image, right next to the Maiden, there are seven other stars, arranged in a triangle by the Lion's tail, which Conon, the mathematician of Samos, and Callimachus describe as being Berenice's hair. When Ptolemy had married his sister Berenice, daughter of Ptolemy and Arsinoe, and set off a few days afterwards to make war against Asia, Berenice vowed to cut off her hair if Ptolemy returned victorious. In fulfilment of her vow, she deposited her hair in the temple of Aphrodite-Arsinoe at Zephyrion,* but on the following day it was no longer to be seen. The king was greatly upset by this, but as was said above, the mathematician Conon, in the hope of gaining the king's favour, claimed to have seen the lock set among the stars; and he pointed to seven stars that did not belong to any constellation, saying that these must surely be the hair.

Some authors, including Callimachus, have said that this Berenice raised horses and used to send them to the Olympic Games.* Others add that when Ptolemy, the father of Berenice, had once been overcome by fear in the face of the overwhelming numbers of the enemy, and had sought safety in flight, his daughter, who was very experienced in horse-riding, jumped on to a horse, rallied the rest of the army, and killed a great many of the enemy and put the rest to flight. For that reason Callimachus called her great-souled.* According to Eratosthenes, she arranged for the Lesbian girls* to be given the dowry that each had been left by her father, but that no one had handed over, and laid a claim meanwhile for restitution. (*Astronomy* 2.24)

COMMENTARY

The Lion

(i) Eratosthenes apparently suggested as his primary interpretation that Zeus placed the lion in the sky because it is the king of the beasts.

(ii) Or else this is specifically the Nemean lion which was killed by Heracles as the first of his twelve labours. Although Eratosthenes said that the hero attacked it unarmed for the sake of glory, it was usually explained that he was obliged to seize hold of it and throttle it because it was invulnerable and could not be pierced by weapons (Pindar, *Isthmian Ode* 6.47–8; full narrative in Ap. 2.5.1); it was no ordinary lion but a child of Echidna (Hes. *Theog.* 327), a notable progenitor of monsters. As was noted by Eratosthenes in his description of the constellation, the lion's skin, which Heracles carried thereafter as one of his attributes, was represented by four stars on the left arm of the constellation of the Kneeler, later known as Hercules. Nigidius offered an account in which Hera raised it on the moon to be an opponent for Heracles, and later placed it in the sky because of her hatred of him (schol. Germ.). It is not known who placed it there in Eratosthenes' account; although Hera may have performed that function there too, as in the case of that other notable enemy of his, the Crab (see pp. 66–7). It is also possible that Zeus was said to have placed it in the sky to commemorate the valour of Heracles, because stress was laid on the glory that he had won by killing it with his bare hands.

Berenice's Hair

Although Ptolemy did not include this among his forty-eight constellations, it has come to be accepted into the modern canon. It is exceptional in being associated with a historical figure. This Berenice (267–221), whose true parents were Mages of Cyrene and Apama, married Ptolemy III Euergetes, king of Egypt (reigned 246–222) soon after his succession, but was then separated from him by the campaign that marked the beginning of the Third Syrian War (246–241). Conon of Samos, who claimed to have rediscovered the lock that she had dedicated for his safe return after it vanished, was an astronomer and mathematician associated with the court at Alexandria (there was no official position of court astronomer). His claim that it could now be seen among the stars was a playful and flattering conceit that would not have been taken any more seriously than was intended. Callimachus wrote a poem about the matter in which the Lock was compared with Ariadne's Crown as a symbol of marital fidelity; although the poem is lost, some idea of its nature can be gathered from the surviving imitation by Catullus (66).

23. VIRGO, THE MAIDEN

EPITOME II. MAIDEN

HESIOD says in his *Theogony* that this is the daughter of Zeus by Themis, whose name is Justice.* Taking up the story from Hesiod, Aratus says that she was immortal and used to live on earth among human beings. When they changed for the worse and no longer held to what is just, she remained with them no longer, but withdrew to the mountains; and when civil strife and wars then broke out among them, she felt complete abhorrence for their injustice, and flew up into the sky. Many other stories too are told about this constellation. For some say that she is Demeter because she is holding an ear of corn, others that she is Isis, others Atargartis, or others Tyche, and for that reason they represent her as headless.

HYGINUS

The Constellation

The Maiden is located under the feet of the Oxherd, and she touches the hind part of the Lion with her head, and the equator with her right hand; but the lower part of her body can be seen above the Crow and the tail of the Water-snake. As she sets, her head precedes the rest of her body.

On her head there is one faint star, and one star on each shoulder, and two on each wing, of which one star set on her right wing near her shoulder is called Protrygeter (Announcer of the Vintage). She has, furthermore, a star on each hand, and one of these, set on her right hand, being of exceptional size and brightness, causes her to be said to be carrying ears of corn. She has ten stars scattered over her clothing, and one on each foot. So she thus has nineteen stars in all. (*Astronomy* 3.24)

The Mythology

According to Hesiod, this is the daughter of Zeus and Themis, but Aratus says that she is thought to be the daughter of Astraios and Eos,* and that she lived at the time of the golden age of human beings, and was their ruler. Because she was so conscientious and equitable, she was called Justice, and in those times no one was impelled to make war against foreign nations, and no one sailed the seas, but people were accustomed to spend their lives tending their fields. Those who were born after the death of this generation, however, proved to be less dutiful and more avaricious, and Justice accordingly spent less time among human beings. In the end matters arrived at such a point that the race of bronze was born, and she could then bear it no longer and flew up into the heavens.

But others have said that she is Fortune, and others again that she is Demeter, and people disagree about her all the more because her head seems so faint. According to some accounts, she is Erigone, daughter of Icarios, whom we have spoken about above,* or in other accounts she is a daughter of Apollo and Chrysothemis, who was given the name of Parthenos (Maiden) during her childhood, and was placed among the constellations because of her premature death. (*Astronomy* 2.25)

COMMENTARY

(i) Aratus (100–136) developed an allegorical tale in which Dike, or Justice personified, withdrew progressively from human company as people's morals declined, until she finally removed herself altogether by flying up into the sky to become the Maiden, where she can still be seen as delivering a silent admonition. The stages of human decline are illustrated by reference to Hesiod's myth of the golden, silver, and bronze races (*Works and Days*, 109 ff.), although Aratus's adaptation is both free and selective.

(ii) In his lost poem, the *Erigone*, Eratosthenes developed a more conventional astral myth to explain the origin of this constellation along with that of Bootes, by identifying the Maiden as Erigone, the daughter of Icarios, who spread Dionysos' gift of wine through Attica; see further under Bootes, p. 37.

(iii) Although Demeter was not a virgin goddess, this constellation-figure came to be identified with her because the Maiden is holding an ear of corn, as represented in the bright star (alpha Virginis) known accordingly as Stachys in Greek or Spica in Latin. The constellation then came to be identified in turn with Eastern fertility goddesses often identified with Demeter, namely Isis, Atagartis, and Cybele.

(iv) Tyche, or Fortuna under her Latin name, made no appearance in myth, but came to be of some importance in urban cult in the insecure Hellenistic world. Since Fortune could naturally be imagined as being blind, some suggested that the Maiden could be identified with her because of the lack of bright stars in her head.

(v) Hyginus is our only source for the rather rudimentary myth of Parthenos (Maiden), daughter of Apollo, who was placed in the sky by her father as a result of her early death.

(vi) Or this is Thespieia, daughter of the river-god Asopos, who was the eponym of Thespiai, a town under Mount Helicon in Boeotia. Apollo granted her three gifts, to give her name to a city on earth, to become the Maiden in the heavens, and to deliver oracles (schol. Arat. 223).

24–25. SCORPIUS, THE SCORPION, and THE CLAWS (or LIBRA, THE SCALES)

EPITOME 7. SCORPION

BECAUSE of its huge size, it is divided between two signs,* one containing its claws, and the other its body and sting. They say that Artemis caused it to emerge from a hill on the island of Chios and sting Orion,* who thus met his death, because he had abandoned all propriety and tried to rape the goddess while they were out hunting. Zeus placed it among the brightest constellations to ensure that people of future generations would recognize its strength and power.

The Vatican Fragments offer a different account of Orion's death:

Because of its huge size, it is divided between two signs, one containing its claws, and the other its body and sting. Orion is supposed to have been killed by Earth because he had proclaimed in front of Artemis that no wild beast would escape him; this constellation appears as a symbol of that event.* They say that the scorpion stung Orion and that he thus met his death; because of Earth's remarkable deed, Zeus placed the scorpion among the stars, to ensure that people of future generations would recognize her nature and power.

HYGINUS

The Constellation

Its front part, known as the Claws, is pressed by the equator in such a way that it seems to hold up that circle. The Scorpion itself lies under the feet of the Serpent-bearer, whom we have talked about above, and it seems to touch the winter tropic with the end of its tail; nor is it far from the star-figure that the Centaur is seen to be carrying as a sacrificial victim. It sets obliquely, and rises vertically, starting with the Claws.

It has two stars on each of its Claws, as they are called, but the first is brightest; and it has three stars, furthermore, at the front, of which the middle star is the brightest, and three on its back, two on its belly, five on its tail, and two set directly on its sting, with which it strikes, so it is thought. It thus has nineteen stars in all. (*Astronomy* 3.25)

The Mythology

Because of the large size of the various parts of its body, it [the Scorpion] has been divided into two signs, and one of them has come to be known among ourselves as the Scales. But the constellation as a whole is supposed to have been placed in the sky for the following reason. Orion was out hunting, and he was so convinced of his supreme skill as a hunter that he went so far as to tell Artemis that he was capable of killing everything that was born from the earth; and Earth was so enraged that she sent forth a scorpion to kill him, so the story goes. But Zeus, admiring the courage of both the one and the other, placed the scorpion among the constellations, so that its image would remind people not to be too self-confident in anything. Artemis for her part, because she was so fond of Orion, asked Zeus to grant him the same favour as he had granted of his own accord to Earth; and he thus placed Orion in the sky in such a way that, as the Scorpion rises, Orion goes down. (*Astronomy* 2.26)

COMMENTARY

This is one of the few constellations which could be said to bear an obvious resemblance to what it is meant to represent: it is a 'natural' constellation. Since Orion sets as the Scorpion rises, it could be imagined that he is under pursuit from it, and that thought provided the basis for the only myth that was put forward to explain its origin, in which it is said to have killed Orion at the will of Earth or of Artemis (see further on p. 101 ff.).

Because of its large size, this constellation was divided between two signs of the zodiac, its claws being regarded as a separate sign. The Claws naturally had no myths of their own, and even in so far as this sign was identified instead as the Scales (libra), only one myth of a very rudimentary character is recorded of it (schol. Germ., following Nigidius). There was a certain 'Mochus', so we are told, who first invented weights and scales for human beings, and because these were thought to be extremely useful to them, he was received among the number of the stars and called Libra. It has been plausibly suggested that the name of this person should properly be Stathmouchos (i.e. Bearer of the Scales), and we are evidently supposed to picture the Scales as being held by him. They were sometimes depicted with a bearer, even if there was never thought to be any corresponding figure among the stars.

26. SAGITTARIUS, THE ARCHER

EPITOME 28. ARCHER

THIS is the Archer, who is a Centaur according to most accounts. Others deny this, however, because he cannot be seen to be four-legged, but is standing upright and drawing a bow; and no Centaur ever made use of a bow. This is surely a man, but one who has the legs of a horse and a tail like that of the Satyrs.* That is why these find it hard to believe that this is a Centaur, but prefer to think that it is Crotos, the son of Eupheme,* nurse of the Muses.

This Crotos lived and passed his life on Mount Helicon. The Muses inspired him to discover the use of the bow, so that he would be able to procure food by hunting wild beasts, as Sositheos* recounts. He mixed with the Muses on familiar terms, and when listening to their performances, he indicated his approval by clapping his hands. Now the sound was feeble with only one person clapping in applause, but when they saw what he was doing, the others too followed his example. For that reason the Muses, when they came to enjoy the delight of fame as a result of his approval, asked Zeus to grant him renown for his piety, and he was thus placed among the constellations because of the use that he had made of his hands, taking his archery there too as a distinguishing sign. This practice of his has been perpetuated among human beings. The presence of the Boat* also serves to indicate that he will be visible to all, not only to those who are on dry land, but also to those who are out at sea. For these reasons, those who write that this is a Centaur are mistaken.

HYGINUS

The Constellation

The Archer, who looks toward the west, is represented with the body of a Centaur, as though about to shoot an arrow; from his feet to his shoulders, he is set within the winter tropic, in such a way that only his head seems to project above the aforementioned circle. His bow is cut through the middle by the milky circle. At his feet there is a crown formed from stars, which we have already talked about. He sets head first, and rises vertically.

He has two stars on his head, two on his bow, one on his arrows, one on his right elbow, one on his front foot, one on his belly, one on his back, one on his tail, one on his front knee, one on his foot, one on his lower knee, and one on his shin. In all, fifteen. The Centaur's crown* for its part has seven stars. (*Astronomy* 3.26)

The Mythology

Many have said that this is a Centaur, but others have denied that on the ground that no Centaur ever made use of arrows. The question is also raised as to why he is represented with horse's legs and has a tail like that of a Satyr. Some say that he is a man called Crotos, who was son of Eupheme and nurse of the Muses. According to Sositheos, the author of tragedies, he had his home on Mount Helicon and used to take pleasure in the company of the Muses, and sometimes also liked to go hunting. And he thus won great acclaim for the zeal with which he pursued these activities, for he had become at once very swift in running through the woods and very skilled in the arts. Because of the efforts that he had made, the Muses asked Zeus to portray him in a group of stars, and he fulfilled their request; but wanting to illustrate all his skills in a single image, Zeus gave him horse's legs, because he had often gone riding, and added some arrows to indicate both his sharpness of mind and his speed. And he attached a Satyr's tail to his body because the Muses had taken no less pleasure in his company than Dionysos in that of the Satyrs. In front of his feet there are a few stars arranged in a circle; some have said that this is his crown, cast off by him as though in play. (*Astronomy* 2.27)

COMMENTARY

(i) There was disagreement as to whether the figure represented in this constellation is four-footed or two-footed, and thus whether it can be regarded as a Centaur. According to the dominant view in the astronomical literature, advanced by Eudoxos and later by Hipparchos, it is four-footed, as Aratus indicates (400) through his reference to its 'forelegs'. But some authors who wrote about astral mythology argued against this, on iconographic and, more playfully, mythical grounds, saying that no Centaur ever used a bow. While this was true of the Centaurs in general, who preferred to resort to cruder weapons such as rocks and uprooted trees, Cheiron could be supposed to differ from them in this as in other respects, and was sometimes explicitly stated to have been a skilful archer. In any case, Eratosthenes himself apparently took the lead in advancing the argument that this could not be a Centaur, because he described the constellation-figure as resembling a Satyr, and appealed to the none too serious myth of Crotos, derived from a Satyr play, to explain its origin. It should be noted that this Crotos, who was no more than Applause personified, was himself shaped like a normal human being, and not like a Satyr, but was said to have been represented in the sky with a horse's legs and tail for symbolic reasons. Incidentally, the word *krotos* could mean either clapping with one's hand or beating with one's foot (which could itself be a sign of approval), and it is not entirely clear which is intended in this narrative, although the former interpretation has generally been assumed.

(ii) When regarded as a Centaur, the Archer was inevitably identified with the noble Centaur Cheiron (cited as an alternative by Nigidius, fr. 97 Sw., cf. Seneca, *Thyestes* 861, Lucan 9.536). In that case, a different interpretation was needed for the constellation of the Centaur (see pp. 120–2).

27. CAPRICORNUS, CAPRICORN

EPITOME 27. CAPRICORN

THIS figure is similar in appearance to Aigipan, and is moreover modelled on him.* His lower limbs are formed like those of a beast, and he has horns on his head. He was honoured in this way because he was suckled together with Zeus, according to Epimenides, the author of the *Cretan Tales*, who reports that he was living on Ida with Zeus when that god set out to attack the Titans. It seems that he discovered the seashell that served as a weapon to the allied gods, because of the so-called panic-making sound that it emitted, which put the Titans to flight. After taking power, Zeus placed him among the stars, along with his mother, the Goat.* He has the tail of a fish to indicate that he discovered the shell in the sea.

HYGINUS

The Constellation

Capricorn looks toward the west and is depicted wholly within the circle of the zodiac; his tail and the whole of his body are cut through the middle by the winter tropic. He lies under the left hand of the Water-pourer. He sets head first, and rises vertically.

He has one star on his nose, one beneath his neck, two on his chest, one on his hind foot, another on the same, seven on his back, five on his belly, and two on his tail. That makes twenty stars in all. (*Astronomy* 3.27)

The Mythology

His [Capricorn's] appearance is similar to that of Aigipan. Zeus, having been suckled with him, wanted to place him among the stars, in the same way as the goat that had been his nurse, which we have already spoken about. It is said too that when Zeus went off to attack the Titans, he was the first to arouse so-called panic fear in the enemy, as Eratosthenes recounts. It is for that reason, and because he hurled seashells at the enemy instead of stones, that the lower part of his body is formed like that of a fish.

Egyptian priests and poets say, however, that when many of the gods had once gathered together in Egypt, Typhon,* a very fierce giant and great enemy of the gods, suddenly appeared there. Overcome by fear, the gods assumed different forms, Hermes turning into an ibis, and Apollo into the so-called Thracian bird, while Artemis took on the appearance of a cat.* It is for that reason, so it is said, that the Egyptians do not allow any ill-treatment to be inflicted on these creatures, because they regard them as being images of the gods. On that same occasion, so the story goes, Pan hurled himself into the river, giving the lower part of his body the appearance of a fish, and the rest of it that of a goat, and thus escaped from Typhon. Zeus so admired his stratagem that he placed an image of him among the constellations. (*Astronomy* 2.28)

Alternative account

When the gods, in Egypt, took fright at the ferocity of Typhon, Pan told them to turn themselves into wild beasts to deceive him the more easily, and Zeus struck him dead with a thunderbolt. By the will of the gods, Pan was placed among the stars because his advice had enabled them to escape from the power of Typhon; and because he had turned himself into a goat on that occasion, he was called Aigōkeros, which we translate as Capricorn. (*Mythical Tales* 196, Pan)

COMMENTARY

(i) This constellation of eastern origin represents a goat-fish, with the foreparts of a goat and the hind parts of a fish. Since there was nothing of that kind in Greek myth, a certain amount of ingenuity was required to develop a myth to account for its origin. Its goat-like features would inevitably call to mind the rustic deity Pan, who was often pictured as having a goat's head or horns and goat's legs. Eratosthenes suggested accordingly that the figure in the constellation is Aigipan (Goat-Pan); it is not entirely clear whether we are intended to regard this as a name for Pan himself, in specific reference to his goat-like features, or to view Aigipan as being a separate being related to Pan, but the former interpretation is perhaps to be preferred. But what of Capricorn's fish-like features? In Eratosthenes' account, they were presented as being merely symbolic. Aigipan came to the assistance of Zeus and his fellow-gods in their war against the Titans by inducing 'Panic' fear in the enemy by blowing a conch-shell horn, and he was then represented in the sky as part-fish to indicate the marine origin of the horn. The seashell horn was originally associated with the minor sea-god Triton, who is indeed mentioned by Hyginus in this connection (see p. 67), and was transferred to Aigipan specifically to allow the development of this astral myth. Aigipan's services in this regard would suffice to justify his transference to the heavens, but as observed in connection with the Goat star (see pp. 42 and 44), there were myths in which Zeus was said to have been suckled by a goat, and through the suggestion that this Goat-Pan had been suckled by it alongside Zeus, not only could additional justification be provided for the catasterism, but it could be suggested that there had been a joint catasterism in which the goat and Aigipan were placed among the stars at the same time.

(ii) As in the case of the Fishes (see p. 83), use could be made of the myth in which the gods were said to have assumed different animal forms to escape the monster Typhon. This myth (the best account is that by Antoninus Liberalis, 40) provided an explanation for why Egyptian gods were portrayed partially or wholly in animal form. For present purposes, the god Pan, who already had goat-like features, could be said to have changed himself into a goat-fish after jumping in the Nile, and to have come to be represented in the sky in the form that he had temporarily assumed.

28. AQUARIUS, THE WATER-POURER

EPITOME 26. WATER-POURER

IT would seem that he owes his name to the action that he is performing; for he is standing with a wine-jar in his hand and is pouring out a large stream of liquid. Some say that this is Ganymedes, thinking to find sufficient proof in the fact that the figure is represented like a cup-bearer pouring wine. They cite the poet Homer as a witness,* because he describes how Ganymedes was carried off to serve as cup-bearer to Zeus because of his exceptional beauty, a service that the gods had judged him worthy to fulfil, and states that he attained immortality, something unknown among human beings. The fluid that he is pouring out represents the nectar that is drunk by the gods, and as evidence of that they adduce the fact that that is supposed to be the beverage of the gods.

HYGINUS

The Constellation

The Water-pourer has his feet set fast on the winter tropic. His left
hand is stretched out toward the back of Capricorn, while his right
hand almost touches the mane of Pegasos. He is looking toward the
east. Because he is depicted in such a way, he necessarily seems to be
almost lying on his back. The stream of water pours out toward the
Fish that is portrayed as being on its own, which we will talk about
below. Both when rising and setting, the head of the Water-pourer
precedes the rest of his body.

He has two faint stars on his head, one bright star on each shoulder, a large star on his left elbow, one on his front hand, a faint one on
each nipple, one on the inside of his thighs, one on each knee, one on
his left leg, and one on each foot. In all, fourteen. The stream of water
and the urn itself have thirty stars, but of all these stars only the first
and last are bright. (*Astronomy* 3.28)

The Mythology

According to many accounts, this is Ganymedes; Zeus snatched him
away from his parents because of his physical beauty, and is supposed
to have made him cup-bearer to the gods.

Or according to Hegesianax, this is Deucalion, because such
quantities of water poured from the sky during his reign that this
is said to have caused a great flood. Euhemerus indicates, however,
that this is Cecrops, commemorating the antiquity of his race, and
showing that water was used in sacrifices to the gods before wine was
revealed to mortals, and that Cecrops ruled before the discovery of
wine. (*Astronomy* 2.29)

COMMENTARY

(i) This constellation was usually identified with Ganymedes, son
of Tros, a young Trojan prince who was snatched away to become
cup-bearer to Zeus on Olympos. This was a very ancient myth, and
Eratosthenes appealed directly to Homer's account (*Il.* 20.232–5),
although the *Iliad* does not in fact say that he was granted immortality, as the Epitome suggests, but that he was taken away to live
with the immortals. That he was abducted by an eagle and that
Zeus became his lover were ideas of later origin (see p. 58).

(ii) Hyginus cites two alternatives from other sources, which may well have been mentioned previously by Eratosthenes. Perhaps this is Deucalion, the hero of the Greek myth of the great flood (Ap. 1.7.2); in that case, he is depicted as a water-pourer for merely symbolic reasons.

(iii) Or this is Cecrops, the earthborn first king of Athens (see Ap. 3.14.1–2), who can be imagined to be pouring a libation to the gods. It could be argued in this connection that he had reigned at such an early period that wine was not yet available to be used for that purpose, and he could thus be imagined as being quite literally a water-pourer, by contrast to Ganymedes, who would have poured nectar, the drink of the gods. In Attica wine was supposed to have been revealed by Dionysos to Icarios (see p. 37), who lived during the reign of a later king, Pandion.

(iv) The scholia to Germanicus report a tradition that identified this constellation with Aristaios, who introduced many useful arts, and above all funded the rites that summoned the Etesian winds to moderate the heat brought by the rising of the dog-star (see further on p. 117, and for the rites, A.R. 2.520–7); for which reason the gods honoured him by granting him a place in the heavens. He is evidently to be pictured as making a libation to Zeus in connection with the cult that he had founded. This Aristaios was a son of Apollo by the nymph Cyrene; for his life and the arts that were attributed to him, see Diodorus 4.81–2.

(v) Or this is the Demon of the Nile, who regulated the flow of that river. Our source (schol. Arat. 283) refers to Pindar, who provided some account of this being, as does Apollonius of Tyre (6.26); he was apparently pictured as standing at the head of the river, here symbolized in the water that he is pouring, and he was supposed to have altered its flow, to bring about the seasonal variations, by shifting the position of his feet.

29. PISCES, THE FISHES

EPITOME 21. FISHES

THESE are the offspring of the large Fish,* whose story we will recount in detail when we get to it. Each lies apart from the other in a different part of the sky, one being known as the Northern Fish and the other as the Southern. They are joined together by a knot which stretches toward the front foot of the Ram.

HYGINUS

The Constellation

One of these is called the southern and the other the northern, because only one of them, the northern, is situated between the equator and the summer tropic, under the arm of Andromeda looking toward the arctic pole, while the other is situated on the edge of the zodiac under the shoulder-blades of the Horse, not far from the equator and looking toward the west. These Fishes are linked together by a series of stars resembling a ribbon, running from the front foot of the Ram. The lower of the two Fishes can be seen to set and rise first. That Fish has seventeen stars, while the northern one has twelve in all.

The connection between them has three stars running north, three on the other side, three toward the east, and three on the knot, making twelve in all. The point where they run together, which can be seen by the front foot of the Ram, is called by Aratus in Greek the *syndesmos hypouranios*, or by Cicero the celestial knot: both want to indicate that it is not only that of the Fishes, but also that of the entire sphere. For at the place in question at the foot of the Ram, the circle of the meridian which indicates the middle of the day, is located just where the meridian joins and cuts across the equator, and at that very point, at the intersection of the two circles, the knot of the Fishes is to be found. And so this can rightly be called not only the knot of the Fishes, but also the celestial knot. (*Astronomy* 3.29)

The Mythology

According to Diognetos of Erythraia, Aphrodite once visited Syria with her son Eros and arrived beside the river Euphrates. All of a sudden, Typhon, whom we mentioned above,* appeared at that very place; Aphrodite hurled herself into the river along with her son, and there they turned themselves into fishes, and so delivered themselves from danger. As a consequence the Syrians who live in the neighbouring regions abstained thereafter from eating fishes, being afraid to catch them lest, in similar circumstances, they might seem to be breaching the refuges of the gods, or might capture them in person. According to Eratosthenes, these fishes are offspring of the fish that we will talk about later. (*Astronomy* 2.30)

COMMENTARY

(i) Since fishes played almost no part at all in Greek myth and cult, it was necessary to look to the East to find an explanation for the two constellations in which they appear. It was known that the mother goddess Derceto, known to the Greeks as the Syrian goddess, had pools containing sacred fish near her temple at Bambyke (Hierapolis), and that the local people honoured cultic images of fishes, and abstained from eating them. Indeed, the goddess was sometimes portrayed as half-piscine in form. All the myths offered for these Fishes and the Southern Fish relate to that goddess (who was known under different names in different parts of the Near East).

We will start with the joint myth that Eratosthenes provided to explain the origin of all three Fishes, as recounted in connection with the Southern Fish. When Derceto fell into the lake mentioned above, she was rescued by a fish, which was placed in the heavens as a consequence as the Southern Fish, along with these two others which were its offspring. The story (i.e. the basic story without the catasterism) is ascribed to Ctesias, a physician of the fifth century who wrote books about India and Persia, but Eratosthenes may have altered it quite drastically; it has been plausibly argued that a very different narrative recorded by Diodorus (3.4.2–6), in which Derceto throws herself into the lake and is turned into a fish, may hold more closely to Ctesias's account.

(ii) According to a well-known myth that was also adapted to explain the origin of Capricorn (see p. 80), the gods transformed themselves into different beasts to escape from the monstrous Typhon. While the standard myth is set in Egypt and involves all the main gods, Hyginus recounts a tale in connection with the Fishes in which Typhon appears to Aphrodite and Eros while they are beside the Euphrates, and they jump into the river and turn themselves into fishes, hence the origin of the local taboos with regard to fishes, and evidently of the present constellation also, although we are not told how the images of the fishes came to be placed in the sky. Aphrodite is appointed to be the heroine of the tale because she could be identified with the Syrian goddess, and her son Eros is included in the story too because there are two Fishes in the constellation. Ovid (*Fasti* 2.451 ff.) offers a hybrid version in which they jump into the river and are rescued by fishes, much as Derceto is said to have been rescued in the preceding tale.

(iii) A further tale, derived from Nigidius, is recorded in the Germanicus scholia. Two fishes discovered an egg of enormous size in the Euphrates and rolled it ashore, where it was brooded by doves until the Syrian goddess hatched out a few days later; at her request, Zeus rewarded the fishes by placing them in the heavens. Doves were also associated with the cult of the Syrian goddess, and they play an important role in the myth recounted about her by Diodorus.

30. TAURUS, THE BULL; with the associated star-clusters of the PLEIADES and HYADES

EPITOME 14. BULL

IT is said to have been placed among the stars because it carried Europa across the sea from Phoenicia to Crete, as Euripides recounts in his *Phrixos*;* for that reason it was granted the honour by Zeus of being one of the most conspicuous constellations. Others say, however, that this is a cow, an image of Io, and that it was for her sake that the constellation was marked out for this honour by Zeus.

The forehead and face of the Bull are delineated by the stars known as the Hyades. Where the back of the Bull is cut off, the Pleiades are set, which consist of seven stars, and are thus called the Seven-starred. Only six are in fact visible, while the seventh is extremely faint.

It is further mentioned in the Vatican Fragments that the Hyades could be identified as nurses of Zeus:

According to Pherecydes of Athens, these are the nurses of Zeus, who are known as the nymphs of Dodona.

EPITOME 23. PLEIADES

The Pleiades lie on the back of the Bull at the so-called cut-off;* the cluster is made up of a group of seven stars, which are said to be the daughters of Atlas, and it is thus called the Seven-starred. One cannot see seven, however, but only six, and the explanation for that goes something like this: six of them had liaisons with gods,* so they say, and one of them with a mortal. Three of them slept with Zeus, namely Electra, who gave birth to Dardanos, Maia, who gave birth to Hermes, and Taygete, who gave birth to Lacedaimon; while two slept with Poseidon, namely Alcyone, who gave birth to Hyrieus, and Celaino, who gave birth to Lycos; and Sterope is said to have slept with Ares, bearing Oinomaos to him. But Merope married a mortal, Sisyphos, and that is why she is wholly invisible. The Pleiades are very highly regarded by human beings because they indicate the changing of the seasons.

HYGINUS

The Constellation

The Bull faces toward the east, and only half of it can be seen; its knees seem to be beginning to sink to the earth, and its head is turned in the same direction. Its knees are divided from the rest of its body by the equator. Its left horn, as we have mentioned above, comes together with the right foot of the Charioteer. Between the edge of its body and the tail of the ram there lie seven stars which have been called the Vergiliae by the people of our country, and the Pleiades by the Greeks. The Bull sets and rises backwards.

It has one star on each horn, of which that on the left is the brighter, one star on each eye, one on the middle of its forehead, and one on the base of each horn; these seven stars are known as the Hyades, although some exclude the two last-mentioned stars, so as to ascribe five stars in all to the Hyades. The Bull has, furthermore, a star on its left hind knee, one above its hoof, one on its right knee, three between its shoulder-blades, the last of which is brighter than the others, and one star on its chest. Which makes eighteen in all, excluding the Pleiades. (*Astronomy* 3.20)

The Mythology

It [the Bull] is said to have been placed among the constellations because it carried Europa safely to Crete, as Euripides recounts. Or according to some authors, when Io was transformed into a cow, Zeus, so as to make amends, placed her among the stars in such a way that the front of her body could be clearly seen in the semblance of that of a bull, while the rest of her body was rather faint.

The bull faces toward the sunrise, and the stars that outline its face are known as the Hyades. According to Pherecydes of Athens, these are the nurses of Dionysos, seven in number, who were formerly known as the nymphs of Dodona. These are their names: Ambrosia, Eudora, Pedile, Coronis, Polyxo, Phyte, and Thyone. Lycourgos is said to have put them to flight* causing all except Ambrosia to take refuge with Thetis, as Asclepiades* recounts. But according to Pherecydes, they took Dionysos to Thebes to entrust him to Ino, and Zeus expressed his gratitude to them by placing them among the stars.

The Pleiades came to be called by that name, according to Musaeus, because fifteen daughters* were born to Atlas and Aithra, daughter of Oceanos, five of whom were called the Hyades, so he points out, because they had a brother Hyas who was greatly loved by his sisters. After he was killed during a lion hunt, the five sisters whom we have just mentioned were so overcome by unremitting grief, so the story goes, that they died as a result; and so, because they grieved most of all at his death, they came to be called the Hyades. The other ten sisters reflected on the death of their sisters, and seven of them committed suicide; and since the greater number of them felt that way, they came to be called the Pleiades.*

Or according to Alexander,* the Hyades were called by that name because they were daughters of Hyas and Boeotia,* and the Pleiades because they were daughters of Pleione, daughter of Oceanos, and Atlas.

The Pleiades are said to be seven in number, but no one can see more than six of them. It has been suggested by way of explanation that, of the seven, six went to bed with immortals—three with Zeus, two with Poseidon, and one with Ares—while the other is indicated to have been the wife of Sisyphos. To Zeus, Electra bore Dardanos, and Maia Hermes, and Taygete Lacedaimon; to Poseidon, Alcyone bore Hyrieus, and Celaino bore Lycos and Nycteus; and to Ares, Sterope bore Oinomaos (although others say that she was the wife of Oinomaos). As for Merope, who married Sisyphos, she gave birth to Glaucos, who was the father of Bellerophon according to many accounts. She was placed among the stars thanks to her other sisters, but because she married a mortal, her star is faint.

According to other accounts, it is Electra who cannot be seen, for the following reason. The Pleiades led the chorus of the stars, so it is thought, but after the fall of Troy and the destruction of all who were descended from her through Dardanos, Electra was overcome by grief and abandoned the company of her sisters to establish herself on the circle known as the arctic, and at long intervals she can be seen in mourning with her hair unloosed; for that reason she has come to be called a comet (long-haired star).

The ancient astronomers placed these apart from the Bull; they were the daughters, as we have already said, of Pleione and Atlas. While Pleione was once passing through Boeotia with her daughters, Orion* grew overexcited and tried to rape her, causing her to flee; but Orion pursued her for seven years without being able to catch her. Taking pity on the girls, Zeus placed them among the stars, and some astronomers have called them the Bull's tail. Thus it is that Orion still seems to pursue them as they flee toward the west. Our countrymen have called these stars the Vergiliae because they rise after springtime (*ver*),* and they enjoy greater honours, indeed, than all other stars because their rising indicates the arrival of summer, and their setting the coming of winter, something that cannot be said of other constellations. (*Astronomy* 2.21)

Alternative account of the mythology of the Pleiades and Hyades

Atlas had twelve daughters and a son, Hyas, by Pleione or an Oceanid. When Hyas was killed by a wild boar or a lion, his sisters grieved for him so desperately that they died of their grief. Of these, the first five were transferred to the stars to take their place between the horns of the Bull, namely Phaisyle, Ambrosia, Coronis, Eudora, and Polyxo, who were called the Hyades after the name of their brother. In Latin they are called the Suculae.* Some say, however, that they are called the Hyades because they are arranged like the letter Y, or others because they bring rain at their rising, for raining is called *huein* in Greek. There are some who think that they appear among the stars because they were the nurses of Dionysos whom Lycourgos drove out of the island of Naxos.* The other sisters who died of grief later were also turned into stars, and they were called the Pleiades because they were more in number (*pleious*). Some think, however, that they owe their name to the fact that they are set close together, that is to say, *plesion*, and they are indeed so tightly clustered that it is not easy to count them, and it is impossible to tell for certain with the naked eye whether there are six or seven of them.

Their names are Electra, Alcyone, Celaino, Merope, Sterope, Taygete, and Maia, and of these, they say that Electra does not show herself because of the death of Dardanos and the loss of Troy; while

others think that Merope seems to blush because she took a mortal for
a husband whereas all the others had liaisons with gods. Driven from
the chorus of her sisters for that reason, she wears her hair unloosed
in sorrow, and is thus called a comet or long-haired star, because she
stretches out for such a distance, or else called *xiphias* because she is
shaped like a sword-point. This star is a portent of sorrow. (*Mythical
Tales* 192, Hyas)

COMMENTARY

The Bull

(i) This was commonly said to be the bull that had carried Europa
across the sea from Phoenicia to Crete. Europa was the daughter of
the Phoenician king Agenor or Phoenix, and Zeus fathered Minos
and other children by her to found the Cretan royal line (Ap.
3.1.1–2). In Eratosthenes' narrative, Zeus was plainly presented as
having sent the bull, but in early sources he is said to have transformed himself into the bull to abduct her (e.g. Hes. fr. 140 MW),
and some Latin authors revert to this tradition when recounting
the astral myth (Ovid, *Fasti* 5.604 ff., cf. Germanicus 536 ff.). In
that case, Zeus would merely have placed an image of the bull in
the sky to commemorate his exploit

(ii) Eratosthenes also cited an alternative in which the constellation represents the transformed Io. This Io was a daughter of the
Argive river-god Inachos, and was of genealogical importance as
the ancestor of the Argive and Theban royal lines. She aroused
the love of Zeus, who subsequently transformed her into a cow to
conceal her from the jealous Hera (or else she was transformed
by Hera herself); she then wandered off to Egypt, where she was
restored to human form and gave birth to Epaphos, her son by
Zeus (Ap. 2.1.3). In that case, the figure in the sky is not a bull at
all, but a cow. No one would know, however, because only the front
half of the animal is represented there; in fuller narratives, it may
have been explained that this was deliberately arranged by Zeus, as
Artemis did for Hippe (see p. 51).

(iii) Two other alternatives are recorded elsewhere without
further detail (schol. Arat. 167). One appeals to another tale from
Cretan myth by suggesting that this is the bull that aroused the
passion of Pasiphae. Her husband Minos had aroused the anger of
Poseidon by failing to offer him in sacrifice a magnificent bull that

he had sent up from the sea, and Poseidon responded by contriving that Pasiphae should mate with it and so conceive the Minotaur (Ap. 3.1.3).

(iv) Or this is the bull of Marathon, which Theseus captured while travelling to Athens to claim his throne, and offered in sacrifice to Athena; since it is identified in our source, as often, with the Cretan bull which was fetched by Heracles as his seventh labour, this story too has a Cretan connection.

The Pleiades

(i) This easily distinguishable star-cluster by the Bull was of calendrical importance from an early period, and is mentioned by Homer (*Il.* 18.486) and Hesiod (*Works and Days* 383). The etymology of its very ancient name remains a matter for speculation. In popular lore, the stars in such clusters tend to be identified either with animals, or with maidens, nymphs, and the like. The Greeks chose to view the Pleiades as maidens, and came to identify them more specifically as the seven daughters of Atlas. Hesiod already refers to them as Atalgeneis (born of Atlas) in his *Works and Days* (383), and they are named explicitly as the daughters of Atlas, with their usual names, in a later 'Hesiodic' fragment (fr. 169 MW, cf. Simonides 555 PMG). The name that was assigned to their mother, Pleione, was evidently suggested by that of the Pleiades themselves. Their nature as beings in the sky and in astral myth, in which they are seen as a group of maidens who are associated together as a unit, is inconsistent with the main function that they serve in ordinary myth, as women who become ancestors of notable heroic lines, mainly as a result of liaisons with gods, and thus stand at the head of the Atlantid genealogies (Ap. 3.10.1, etc.)

It was only relatively late that any story came to be offered to explain how these daughters of Atlas came to be placed in the sky. The main story was suggested by the position that they occupy there in relation to the constellation Orion. Since they lie quite close to him and set ahead of him, the notion could arise that he is pursuing them through the sky. When Hesiod remarks that they plunge into the sea to escape him (*Works and Days* 619–20), it is no more than a poetic expression (cf. Pindar, *Nemean Ode* 2.10–12), but that thought provided the starting-point for the development of an astral myth. They wanted to remain virgins, so we are told, and to hunt with Artemis, but they came under pursuit from Orion and appealed to Zeus to transfer them to the stars (schol. *Il.* 18.486). Or in the version recorded by Hyginus, it is their mother Pleione who arouses the lust of Orion, and they come under pursuit too because they are with her. It does seem odd that they should be the ones who are snatched away to become stars, but this version may have been based on an earlier tradition in which Orion was said to have pursued their mother (such a story is ascribed to Pindar, schol. *Nem.* 2.10–12). Although the Epitome makes no mention of such a myth, Eratosthenes would presumably have recounted it in some version, not necessarily that of Hyginus.

(ii) Hyginus also recounts a myth that they shared with the Hyades, in which the members of both groups are sisters who are transferred to the sky after the death of their brother Hyas (see below).

(iii) There is a fragment from Aeschylus (fr. 312N) in which we are told that the Pleiades were so distressed by the sufferings of their father Atlas—who had to hold up the world—that they appear in the heavens as wingless doves (*peleiades*, in reference to a folk etymology for their name). This could be more a poetic fancy than a reference to an astral myth in the proper sense.

(iv) According to a fragment from Moiro (cited by Athenaeus, 491b), a woman poet of the early Hellenistic period, some doves (*peleiades*!) brought ambrosia to the infant Zeus from the waters of the Ocean, while a large eagle brought nectar from a cliff, and Zeus placed both the doves and the eagle in the heavens after rising to power, i.e. as the Pleiades and Eagle, awarding the special honour to the former of announcing the coming of summer and winter.

(v) Otherwise there were myths that were offered to explain why only six of the seven Pleiades are clearly visible. Merope, who married Sisyphos, king of Ephyra/Corinth, hides herself away (Ovid, *Fasti* 4.175–6) or shines faintly as though blushing, because she is ashamed to have been the only sister who married a mortal. Or Electra, the mother of Dardanos and ancestor through him of the Trojan royal line (Ap. 3.12.1), was so distressed by the fall of Troy and the destruction of the Trojan family that she veiled her face with clouds, or ceased to shine, or departed elsewhere to become a comet or the little fox-star (Alcor, Ursa Majoris 80) by the large Bear.

The Hyades

(i) A connection with Dionysos was suggested by the god's cultic title of *Hues*. He was a son of Zeus by the Theban princess Semele, daughter of Cadmos, and was born in peculiar circumstances, because his father stitched him into his thigh after inadvertently causing the death of his pregnant mother, and brought him to birth in due time from his own body (see Ap. 3.4.3); there were two main traditions about what happened to him next, that he was reared either by nymphs or by his mother's sister, Ino, at Thebes, but the two versions could be combined as in Hyginus's narrative. The Hyades are identified there as the nymphs who were initially charged with his care, but these nymphs are said to have handed him over to Ino at some point (presumably because they and the child were coming under threat from the jealous Hera; the Lycourgos story is inserted from another source). The Hyades were already personified as nymphs in the Hesiodic *Astronomy* (fr. 219 MW), which cited five names for them, but it was the early mythographer Pherecydes (fifth century) who developed this story in which they were identified as the Dodonian nymphs who looked after the infant Dionysos; Pherecydes took over the Hesiodic names with additions and an alteration, so that there were now seven. The number of the Hyades varies from two to seven in different sources. A reference to the Dodonian nymphs in the *Vatican Fragments* confirms that Eratosthenes took over the story from Pherecydes. Dodona was in Epirus in north-western Greece, far away from Ino's home-city of Thebes.

(ii) In a joint myth with the Pleiades, they and the Hyades are sisters, and they have a brother Hyas, who was invented to provide an explanation for the name of the Hyades. The sisters became divided into two groups, and so acquired their separate names, as a result of the differing degrees of grief that they felt when Hyas met a premature death during a hunting-trip. Five died quickly of their grief, and so came to be named the Hyades after their brother, while seven died more slowly, and were called the Pleiades because there were more of them (*pleious*). There is an error in the present text of Hyginus's *Astronomy*, which states that there were fifteen sisters rather than twelve, and then compounds the error with an idiocy through the explanation that it offers for the name of the

Pleiades, by presenting them as having formed the more sensitive majority *within* the second group; since the correct number is given for the sisters in Hyginus's other reference to the myth, in *Fabulae* 192, also translated above, the author himself may not have been responsible for this.

(iii) These are the daughters of Cadmos (schol. Arat. 172). There were four of these in the usual tradition, Agave and Autonoe being named in addition to Semele and Ino. Although no details are offered in our source, they were evidently placed in the sky because of their connection with Dionysos, since reference is made once again to the notion that they owed their name to his cultic title of *Hues*.

(iv) Or these are the three daughters of Erechtheus (schol. Arat. 172). When Eumolpos and the Thracians launched an attack against Athens, Erechtheus, an early king of Athens, received an oracle saying that victory could be achieved only through the sacrifice of one of his daughters; he put the youngest to death, but the others then committed suicide because they had sworn to die a common death (Ap. 3.15.4). Our source refers to a lost play about this episode by Euripides, the *Erechtheus*, but that play could hardly have suggested that they became the Hyades, because we know that it indicated that they became the Hyacinthides (fr. 65 Austin), heroines who were honoured in an Athenian cult.

(v) These are the Heliades, the sisters of Phaethon (Claudian 28, 170 ff.). It was said that they so wept for their dead brother (see p. 127 for the circumstances) that they were turned into poplar trees, and their tears became the source of amber (Hyginus, *Fab.* 154). If the Charioteer, who is separated from the Bull and Hyades only by the Twins, was identified with Phaethon, the thought could naturally arise that these star-maidens could be identified as his sisters.

31. ARIES, THE RAM

EPITOME 19. RAM

THIS is the ram that carried away Phrixos and Helle; it was immortal and was given to them by their mother Nephele.* As Hesiod and Pherecydes report,* it had golden fleece. As it was carrying the children over the narrowest strait of the sea, which came to be called the

Hellespont after Helle, it let her fall off, but Poseidon came to her rescue, and slept with her, fathering a son by her, Paion* by name. As for Phrixos, the ram carried him safely to the Black Sea, to the land of Aietes.* Removing its golden fleece, the ram gave it to Aietes as a memento, and then ascended to the stars; for that reason, this constellation looks somewhat faint.

HYGINUS

The Constellation

The Ram stands on the equator* with its head turned toward the east. It sets feet-first, and rises with its head under the Triangle, as mentioned above. Its feet are almost in contact with the head of the Sea-monster. It has one star on its head, three on its horns, two on its neck, and one on its front foot, four between its shoulder-blades, one on its tail, three under its belly, one on its side, and one on its hind foot. That makes seventeen stars in all. (*Astronomy* 3.19)

The Mythology

This is thought to be the ram that carried Phrixos and Helle across the Hellespont. According to Hesiod and Pherecydes, it had a golden fleece; we will speak about that at greater length elsewhere. Helle fell into the Hellespont, was raped by Poseidon, and gave birth to a child who is usually named as Paion, or sometimes as Edonos. Phrixos for his part arrived safely in the land of Aietes, where he sacrificed the ram to Zeus and hung its fleece in the temple; the image of the ram, placed among the constellations by Nephele, marks the time of year when grain is sown, that grain which Ino had previously sown when parched dry, which had been the main cause of the flight [of Phrixos and Helle]. According to Eratosthenes, the ram itself removed its golden fleece and gave it to Phrixos as a memento, and then made its way up to the sky of its own accord; and that is why the constellation, as was remarked above, looks somewhat faint.

According to some accounts, Phrixos was born in the town of Orchomenos in Boeotia; or according to others, he entered the world in the land of the Salonians in Thessaly. Others say that Cretheus and Athamas were sons of Aiolos, along with many others; and some even say that Salmoneus was a son of Athamas and grandson of Aiolos. Cretheus married Demodike,* or in other accounts, Biadike. Seduced by the physical attractions of Phrixos, son of Athamas, she fell in love with him, but could not induce him to respond to her advances; and so, under force of necessity, she made allegations against him to Cretheus, claiming that he had tried to rape her, and making other such charges of the kind that women are accustomed to make. Cretheus was greatly upset by this, as befitted a loving husband and a king, and persuaded Athamas to inflict due punishment on him. But Nephele intervened by snatching away Phrixos and his sister Helle, and placing them on a ram, ordering that they should flee as far as possible across the Hellespont. Helle fell off and paid her debt there to nature, with the result that the Hellespont came to be named after her. Phrixos made his way to Colchis, where, as has already been mentioned, he sacrificed the ram and hung its fleece in a temple. Hermes brought him back to Athamas to convince his father that he had taken flight trusting in his own innocence.

Hermippos recounts, however, that Dionysos, at the time when he was attacking Libya, arrived with his army at a place which is called Ammodes* because there is so much sand there. He thus fell into very grave danger, because he could see that he would have to continue on his way and he was running extremely short of water; as a consequence, the army was falling into a desperate state. As they were considering what they should do, a ram happened to appear in front, roaming around on its own; and at the sight of them, it sought refuge in flight. But the soldiers had noticed it, and even though their progress was made difficult by the dust and heat, they set off in pursuit of the ram, as if trying to snatch booty from the flames, and followed it to the place which would be named after Zeus Ammon after his temple was erected there. When they arrived there, they could find no sign of the ram that they had been following, but they did find what was more to their desire, a plenteous supply of water; and they recovered their strength and immediately reported the matter to Dionysos. At the news, he took his army to that spot* and raised a temple there to Zeus Ammon, with a statue adorned with ram's horns; and he represented the ram among the constellations, placing it such that when the sun is in that sign, all growing things should acquire new vigour, as comes about in springtime, principally because the flight of the ram had given new strength to the army of Dionysos. And furthermore, he wanted to make this the first of the twelve signs because the ram had been the best of guides for his army.

But Leon,* who wrote a history of Egypt, has the following to say

about this statue of Ammon. When Dionysos was ruling over Egypt and the other lands, and was said to have revealed all the arts to the human race, a certain Ammon arrived from Africa and brought him a large flock of sheep, so as to win his favour the more easily and gain a reputation as an inventor. And so Dionysos rewarded him, so it is thought, by granting him a stretch of land lying opposite Egyptian Thebes; and those who make statues of Ammon portray him with a horned head to recall to human memory that he first showed people how to keep sheep. But those who have wished to credit that deed to Dionysos, as something that he did of his own accord without asking it of Ammon, have made horned images of Dionysos, saying that the ram was placed among the constellations in memory of him.*
(*Astronomy* 2.20)

COMMENTARY

(i) This was usually identified as the famous golden-fleeced ram that carried Phrixos to Colchis, at the far end of the Black Sea; the story is recounted at some length by Hyginus (cf. Ap. 1.9.1). Its fleece was hung up in a grove or temple at Colchis, and the fetching of it would provide the motive for the voyage of Jason and the Argonauts. Although some scholars have tried to reinterpret the relevant passage in the Epitome, it seems that Eratosthenes said that the ram stripped itself of its glittering fleece before flying up to the heavens, so providing an explanation for the faintness of the constellation. A conceit of that kind does not seem out of place in this playful genre of myth, and the ram itself was a semi-divine creature that might be thought capable of such an action. In this version there is thus no need for a god to intervene to place the ram in the sky, but Hyginus also cites another in which it was placed there by Nephele (Cloud), the mother of Phrixos, who would have been regarded as a minor goddess. The latter version was introduced to explain why this sign of the zodiac marks the coming of spring, when grain is sown, since its presence could be said to commemorate Ino's parching of the grain, through which she had plotted to cause the death of Nephele's son (see note to p. 94).

(ii) The Egyptian god Amun, who had an important oracle and cult at the oasis of Siwa, was honoured by the Greeks as Zeus Ammon, who was generally portrayed as having ram's horns. In accordance with a common motif in foundation myths, a tale of an animal guide was developed to explain the origin of the god's cult at Siwa and of his horned image. Dionysos represented this guide among the stars as the first and leading sign of the zodiac, and as a spring sign, because the story associated the ram with the bringing of refreshment, in so far as it had guided Dionysos and his army to the oasis; or else Dionysos asked Zeus to place it in the heavens (Hyginus, *Mythical Tales* 33, and various Latin scholia). Servius (on *Aen.* 4.196) records a somewhat different version in which Dionysos prayed to his father Zeus for help in the desert, prompting him to send the ram, and the ram first created the spring at Siwa with a stamp of its hoof (just as Pegasos was said to have created Hippocrene: see p. 50).

32. GEMINI, THE TWINS

EPITOME 10. TWINS

THESE are said to be the Dioscuri. They grew up in Laconia and rose to glory. Surpassing all others in brotherly love, they never contended with one another for anything, whether the throne or anything else; and wanting to commemorate them for the fellowship that united them, Zeus named them the Twins and placed the two of them together in the same place among the stars.

HYGINUS

The Constellation

The Twins can be seen to the right of the Charioteer, above Orion, but in such a way that Orion is positioned between the Bull and the Twins. Their heads are separated* from the rest of their body by the circle which marks the summer, as described above. Holding themselves in an embrace, they set vertically feet-first, but rise obliquely, as though lying down.

The Twin who is set closest to the Crab has one bright star on his head, one bright star on each shoulder, one star on his right elbow, one on each knee, and one on the tip of each foot. The other Twin has one star on his head, one on his left shoulder, another on his right shoulder, one on each nipple, one on his right knee, one on his left knee, one on each foot, and one beneath his left foot, called Propous. (*Astronomy* 3.21)

The Mythology

Many astronomers have said that these are Castor and Pollux, pointing out that, of all brothers, they had the greatest love for one another, for they never contended with one another for supreme power, and never undertook anything without prior agreement. As a reward for their dutiful behaviour, Zeus is supposed to have placed them in the sky as one of the most illustrious constellations. Poseidon rewarded them as a result of the same consideration, giving them horses to ride, and granting them the power to save those who suffer shipwreck.

According to other accounts, these are Heracles and Apollo, and some say indeed that they are Triptolemos (whom we have already mentioned*) and Iasion, who aroused the love of Demeter and were transferred to the sky.

Those who recount the tales of Castor and Pollux add that Castor was killed in front of the town of Aphidnai* when the Spartans were at war with the Athenians. Or others say that he met his death at Sparta when it was under attack from Idas and Lynceus.* According to Homer,* Pollux granted his brother half of his own life; and they thus shine on alternate days.* (*Astronomy* 2.22)

COMMENTARY

(i) The Twins were usually identified as the most famous twins in heroic myth, the Dioscuri (or Dioskouroi in the original Greek form), that is to say, Castor and Pollux (Polydeukes in Greek), the brothers of Helen, Spartan heroes who were also widely honoured in cult. No specific story was recounted in connection with their transference to the sky, Eratosthenes merely stated that Zeus placed them there as exemplars of brotherly love. For a brief account of their adventures and death, see Ap. 3.12.2.

(ii) But some preferred to identify them as another notable pair of twins, Zethos and Amphion (schol. Germ.), the second founders of Thebes. While Cadmos was regarded as the original founder, they were supposed to have founded the lower city, building the celebrated wall with the seven gates (Ap. 3.5.5–6, Pausanias 9.5.3 ff.). Amphion helped his more practical brother to build the wall by moving the stones through the power of his music, and in the present connection the neighbouring Lyre could be seen as his attribute.

(iii) According to three other traditions, two of them recorded by Hyginus, the Twins could be seen as pairs of heroes rather than twins in the strict sense. The first notion, that they are Heracles and Apollo, is also prominent in the astrological and Hermetic literature; its significance is wholly uncertain.

(iv) Or they were Triptolemos and Iasion, two associates of Demeter, the one an Eleusinian whom she appointed to spread her gift of grain (see pp. 39 and 41), the other the lover to whom she bore Ploutos, who symbolized the wealth of the earth (see p. 60 ff.). They would presumably have been placed in the sky by Demeter, in connection with the agricultural benefits that they helped her to confer.

(v) Or Heracles and Theseus (schol. Germ.), two great heroes who performed labours for the benefit of humanity.

(vi) Some said that they were the gods of Samothrace (schol. Germ.), who were thought to bring aid to sailors in distress. Since this was a function also performed by the Dioscuri, the gods of Samothrace were often confused or identified with them, and this account can thus be regarded as a variation on the first.

33. ORION

HESIOD says* that he was the son of Euryale, daughter of Minos, and of Poseidon, and that he was granted the gift of being able to walk over the waves just as though he were on dry land. He came to Chios and raped Merope, daughter of Oinopion,* while drunk; Oinopion learned of this, and in his fury at the outrage, he blinded Orion and expelled him from the land. In the course of his wanderings, Orion arrived at Lemnos, where he made friends with Hephaistos,* who took pity on him and gave him his own servant, Cedalion, as a guide. Orion took him on to his shoulders for him to point the way. Travelling to the east, he made friends with Helios, and was apparently cured by him.* He then returned to Oinopion to take revenge on him, but Oinopion had been hidden beneath the ground by the people of the land; abandoning all hope of being able to find him, Orion went off to Crete, where he devoted himself to the hunt, pursuing wild beasts in the company of Artemis and Leto.* It seems that he threatened to kill every wild beast that appeared on the earth, so angering Earth that she sent out an enormous scorpion, which struck him with its sting, causing his death. And so Zeus set him among the constellations out of regard for his bravery, at the request of Artemis and Leto, also placing the scorpion there to commemorate this episode.

Others say that when Orion grew up, he conceived a passion for Artemis, and that it was she who sent the scorpion against him which stung him and caused his death. The gods, taking pity on him, represented him in the sky as a constellation along with the scorpion, in commemoration of the episode.

HYGINUS

The Constellation

Orion. His belt and the rest of his body are separated [from the upper part of him] by the equator. He is placed as though in confrontation with the Bull, holding a club in his right hand, and with a sword at his waist; he is looking toward the west. He sets at the rising of the hind part of the Scorpion, and rises with his whole body at the same time as the Crab. He has three bright stars on his head, one star on each shoulder, a faint star on his right elbow, a similar star on his hand, three stars on his belt, three faint ones where his sword is depicted, and one bright one on each knee. In all, seventeen. (*Astronomy* 3.33)

The Mythology

According to Hesiod, this is the son who was borne to Poseidon by Euryale, daughter of Minos; he was granted the power to run over the waves as though he were on dry land, just as Iphiclos* is supposed to have been able to run over ears of corn without breaking them.

Aristomachos says for his part that there was a certain Hyrieus* who lived at Thebes (although Pindar places him on the island of Chios), who asked Zeus and Hermes, when they were once visiting him, that he might have a child. So that his request might have more prospect of success, he sacrificed an ox and served it up to them at table. Afterwards, Zeus and Hermes asked that the hide should be removed from the ox, and they shed their semen* on the hide, and ordered that it should be buried beneath the ground. And from it there was later born a child, whom Hyrieus named Urion because of his origin; but euphony and custom have brought it to pass that he is called Orion.

He went from Thebes to Chios, so the story goes, where he raped Merope, daughter of Oinopion, while his passions were inflamed by wine. As a result of that action he was blinded by Oinopion and expelled from the island. He is then supposed to have visited Hephaistos on Lemnos, and from him he received a guide named Cedalion. Carrying this Cedalion on his shoulders, he made his way to Helios, so the story goes, who cured him [of his blindness]; and he then returned to Chios to seek revenge. But Oinopion was kept safe underground by the citizens of his land. Giving up hope of being able to find him, Orion went off to the island of Crete, where he went hunting with Artemis, and he made the boast that we mentioned above and thus came to be transferred to the stars. According to other accounts, however, Orion lived with Oinopion on all too friendly terms, and wanting to prove to him what a great passion he had for hunting, he made the boast to Artemis that we mentioned above, and so met his death. Others, including Callimachus, say that he tried to rape Artemis, who transfixed him with her arrows, and he was depicted in the sky because of the passion that they shared for hunting.

According to Istros,* Artemis loved Orion and is supposed to have come close to marrying him. But Apollo was annoyed by this, and reproached the goddess repeatedly but to no effect. On noticing Orion swimming so far out one day that only his head could be seen, he bet Artemis that she would be unable to shoot an arrow into the dark object that could be seen in the sea. Since she was anxious to be regarded as a most skilful archer, she shot off an arrow and pierced Orion's head. When the waves washed his body ashore, Artemis felt great remorse at having shot him, and shedding many a tear over his death, she placed him among the constellations, so it is thought. As to what Artemis did after his death, we will speak of that when recounting her stories. (*Astronomy* 2.34)

COMMENTARY

This imposing figure in the sky is already identified as Orion in the Homeric epics. 'Mighty Orion' is mentioned among the constellations on the shield of Achilles (*Il.* 18.486), and the neighbouring star Sirius is described as his dog (*Il.* 22.27–9). Both then and later, he was renowned above all as a hunter. Odysseus sees him in the Underworld driving ghostly beasts over the asphodel, with a bronze cudgel in his hands (*Od.* 11.572 ff.), and the Bear in the heavens is said to be keeping a wary eye on him (*Od.* 5.273–4). Starting with the dog-star and then the constellation of which it came to form part, a hunting-scene was constructed in which he can be seen continuing his favourite activity in the sky too, as he chases after admittedly modest prey, the Hare.

During his life on earth, Orion was associated primarily with Boeotia in east-central Greece, but he was also said to have gone hunting on the Greek islands, and indeed to have benefited the inhabitants of many places by clearing them of wild beasts (Corinna 673 PMG). In the course of time, his main stories were ordered into a biographical narrative, as summarized in similar terms by Hyginus and Apollodorus (1.4.3–4): he starts his life in Boeotia, and then travels to the island of Chios and further abroad, before becoming a hunting-companion of Artemis on Crete, where he finally meets his death. His myths centre around his activities as a hunter, and around the most notable features of his character, a tendency to violence and lack of self-control, for he always continued to be pictured as a rather crude and primitive figure, by comparison to more sophisticated heroes like Perseus and Theseus. On Chios, he thus clears the island of wild beasts and snakes, but goes on to rape the king's daughter; in the version that may well come closest to the earliest tradition, she is promised to him in marriage as a reward for his services, and he finally turns to violence when the king shrinks from fulfilling his side of the bargain, being revolted at the thought of having such a man as his son-in-law (Parthenius 30).

This tendency to excess is also a central factor in the stories relating to his death, which are our main concern in the present context. For he provokes his own death, either by taking his ambitions as a slayer of wild beasts to such an extreme that he boasts that he will slay every one of them, or because he dares to lay hands on the goddess Artemis. Although the *Odyssey* (5.121–4) states that she killed him with her arrows because the gods disapproved of his love affair with the goddess Eos, he becomes a hunting-companion of Artemis in the subsequent tradition, and that is a vital element in the accounts of his death, which fall into three categories.

(i) While he is hunting on Crete with Artemis and her mother Leto, he threatens to kill every wild beast on the earth, provoking Earth to cause his death by sending a huge scorpion against him; but he is then placed in the sky by Zeus at the request of Artemis and Leto. Such was the account offered by Eratosthenes, who apparently used the Hesiodic *Astronomy* (a work written after Hesiod's lifetime) as the source for his narrative, although we cannot be certain that the catasterism was already included in that work. This remained the dominant tradition thereafter. The idea that Orion was killed by a scorpion was not derived from anything in his standard mythology, but was suggested by the position that his constellation occupies in relation to the Scorpion in the sky, which rises as Orion sets, and thus seems to pursue him through the sky. In Ovid's version (*Fasti* 5.537 ff.), the scorpion attacks Leto, and Orion meets his death when he stands in the way to protect her; and it is Leto who places him in the heavens. There were also versions in which Artemis and Leto share Earth's anger at Orion's boast (schol. Germ.), or even send the scorpion them-selves (schol. Nicander *Ther.* 15).

(ii) Or else Orion provoked his death by trying to rape Artemis. Hyginus mentions that Callimachus described her as having shot him with her arrows for that reason, but does not make clear whether that poet went on to explain how he came to be placed in the sky. Aratus (635 ff.) recounts that Artemis punished him by splitting open a hill to send the scorpion against him, just as Earth was supposed to have done, but he was apparently not the inventor of this hybrid version of the myth, if the mythographer Palaiphatos, who also reports it (*Incredible Stories* 51), can be rightly dated to the fourth century. Although Aratus remarks that Orion can be seen fleeing from the scorpion in the sky, he does not explain how Orion came to be placed there. Eratosthenes cited Aratus's story as an alternative account of the death of Orion, add-ing that the gods had commemorated the episode by placing him and the scorpion in the sky.

(iii) Hyginus also records an exceptional account in which Orion commits no offence, at least in the conventional sense of the word, and the scorpion makes no appearance. In this deliberately unconventional version, invented by the poet Istros (mid third century), Artemis is said to have fallen in love with Orion, much to the disapproval of her brother Apollo, who incited her to shoot him without realizing what she is aiming at; and filled with remorse afterwards, she placed him in the sky.

34. CETUS, THE SEA-MONSTER

EPITOME 36. SEA-MONSTER

THIS is the monster that Poseidon sent to Cepheus because Cassiepeia had claimed to rival the Nereids in beauty. Perseus killed it, and that is why it was set among the constellations to commemor-ate his exploit. Sophocles, the author of tragedies, tells the story in his *Andromeda*.

HYGINUS

The Constellation

The Sea-monster, which is cut through the middle of its tail by the winter tropic, looks toward the east and almost touches the hind foot of the Ram with its mouth. The front of its body, which faces toward the east, seems almost to be washed by the river Eridanos. It sets at the rising of the Crab and the Lion, and rises with the Bull and the Twins. It has two faint stars at the end of its tail, five from there up to the curve of the rest of its body, and five under its belly, making thirteen in all. (*Astronomy* 3.30)

The Mythology

Poseidon sent it [the Sea-monster] to attack Andromeda, whom we have already discussed; but it was killed by Perseus, and it was then placed among the constellations because of its enormous size and that hero's courage. (*Astronomy* 2.31)

COMMENTARY

This is the final constellation in the Perseus–Andromeda group (see p. 15), set at a safe distance from the others in the southern sky.

35. DELPHINUS, THE DOLPHIN

EPITOME 31. DOLPHIN

IT is said to have been placed among the constellations for the following reason. When Poseidon wanted to take Amphitrite as his wife, she stole away and fled to Atlas,* being anxious to preserve her virginity; and when she had hidden herself away, most of the Nereids* followed her example. Poseidon sent many out in search of her, the dolphin among them. In the course of its wanderings, it arrived at the islands of Atlas, and coming across Amphitrite there, it sent news of this to Poseidon, and carried her to him. Poseidon married her and granted the dolphin the highest honours of the sea; he declared it to be sacred, and placed an image of it among the constellations. And all who want to give pleasure to Poseidon portray him with a dolphin in his hand, so conferring the highest honour on it for its good deed.

HYGINUS

The Constellation

The Dolphin is represented not far from the constellation of the Eagle, and it touches that circumference of the equator with the tip of the curve of its tail, while its head almost touches the muzzle of the horse Pegasos.* It rises with the first part of the Archer, and sets when the Maiden has risen as far as her head.

It has two stars on its head, two stars above its head in the direction of its neck, three stars on its belly, where something like fins can be seen, one on its back, and two on its tail. In all, nine stars. (*Astronomy* 3.16)

The Mythology

The reason for its [the Dolphin's] presence among the stars is explained as follows by Eratosthenes and others: when Poseidon wanted to take Amphitrite as his wife, and she wanted to retain her virginity and fled to Atlas, he sent out many men in search of her, including one called Delphinus,* who, after having roamed from isle to isle, finally came upon the girl, and persuaded her to marry Poseidon, arranging the wedding in person. By way of a reward, Poseidon placed an image of a dolphin among the constellations. And furthermore, we see that those who make statues of Poseidon place a dolphin either in his hand or beneath his foot, thinking that this will be most pleasing to that god.

According to Aglaosthenes, the author of the *Naxica*, there were some Tyrrhenian shipmasters* who took Dionysos away when he was still a child, along with his companions, to convey him to Naxos and entrust him to the nymphs who were to be his nurses. For as our authors and many Greeks too have said in their theogonies, he was brought up by those nymphs. But to return to the matter in hand, the shipmasters were induced by hope of gain to want to turn the ship on to another course. Dionysos gained wind of their plan, however, and told his companions to sing together in a common strain, and the unaccustomed sounds so enchanted the Tyrrhenians that they began to dance, and in their desire to leap around, they unwittingly threw themselves into the sea, and there they were turned into dolphins. Wanting to recall their actions to human memory, Dionysos placed an image of them among the stars.

Others say, however, that this is the dolphin that carried the citharode* Arion from the Sicilian Sea to Tainaron.* As a musician who surpassed all others in his skill, he was travelling around the islands to make money, but his young slaves, thinking that it would suit their advantage better to gain freedom through treachery than continue in tranquil servitude, devised a plan to throw their master into the sea and divide his property between them. On recognizing their intent, Arion asked them, not as a master might ask his slaves or an innocent man might ask criminals, but as a father would ask his sons, to be allowed to wear the robes that he had often worn as a victor, because there was no one other than himself who would be better able to mark his own end with a fitting lament. When his request was granted, he immediately picked up his lyre and began to lament his own death, and attracted by the harmonies, dolphins came swimming from every part of the sea to listen to the singing of Arion. Invoking the power of the immortal gods, he hurled himself down among them, and one of them took him on to its back and carried him to the shore at Tainaron. In commemoration of this episode, an image of a dolphin can be seen to be attached to the statue of Arion* that was erected there. As for the slaves who supposed they had gained freedom from their servitude, they were driven by a storm to Tainaron, where they were captured by their master and subjected to no slight punishment. (*Astronomy* 2.17)

Alternative account

Since Arion of Methymna was very skilled in the art of singing to the cithara, Pyranthus,* king of Corinth held him in very high regard. After he had asked the king's permission to display his art from city to city, and had acquired a considerable fortune, his servants and the sailors [on the ship on which he was travelling back from Sicily] plotted together to kill him. Apollo appeared to him in his sleep and told him to sing in his robes and crown, and to entrust himself to those who would come to his aid. So when the servants and sailors were about to kill him, he asked that he should be allowed to sing beforehand. On hearing the sound of his lyre and his voice, dolphins began to gather around the ship, and when Arion caught sight of them, he hurled himself into the waves. They took him on to their back and carried him to Corinth, to King Pyranthus. When he was set ashore, he was so eager to proceed on his way that he failed to push the dolphin back into the sea, and it died there. After he had recounted his misfortunes to Pyranthus, the king ordered that the dolphin should be buried, and that a monument should be raised to it.

Shortly afterwards Pyranthus was informed that the ship on which Arion had been travelling had been driven to Corinth by a storm.

He ordered that the sailors should be brought to him, and asked them about Arion, but they said that he had died and that they had seen to his burial. The king replied, 'You can swear to that tomorrow in front of the dolphin's monument.'* He then ordered that they should be kept under guard, and told Arion to hide himself away in the dolphin's monument early on the following day, dressed as he had been when he had thrown himself into the sea. When the king brought the sailors there and told them to swear by the departed spirit of the dolphin that Arion was dead, Arion emerged from the monument in front of their eyes. Wondering to what divine intervention he had owed his rescue, they were unable to utter a word. The king ordered that they should be crucified* on the dolphin's monument, while Apollo for his part arranged that Arion, because of his skill in the art of the cithara, should be placed among the stars along with the dolphin. (*Mythical Tales* 174, Arion)

COMMENTARY

(i) Dolphins were associated with the sea-god Poseidon as his special beast, and he was often represented with them in works of art. To provide a more specific explanation for why he should have wished to place a dolphin in the sky, Eratosthenes provided a myth, quite possibly of his own invention, in which a dolphin helped him to win his reluctant bride, the Nereid Amphitrite. She is mentioned as his consort by Hesiod (*Theogony* 390), but there is no earlier record of the present story; there is otherwise a tale in which Poseidon is said to have abducted her from the island of Naxos, when she emerged from the sea to dance there with her sisters (schol. *Od.* 3.91). Hyginus offers what is in effect a rationalized version of the myth, by attributing the relevant actions to a man called Delphinus (Dolphin), evidently as the result of a misinterpretation of the Greek text on which his narrative was founded.

(ii) There was a famous myth of early origin in which some sailors tried to abduct the young Dionysos, who responded by driving them into a frenzy, and causing them to leap into the sea and turn into dolphins (*Homeric Hymn* 7, to Dionysos, cf. Ovid, *Metamorphoses* 3.528–691); a catasterism could easily be added through the suggestion that Dionysos commemorated the episode by placing an image of a dolphin in the sky.

(iii) Tales in which dolphins make friends with human beings or come to their rescue had the same appeal in ancient times as they do nowadays (e.g. Pliny, *Natural History* 9.28 ff.). The most famous story of that kind, though admittedly not the most authentic, was that in which Arion of Lesbos, a lyric poet of the seventh century who worked at the court of Periandros, tyrant of Corinth, was rescued by a dolphin in the circumstances described by Hyginus; the tale was recounted by Herodotus (1.23–4), and then retold with many variations thereafter. Hyginus records two versions of the catasterism that could be added to explain the origin of the constellation—a rationalistic account in which the constellation-figure was devised by astronomers to commemorate the incident, and a mythical account in which the dolphin itself was set in the sky by Apollo, who could be thought to have taken an interest in Arion as the god of music. When Hyginus suggests in his *Mythical Tales* that Arion was placed in the sky along with the dolphin, he has clearly fallen into error, for it was his musical instrument that was placed there, as the neighbouring constellation of the Lyre (Serv. *Ecl.* 8.55). He would have sung his poems to the cithara, a form of lyre.

36, 37, 38. HYDRA, THE WATER-SNAKE, with CRATER, THE BOWL, and CORVUS, THE CROW

EPITOME 41. WATER-SNAKE, ON WHICH THE BOWL AND CROW ARE SET.

THIS constellation is combined with others because of a remarkable episode. The crow is honoured in association with Apollo, for each of the gods has a bird that is consecrated to him. When the gods were once preparing to offer a sacrifice, the crow was sent to fetch water for use in a libation, and on seeing a fig-tree by the spring which bore figs which were not yet ripe, the crow waited for them to ripen. When, after a certain length of time, the figs had ripened and the crow had eaten them, it realized that it had committed a fault, and snatching up the water-snake that was in the spring, the crow carried it off along with the cup, and claimed that the snake had drunk all the water that the spring had brought forth each day. But Apollo, who realized what had really happened, imposed due punishment on the crow, by causing it to suffer thirst among men during that time of year, as Aristotle has recorded in his treatise *On Animals*.* To ensure that the offence that the crow had committed against the gods would be clearly remembered, Apollo represented amongst the constellations the Water-snake, the Bowl, and the Crow, which can neither drink [from the Bowl] nor approach it.

HYGINUS

The Constellation

The Water-snake, which extends over the length of three constellations, the Crab, Lion, and Maiden, is located between the equator and the winter tropic, in such a way that its head—which stretches toward the constellation known as Procyon—and almost a quarter of the entire snake can be seen between the winter tropic and the equator. The end of its tail almost touches the head of the Centaur, and [on its back] it carries the Crow, which pecks at it with its beak and stretches out its entire body toward the Bowl, which is set some distance away, almost between the Lion and the Maiden, leaning somewhat toward the head of the Water-snake. The Snake sets at the rising of the Water-pourer and the Fishes, and rises with the signs that we have just mentioned above.

It has three small stars on its head, six on the first curve after its head, of which the last is the brightest, and three stars on the second curve, four on the third, two on the fourth, and nine on the fifth up to the end of its tail, all of them faint. In all, twenty-seven.

The Crow has one star on its throat, two on its wing, two below the wing toward its tail, and one on each foot. In all, seven.

The Bowl, positioned above the first coil from the snake's head, has two stars on its rim, two faint stars on its handles, two in the middle of the cup, and two at its base. That makes eight in all. (*Astronomy* 3.39)

The Mythology

On [the Water-snake] the Crow is perched and the Bowl is set, so it is thought; the following story has been handed down in explanation of it. When Apollo, under whose protection the crow stands, was once offering a sacrifice, he sent the bird to a spring to fetch some pure water. On seeing several fig-trees there whose fruit was not yet ripe, it settled on one of the trees to wait for it to ripen; and some days later, after the figs were ready and the crow had eaten a good number of them, Apollo, who was waiting, saw it arrive in all haste with a bowl full of water. To punish it for its fault in having delayed for so long, Apollo, who had been obliged to use other water because of what the crow had done, inflicted the following disgrace on it, so the story goes: throughout the period while figs are ripening, the crow is unable to drink, because it has a sore throat during that time of year. So wanting to portray the thirst of the crow, the god placed the bowl among the constellations, setting the water-snake beneath it to hold back the thirsty crow. For the Crow seems to be pecking at the end of its tail, so as to be granted access to the Bowl.

According to Istros and several others, Coronis* was the daughter of Phlegyas, and she bore Asclepios to Apollo, but Ischys, son of Elatos, later slept with her; and the crow saw this, and reported the matter to Apollo. As a bearer of bad news, Apollo turned it black, instead of white as before, and he transfixed Ischys with his arrows.

As regards the Bowl, Phylarchos* recounts the following tale about it. In the Chersonnese, near Troy, where many authors have said that the tomb of Protesilaos* is to be found, there lies a city called Elaiousa. While it was under the rule of a certain Demophon, it was suddenly struck by a plague which caused the citizens to die in extraordinary numbers. Demophon, being greatly disturbed by this, sent a deputation to the oracle of Apollo to seek a remedy for the devastation; and the oracle responded by saying that a maiden of noble birth should be sacrificed to the guardian deities of the city each year. Demophon chose them by lot from all the girls apart from his own daughters, and had them killed, until the day came when a citizen of very noble birth took exception to Demophon's procedure, and refused to allow his own daughter to be entered into the draw unless the daughters of the king were also included. This so enraged the king that he had the man's daughter put to death without drawing any lots. Mastousios (for that was the name of the girl's father) pretended not to take offence at this for the present out of patriotic feeling, since she might have been drawn by lot afterwards and put to death; and by degrees that king came to forget the episode. And so when the father of the young girl had made a show of being just about the best friend of the king, he said that he was going to offer an annual sacrifice and invited the king and his daughters to the ceremony. Suspecting nothing untoward, the king sent his daughters on ahead; being held back for his own part by affairs of state, he would come along later. Everything worked out just as Mastousios had hoped, he killed the king's daughters, mixed their blood in with some wine in a bowl, and when the king arrived, had this served up to him as a drink. When the king asked after his daughters and discovered what had happened to them, he ordered that Mastousios should be thrown into the sea together with the bowl. As a consequence, the sea into which he was thrown was named the Mastousian Sea in memory of him; and the harbour is known as Crater (the Bowl) to this day. The ancient astronomers represented it in the sky to remind people that no one can profit with impunity from a crime, and that personal hatreds cannot usually be forgotten.

Others claim, along with Eratosthenes, that this is the bowl that Icarios made use of when he revealed wine to human beings; and others that it is the jar into which Ares was thrown by Otos and Ephialtes. (*Astronomy* 2.40)

COMMENTARY

(i) The crow was regarded as a messenger of Apollo from an early period (Hes. fr. 40), and it had a well-known myth associated with it, a 'just-so story' in which the god was said to have turned the bird black for reporting bad news (Ap. 2.5.2). The hoarse croaking of crows was interpreted as a sign of thirst, and a story of similar nature was devised to account for that too, in which Apollo was said to have punished it with that thirst because it had once delayed to feed when it was sent to fetch water for a sacrifice (Aelian, *Nature of Animals* 1.47; in this version it waited for some corn to ripen, and then claimed that a snake had blocked the spring). Eratosthenes made use of this story, which was plainly not of his own invention, to provide a joint mythical explanation for the origin of this group of three constellations, the Water-snake along with the Crow and Bowl (which Aratus had already described as being closely inter-connected, 448–9), by suggesting that Apollo had placed the entire group in the sky to commemorate the disgrace of the crow. The crow had compounded its fault by trying to lie to the god of prophecy, a point that is underlined in Ovid's account (*Fasti* 2.243 ff.).

(ii) Two further explanations were offered for the origin of the Water-snake, taken on its own, both reported in schol. Arat. 443. (*a*) It is the hydra of Lerna which was killed by Heracles as his second labour (see pp. 66–7), an idea that seems to have found little favour, probably because that beast differed from the constellation

figure in being pictured as a many-headed monster. (*b*) As a figure with a winding course, this could also be interpreted as being
a river, and it was suggested accordingly that it represents the Nile;
in support of that notion, an ingenious scheme was developed in
which different sections of the constellation were aligned to different signs of the zodiac, and thence to the changes in the level of the
Nile at different times of the year.

(iii) As for the Bowl, Hyginus records three alternative myths
for that constellation taken in isolation. (*a*) One is an obscure
local legend set in the city of Elaiousa at the southern end of the
Chersonnese opposite Troy, a tale devised to explain the name
of the harbour there, which was called the Bowl of the Achaeans
(pseudo-Scylax 96), evidently because of its bowl-like shape. This
was a revenge-tale with no pretence to originality, following the
pattern of the famous myth of Atreus and Thyestes (Ap. Epit.
2.10–13). To work the bowl-like constellation into that legend, it
was suggested that ancient astronomers had devised the figure in
the sky to point the moral of the tale. (*b*) Or this is the bowl that
was used by Icarios when he was spreading Dionysos' gift of wine;
in that case, this constellation is worked into the astral myth that
identified Bootes and the Maiden with Icarios and Erigone (see
pp. 37–8). (*c*) Or this was the vessel, strictly a large bronze jar, in
which Otos and Ephialtes—two giants who entered into conflict
with the gods, trying to storm Olympos among other things (Ap.
1.7.4)—had once imprisoned the god Ares for thirteen months, an
episode that was recorded by Homer, though without any explanation of the circumstances (*Il.* 5.385–91).

39. CANIS MAJOR, THE GREAT DOG

EPITOME 33. DOG

IT is recounted that this is the dog that was given to Europa* for her
protection, along with the lance.* Minos came to possess both of them,
and later, when he was cured of an illness by Procris, he passed them
on to Procris as a gift; and subsequently Cephalos gained possession
of both of them, as the husband of Procris. He went to Thebes, taking
the dog with him, to hunt the fox,* which, so an oracle had declared,
could not be killed by anyone whatever. Zeus, being at a loss as to what

to do, turned the fox to stone, and raised up the dog to set it among the constellations, judging it to be worthy of that honour.

But others say that this is the dog of Orion, which accompanied him when he was out hunting, in accordance with the general opinion that such an animal protects all hunters against wild beasts. The dog was raised up to the stars when Orion ascended there, and that doubtless came about because it had never abandoned Orion in any of his adventures.

HYGINUS

The Constellation

The Dog, which is pursuing the fleeing Hare, has its hind feet cut off by the winter tropic. The right foot of Orion almost comes into contact with its head, which looks toward the west but is turned toward the equator. It sets at the rising of the Archer, and rises with the Crab. This Dog has one star on its tongue, which is called the dog-star, and on its head another star which some people call Sirius, which we have already spoken about. It has, furthermore, a faint star on each ear, two stars on its chest, three on its hind foot, three between its shoulder-blades, one on its left hip, one on its hind foot, one on its left foot, and four on its tail. In all, nineteen. (*Astronomy* 3.34)

The Mythology

It is said that Zeus appointed [the Dog] to be a guard for Europa, and that it later came into the possession of Minos. When Minos fell ill, he was cured,* so they say, by Procris, the wife of Cephalos, and he gave her the dog as a reward for her services, since she was very fond of hunting and the dog had been granted the power of never failing to catch its prey. After her death the dog came to be owned by Cephalos, because Procris had been his wife. He took it with him when he went to Thebes.* There was a fox there which had been granted the power, so they say, of being able to escape from all dogs; and so when the two animals were brought together, Zeus was at a loss as to what to do, so Istros recounts, and turned both of them to stone.*

Or according to other accounts, this was Orion's dog, and because Orion had such a passion for hunting, it was placed among the constellations along with him. Others again say that this was the dog of Icarios,* whom we have already discussed. These many suggestions have their proponents.

Now the Dog has a star on its tongue which is itself called the Dog, and on its head another star* which Isis is supposed to have placed there under her own name, calling it Sirius because of the brilliance of its light, for it is of such a nature that it seems to outshine all other stars. And so, to make it more easily recognizable, she called it Sirius. (*Astronomy* 2.35)

COMMENTARY

The Great Dog

(i) This is Orion's dog. The brightest star in the constellation, Sirius, was initially identified as such, and the constellation was then constructed by adding other stars from the same region. With the addition of the Hare, a hunting-scene was built up in the sky, so that Orion could be seen still pursuing his favourite activity there, as Homer had portrayed him as doing in the Underworld (*Od.* 11.572 ff.). No specific story was developed to explain how the dog came to be placed in the sky, it was simply assumed that it was transferred together with its master, as a kind of attribute. Eratosthenes favoured the other Dog for this role (see pp. 64–5), and looked elsewhere to provide a proper astral myth for this greater one.

(ii) According to a myth that goes back to early epic (*Epigonoi* fr. 5 PEG; full later accounts in Antoninus Liberalis 41, Ovid, *Metamorphoses* 7.763 ff.), the Thebans were once persecuted by the fearsome Teumessian fox, which was fated never to be caught, and an intolerable contradiction arose when Cephalos, son of Deion, arrived from Athens with a dog which was fated always to catch its prey and set it in pursuit of the fox; so Zeus was obliged to resolve the problem by turning both beasts to stone. Eratosthenes needed to make only a slight alteration to the story, by saying that Zeus may have turned the fox to stone but judged the dog worthy of being transferred to the heavens, presumably because it was a wondrous beast that he himself had once assigned to protect his mistress Europa. Hyginus fails to make any mention of the catasterism, merely citing a Hellenistic poet for the traditional version in which the dog too was turned to stone; the present version is found only in literature relating to astronomy. We are told elsewhere that Procris was already married to Cephalos when she met Minos, having fled to Crete when her husband discovered that she had been unfaithful to him, and she passed the wonder-dog on to him when they later became reconciled, after she had engaged in a love affair with Minos (Ap. 3.15.1, Antoninus Liberalis 41). Cephalos was subsequently invited to bring his dog to Thebes to hunt the fox, or else he settled there when he was obliged to leave his native Attica after accidentally killing his wife in a hunting-accident.

Sirius

Although the dog-star Sirius (or Seirios in Greek form) was the original dog of Orion before the constellation was devised, and it was later said that the myths of that constellation could be applied to that star too (schol. Arat. 2.517), there was an important myth that was applied to this star in its specific nature as a heat-bringing star. For it was imagined to exert that effect because the period that followed its early rising was the hottest time of the year. In the myth of Icarios, as developed by Eratosthenes, the dog of Icarios led his daughter Erigone to his body, and jumped into a well after she killed herself (see p. 38). It is stated in that narrative that the dog was called Maira (a name that was applied to Sirius during the period of its greatest heat), and that it was finally transferred to the heavens to become the dog-star.

During the dog-days of summer, the heat was moderated to some extent in the Aegean region by the Etesian (i.e. Annual) winds, northerlies which were supposed to blow for forty days. On the small island of Ceos, to the south-east of Attica, annual rites were conducted to summon these winds, involving sacrifices to Zeus Ikmaios ('of Moisture') and to Sirius itself. Legend claimed that the rites had been introduced by Aristaios, son of Apollo and Cyrene, a culture hero from Boeotia, who had sailed to Ceos at the bidding of his father's oracle at Delphi (A.R. 2, 516 ff., Diodorus 4.82); and in a coda to the tale of Icarios and Erigone, Eratosthenes wove this originally independent myth into theirs. He explained the heat of the dog-days by saying that the men of Attica who killed Icarios took refuge in Ceos, and that his dog, in its new nature as a star, scorched the island because the Ceans had harboured them, causing famine and disease. When Aristaios—who is already there as their king in this version—consulted the Delphic oracle, he was told to atone for the death of Icarios through sacrifices, and to found the aforementioned cult to bring the cooling winds (see Hyginus's narrative on pp. 38–9).

40–46. CONSTELLATIONS BETWEEN THE WINTER TROPIC AND THE ANTARCTIC CIRCLE

40. ARA, THE ALTAR

EPITOME 39. ALTAR

THIS is the altar on which the gods swore alliance for the first time when Zeus was about to wage war against Cronos. After succeeding in their enterprise, the gods placed the altar in the sky in commemoration. Men also bring an altar to their banquets, and offer sacrifice on it when they have decided to swear an agreement with one another; they touch it with their right hand, regarding this as a guarantee of their good faith.

The Vatican Fragments add after the first sentence:

The Cyclopes had fashioned it, covering the flame to ensure that the power of the thunderbolt* should not be seen.

HYGINUS

The Constellation

The Altar, which almost touches the antarctic circle, is located between the head of the Victim and the end of the Scorpion's tail. It sets at the rising of the Ram, and rises with Capricorn. It has two stars on top of the incense-burner that is depicted on it, and two others at the bottom, so four in all. (*Astronomy* 3.38)

The Mythology

It was on this altar that the gods are supposed to have offered the first sacrifice, and to have sworn their alliance when they were about to make war against the Titans; it was made by the Cyclopes. This was the origin, so it is said, of the practice among human beings, when they are contemplating any enterprise, of offering sacrifice before they embark on it. (*Astronomy* 2.39)

COMMENTARY

(i) The Altar was of some importance as a weather-sign, and Aratus (408 ff.) tells us that the goddess Night placed it in the sky for that purpose, out of pity for human sufferings, but that is no more than a manner of poetic expression, and the only proper astral myth recorded for it is that in which it is said to be the archetypal altar, built by the Cyclopes, on which Zeus and his fellow gods swore their alliance before setting out to confront the Titans, in the war that led to the establishment of the present order of the world. This tale, which is of the simplest kind, was almost certainly devised by Eratosthenes. These Cyclopes were not the one-eyed giants encountered by Odysseus, but primordial deities, sons of Sky and Earth, who carried out work for gods of later birth as smiths: see also p. 53.

(ii) The Altar could otherwise be regarded as an attribute of the Centaur, a neighbouring constellation usually identified as Cheiron. That Centaur is pictured as holding a beast or sacrificial victim in his hands, and it could be supposed that the pious Cheiron is bringing the Beast forward to sacrifice it on the Altar (thus schol. Arat. 408, citing *Il.* 11.833, where Cheiron is described as the most righteous of the Centaurs). Or alternatively (schol. Arat. 408) the Beast could be said to symbolize the hunt, for Cheiron was a great hunter too, and the Altar to symbolize the marriage of Peleus and Thetis (the parents of Achilles), which was celebrated in Cheiron's cave in the presence of both gods and mortals. Or because the Centaur Pholos, who was sometimes said to be represented in the constellation of that name, was skilled in divination, he was depicted bringing a victim to the Altar when he was placed among the constellations (see Hyginus on p. 121)

41, 42. CENTAURUS, THE CENTAUR, and LUPUS, THE WOLF, originally known as THE BEAST

EPITOME 40. CENTAUR

It would seem that this is Cheiron who lived on Mount Pelion; he surpassed all human beings in righteousness, and was the tutor of Asclepios and Achilles. Heracles is supposed to have visited him because of the love that he felt for him, and to have lived on intimate terms with him in his cave, honouring Pan. He was the only Centaur whom he did not kill, paying heed instead to what he had to say, as Antisthenes,* the follower of Socrates, recounts in his *Heracles*. After they had been living together for quite a long time, an arrow slipped out of Heracles' quiver and fell on to Cheiron's foot, causing his death. On account of his piety and unfortunate end, Zeus placed him among the constellations.

In the Centaur's hands, near the Altar, there lies the Beast, and the Centaur seems to be bringing it forward for sacrifice, which serves as a most conspicuous indication of his piety.

HYGINUS

The Constellation

He is depicted in such a way that he seems to be pressing against the antarctic circle with his feet and supporting the winter tropic with his shoulders. With his head he almost touches the tail of the Water-snake. In his right hand he is holding a beast killed for sacrifice, which is hanging down and touches the winter tropic with its feet and the end of its muzzle, being situated between that and the antarctic circle. The Centaur's shins are separated from the rest of his body by the milky circle. He looks toward the east, and sets entirely at the rising of the Water-pourer and the Fishes, while he rises with the Scorpion and the Archer.

He has three faint stars above his head, one bright star on each shoulder, one star on his left elbow, one on his hand, one in the middle of his equine chest, one on each hind knee-bend, four between his shoulder-blades, two bright ones on his belly, three on his tail, one on his equine rump, one on each back knee, and one on each shin. In all, twenty-four.

The sacrificial beast for its part has two stars on its tail, one on the first of its back paws and one between the two paws, a bright star between its shoulder-blades, one on the front of its paws, another below, and three distributed across its head. In all, ten. (*Astronomy* 3.37)

The Mythology

This is said to be Cheiron, son of Cronos and Philyra, who surpassed not only the other Centaurs in righteousness, but also human beings, and is supposed to have reared Asclepios and Achilles. And so as a result of his piety and diligence, he came to be included among the constellations. One day, when Heracles was staying with him, and was examining his arrows while sitting with him, one of them fell on to Cheiron's foot, so the story goes, and caused his death. Others say, however, that the Centaur was amazed that Heracles had been able to kill creatures as heavily built as the Centaurs with such small arrows, and tried for his own part to shoot with the bow; and as he was doing so, the arrow slipped from his hand and fell on to his foot. Pitying him for his misfortune, Zeus placed him among the constellations, with a victim which he seems to be holding above the Altar for sacrifice.

According to other accounts, this is the Centaur Pholos, who was unequalled for his skill in divination; and so, by the will of Zeus, he was portrayed as approaching the Altar with a victim. (*Astronomy* 2.38)

COMMENTARY

(i) Although the Centaurs were not only half-animal in form, but also violent and uncivilized in character, there were two who departed from the usual pattern, Cheiron and Pholos, who were said accordingly to be of higher birth; and it was the one or the other who was thus said to be the Centaur represented in this constellation. Cheiron, who lived in a cave on Mount Pelion in Thessaly, was skilled in music, medicine, and other arts, and was supposed to have acted as tutor to various heroes, so it could be suggested (schol. Arat. 436) that he deserved a place in the heavens because of his righteous character and services in educating Asclepios and Achilles. In the usual tradition he had nothing to do with Heracles, who was not noted in any case for his cultivation, but when developing a myth for this constellation, Eratosthenes made use of a book written by the Socratic philosopher Antisthenes, in which the hero was presented as exemplifying what would come to be regarded as the Stoic virtues, and as having benefited from the company of the wise Centaur. According to an apparently quite old tradition, Heracles accidentally shot Cheiron during his battle with the Centaurs, a mishap that was sometimes said to have become the cause of Cheiron's death; but Eratosthenes' account of his death, in which he wounds himself by accidentally dropping one of the hero's arrows on to his foot, is based on a story which was originally told about Pholos (see below). Heracles' arrows were particularly dangerous because they had been smeared with poison from the Lernaian hydra.

(ii) Those who preferred to regard the Archer as a Centaur, unlike Eratosthenes, and identified him with Cheiron (see p. 78), had to find another identification for the present constellation, and it is thus not surprising that Hyginus should report that some authors claimed that it represents the other noble Centaur, Pholos. He was the eponym of Pholoe in Arcadia, and Heracles was said to have visited him when he was travelling south to catch the Erymanthian boar, as his fourth labour; when Pholos opened a jar of wine for him, the other Centaurs were enraged because it was their common property, or else were sent into a frenzy by the smell of the wine, and a battle broke out in which Heracles slaughtered the Centaurs with his arrows. Amazed that such small arrows could kill such large and powerful creatures, Pholos picked up an arrow to examine it, and accidentally dropped it on to his foot, causing his own death. For full narratives, see Ap. 2.5.4 and Diodorus 4.12.3–8. The skill in divination that Hyginus ascribes to Pholos is not mentioned in any other source.

(iii) The Centaur is holding a Beast, and whether he is identified as Cheiron or as Pholos, he could be imagined to be bringing it to sacrifice on the neighbouring Altar, forming a picture in the sky which illustrates his piety (see further on p. 119).

43. LEPUS, THE HARE

EPITOME 34. HARE

THIS is the Hare that forms part of the so-called hunting-scene. Hermes is supposed to have placed this animal among the constellations because of its speed. It is thought to be the only four-footed creature that can be pregnant with several litters at one time, giving birth to one set of young while carrying another in its womb, according to what Aristotle reports in his treatise *On Animals*.*

HYGINUS

The Constellation

The Hare is fleeing under the left foot of Orion along the winter tropic, which passes through the lower part of its body. It sets at the rising of the Archer, and rises with the Lion. It has one star on each ear, two spread out over its body, and one on each hind foot. There are thus six in all. (*Astronomy* 3.32)

The Mythology

It is said that this Hare is fleeing the dog of Orion in the hunt; for since Orion was depicted as a hunter, as was right and proper, they also wanted to show what he was hunting, and so placed the hare in flight at his feet. Some say that it was Hermes who placed it there, and that it has been granted the capacity, shared by no other kind of four-footed beast, of being able to give birth to young while already being pregnant with others. But those who reject the preceding explanation say that it is hardly fitting that a hunter as mighty and renowned as Orion, whom we have already discussed in connection with the sign of the Scorpion, should be portrayed in pursuit of a hare. Callimachus too comes under reproach for having said, when writing in praise of Artemis, that she delighted in the blood of hares* and used to hunt them. They have consequently pictured Orion as confronting the Bull.

With regard to the hare, the following tale has been handed down to us. In ancient times there were no hares on the island of Leros,* but a young man of that land, who had a special fondness for the creature, brought in a pregnant female from abroad and took great care of her as she gave birth to her young. After she had done so, many of his fellow-citizens developed the same enthusiasm, and some acquiring hares through purchase, and some as gifts, they all began to rear them. And so, before long, hares came to be born in such huge numbers that the whole island is said to have been invaded by them. Since they were given nothing to eat, they attacked the corn-fields and devoured everything. Facing disaster as a result, being struck by famine, the whole body of citizens reached a common decision, and with great difficulty, so the story goes, they eventually drove the hares from the island. And afterwards, the image of a hare was thus placed in the heavens to remind people that, in this life, nothing is so desirable that one cannot subsequently derive more sorrow from it than joy. (*Astronomy* 2.33)

COMMENTARY

(i) This constellation was devised to provide Orion's dog with suitable prey, and so create a hunting-scene. No specific myth was devised in that connection to account for its transference to the sky. This identification was subjected to playful criticism, on the ground that hares would be unworthy prey for such a mighty hunter; although hare-hunting was in fact regarded as a notable test of skill (e.g. Xenophon, *On Hunting* 5) because of the animal's speed, agility, and irregular pattern of flight.

(ii) Eratosthenes suggested that Hermes, as the deity who organized the heavens, placed the hare there because of its speed and agility. It is not clear whether he put this forward as an alternative account of its origin, or as further justification for it having been included in the hunting-scene.

(iii) Otherwise there is the local tale of a hare-plague. Such stories seem to have been commonplace in antiquity, especially in connection with islands (Athenaeus 400d ff., with regard to Astypalaia; Pliny, *Natural History* 8.218, the Balearic islanders petitioned Augustus for military assistance against hares). In the present case we are to imagine that astronomers devised the constellation-image to point a moral, as in the case of the Bowl (see p. 113).

44. ARGO

EPITOME 35. ARGO

SHE was placed among the constellations by Athena, to serve as a very clear example to future generations, because she was the first ship to be constructed, was endowed with the power of speech, and was the first to cross the open sea, which had been impassable up until then. Its image was placed among the constellations not in a complete form, but only the part of it that extends from the helm to the mast, including the steering-oars, so that those who engage in navigation, when they look up at it, may have confidence in their work, and so that its presence among the gods may ensure that its renown remains imperishable.

HYGINUS

The Constellation

Argo. Its poop touches the winter circle and tail of the large Dog, and with the lower part of the very end of its hull, it touches the antarctic circle obliquely. It sets at the rising of the Archer and Capricorn, orientated as it would be if it were on the sea, and it rises with the Maiden and the Claws. The ship has [four stars] on its poop, four on its first steering-oar, four on the second, five around its keel, five below its hold, and three near its mast. In all, twenty-six stars. As to why it appears incomplete in the sky, that is something that we have already explained. (*Astronomy* 3.36)

The Mythology

Some have said that she was called Argo in Greek because of her speed,* while others say that it was because Argos was her builder.* She was the first ship on the sea according to many accounts, and it was for that reason above all that she was portrayed in the stars. Pindar says that this ship was constructed in a town in Magnesia called Demetrias,* while according to Callimachus,* in that same region near the temple of Actian Apollo, which the Argonauts are supposed to have erected on their departure, at a place called Pagasai, which is said to owe its name to the fact that the Argo was first 'constructed' there, *pagasai* being the Greek word for that. Homer says that this same place lies in a region of Thessaly, while Aeschylus and some others report that Athena attached a piece of timber* there which was endowed with the power of speech. A complete image of this vessel cannot be seen, however, among the stars, but only the part of it that extends from the stern to the mast, to indicate that people should not give way to terror if their ship is wrecked. (*Astronomy* 2.37)

COMMENTARY

The ship in the heavens was inevitably identified with the *Argo*, on which Jason and the Argonauts travelled when they sailed to the far end of the Black Sea to fetch the golden fleece (Ap. 1.8.16 ff.; for the origin of the fleece, see p. 94 ff.), and Aratus (348) already names the constellation as Jason's *Argo*. Eratosthenes added that Athena placed it in the sky as the first large sea-going ship, an appropriate action for her as the goddess of handicrafts; it was indeed said that the *Argo* had been built under her guidance (A.R. 1.19). A possible alternative would have been the ship that carried the fifty Danaids from Egypt to Greece (Ap. 2.4.4), which was in fact built at an earlier period of mythical history, but although that is suggested in a late marginal note to Germanicus, that is strictly a medieval rather than ancient source.

Eratosthenes apparently failed to explain why the image of the ship is incomplete, showing only about half of it; the quaint suggestion by Hyginus that it is represented in that way to reassure sailors in case of shipwreck is almost certainly derived from a misunderstanding of his Greek source. Germanicus alludes (350) to the episode in which part of the *Argo* was clipped off by the Symplegades or Clashing Rocks (see Ap. 1.9.22, A.R. 2.549 ff.), but this was not a happy inspiration because only the very tip of the stern was lost, whereas a large section of the front is missing from the constellation figure, and more than enough to sink any ship.

45. ERIDANUS

EPITOME 37. RIVER

THIS river begins from the left foot of Orion. It is called Eridanos according to Aratus,* although he provides no evidence to support that identification; but others say that it can be most properly identified with the Nile, because that is the only river that takes its start from the south. It is adorned thoughout with numerous stars.

Beneath it there lies the star known as Canopos, which is situated near the steering-oars of Argo; no star is visible to us at any lower position, and that is why it is called Perigeios (Near-the-Earth).

HYGINUS

The Constellation

The Eridanos, starting from the left foot of Orion, reaches the Sea-monster and then flows back toward the feet of the Hare, and heads straight toward the antarctic circle. The image of it is cut by the winter tropic at the point where it almost touches the Sea-monster. One sees it setting with the rising of the Scorpion and Archer, and rising with the Twins and Crab. It has three stars on its first bend, three on the second, and seven on the third up to the last. In all, it has thirteen stars. (*Astronomy* 3.31)

The Mythology

Some have said that this is the Nile, although many others say that it is the Ocean. Those who prefer to regard it as the Nile point out that this is most fitting because of its great length and its usefulness; there is a star in it, furthermore, which is brighter than all others and is known as Canopos, and Canopos is an island which is washed by the Nile. (*Astronomy* 2.32)

COMMENTARY

Eridanus

(i) The heavenly river is already named by Aratus as the Eridanos (360), a semi-mythical river of the far west which came to be identified with the Po. Aratus alludes to the main myth associated with it, in which Phaethon was said to have plunged down into it after being struck with a thunderbolt by Zeus when he attempted, with disastrous consequences, to drive across the sky in the chariot of his father, the sun-god Helios (e.g. A.R. 4.596 ff.). Only the 'poor remains' of the river remain visible in the sky (360), evidently because the rest was burned up when Phaethon fell into it, perhaps accompanied by fragments from the thunderbolt that killed him; Apollonius refers correspondingly to its steaming waters (4.595–600). And it was a 'river of many tears' (360) because the fate of Phaethon became the cause of much mourning among his relations and friends, especially his sisters the Heliades, whose tears became the source of amber after the gods turned them into trees out of pity (A.R. 4.603 ff., Ovid, *Metamorphoses* 2.340 ff.; see also p. 94).

(ii) Eratosthenes made a show of being sceptical about the preceding identification, saying that Aratus had failed to provide any evidence, and apparently put forward the Nile as the identification that he personally favoured. In that case it could be argued that it runs appropriately from south to north, and that it has Canopos (see below) at the end of it.

(iii) Hyginus mentions that some identified this constellation with the ocean, the great river that was supposed to encircle the earth, although that seems less appropriate in view of the fact the ocean runs round in a circle.

Canopos

The star Canopos, which was mentioned by Eratosthenes in connection with this constellation, was the southernmost star of the first magnitude known to the ancient Greeks. It could not be seen from the Greek mainland, but it rose in the sky as sailors proceeded south, providing evidence of the sphericity of the earth, and was clearly visible from Egypt. The name that came to be applied to it was that of the town of Canopos which lay in the Nile delta, by the westernmost or Canopic mouth of the river. The Greeks claimed that it was named after a Canopos who had been the steersman of Menelaos, king of Sparta, during his voyage to Egypt after the Trojan War. This was a post-Homeric tradition; in the *Odyssey* (3.278 ff.) his original steersman, Phrontis, is said to have died beforehand off the coast of Attica, and that allowed room for this new steersman to be inserted. In Egypt, so the story went, Theonoe, the daughter of the king and diviner Proteus, fell in love with this Canopos, but he failed to return her love, and then suffered a fatal snakebite just as Menelaos was planning to sail onward; Menelaos buried him at the place where he died, and the town that was subsequently built there was named Canopos after him (Conon, *Narrations* 6; or in some accounts Menelaos actually founded the town). The story may well have been recounted by Apollonius of Rhodes in a lost poem of his, the *Kanobos*, and it may indeed have been invented by him. There is no definite evidence to show that Canopos was ever said to have been transferred to the heavens to become this star, even if the idea naturally suggests itself. This was in any case a very appropriate name for a star that rises ever higher during the voyage south to Egypt.

46. PISCIS AUSTRINUS, THE SOUTHERN FISH

EPITOME 39. FISH

THIS is the so-called great Fish, which is said to swallow down the water that is poured out by the Water-pourer. It is recounted of it, so Ctesias says, that it once lived in a lake near Bambyke;* Derceto, who is called the Syrian Goddess by the inhabitants of that region, fell into the lake one night, and it would seem that this fish came to her rescue. They also say that the two Fishes are its offspring, and all three were granted the honour of being placed among the constellations.

The account in the Vatican Fragments is slightly fuller at the end:

They also say that the two fishes are its offspring, and it is because of her [Derceto], since she is a daughter of Aphrodite, that all three were granted the honour of being placed among the constellations. The inhabitants of this land make fishes from gold and silver, and honour them as sacred.

HYGINUS

The Constellation

The fish known as the Southern fish, situated midway between the winter tropic and the antarctic circle, seems to look toward the east, between the Water-pourer and Capricorn, taking into its mouth the water that is poured out by the Water-pourer. It sets with the rising of the Crab, and rises with the Fishes. In all it has twelve stars. (*Astronomy* 3.40)

The Mythology

With its mouth it [the Fish] seems to be taking in the water that is poured by the constellation of the Water-pourer. It once saved Isis when she was in danger, so it is thought. As a reward for this good deed, the goddess placed an image of the fish among the constellations, and also images of its offspring, which we have already talked about. And so many Syrians never eat fishes, and they honour gilded images of them as their household gods. Ctesias* too has written about this matter. (*Astronomy* 2.41)

COMMENTARY

This Fish shared a joint myth with the two Fishes in the zodiac: see further on pp. 83–5.

47–50. THE MILKY CIRCLE, PLANETS, AND CONSTELLATIONS OF LATE ORIGIN

47. THE PLANETS

EPITOME 43. PLANETS

REGARDING the stars that are known as planets (wandering stars) because each has its own specific motion.

They are said to be connected with five gods. The first, Phainon (the Brilliant), is said to be that of Zeus and it is large in size.

The second is called Phaethon (the Radiant), and is of no great size; it takes its name from Helios.*

The third is that of Ares; it is known as Pyroeides* (the Fiery). It is not large, and it is similar in colour to that which is found in the Eagle.*

The fourth, Phosphoros, is that of Aphrodite; it is white in colour, and it is the largest of all these stars. It is called both Hesperos and Phosphoros.*

The fifth is that of Hermes, Stilbon* (the Glittering), which is bright and small. It has been assigned to Hermes because he was the first to determine the ordering of the heavens* and position of the stars, and to regulate the seasons, and provide signs to indicate the proper time to do things. It is called Stilbon because of the ingenuity that Hermes showed in bringing that about.

HYGINUS

The Mythology

It remains for us to speak about the five stars which many have called wandering stars, and the Greeks call planets.

One of them is the star of Zeus (Jupiter), named Phainon (the Brilliant); Heracleides of Pontos* says that when Prometheus was creating men, he created this Phainon as one who surpassed all others in beauty, and when he tried to hide him away rather than hand him over to Zeus like all the rest, Eros reported the matter to Zeus; whereupon Hermes was sent to Phainon to persuade him to come to Zeus and acquire immortality. And so he was placed among the stars.

The second star is said to be that of Helios,* or according to others, that of Cronos (Saturn). According to Eratosthenes, it is called Phaethon, after the son of Helios. Many authors have written about him, describing how, in his ignorance, he drove his father's chariot and set fire to the earth. Zeus responded by striking him with a thunderbolt, and he was thrown down into the Eridanos, and then raised up to the heavens by Helios.

The third star is that of Ares (Mars), which others call the star of Heracles. It follows the star of Aphrodite (Venus) for the following reason, as Eratosthenes recounts: Hephaistos had married Aphrodite and kept such close watch on her that Ares was unable to achieve his desire, and won nothing more from her, so it would seem, than that his star should forever follow hers. And because he burned with such ardent love for her, she then called his star Pyroeis (the Fiery) in reference to that.

The fourth star is that of Aphrodite (Venus), known as Phosphoros; though some say that it is the star of Hera. It is also called Hesperos in many tales that have been handed down to us. Of all stars, this seems to be the largest. Some have said that it is the son of Cephalos and Eos,* who surpassed many others in beauty. In that regard he even rivalled Aphrodite, so it is said, and Eratosthenes says, indeed, that that is why it is called the star of Aphrodite, and it can be seen at both sunrise and sunset. It is thus fitting that, as we remarked above, it should be named both Lucifer (Light-bringer) and Hesperos (the evening star).

The fifth star is that of Hermes (Mercury), known as Stilbon (the Glittering); it is small and bright. It is assigned to Hermes, so it is thought, because he first established the months and determined the courses of the stars. But according to Euhemerus, it was Aphrodite who determined the courses of the stars, and she made them known to Hermes. (*Astronomy* 2.42)

COMMENTARY

The ancient Greeks knew of five planets, and referred to them either by descriptive names, or as being the star of the god who was thought to preside over each of them. It is as a result of the latter practice that we refer to them by the names of gods, referring to the star *of* Jupiter, for instance, simply as Jupiter; but one should not be misled by that into thinking that the planets were actually identified with gods. The descriptive names, which reflect the variations in the intensity and quality of the light emitted by the planets, were of scholarly rather than popular origin, and were probably devised in the Hellenistic period. If they were introduced for the purpose of achieving a consistent terminology, that aim was imperfectly achieved, because the names Phainon and Phaethon were not consistently applied to Saturn and Jupiter, but sometimes to Jupiter and Saturn instead. Eratosthenes departed from common practice by choosing the latter option, and was apparently followed by Hyginus (although there is some muddle in the manuscripts over the name of the first constellation).

Jupiter is the only planet to be provided with a full astral myth including a catasterism, in the form of a rather facile story which was developed by inserting a new element into the myth of Prometheus' creation of man. In so far as the name Phaethon (Radiant) was applied to a planet, to Saturn in Eratosthenes' account, the planet could be said to have been named after the famous son of Helios, but it was apparently never suggested that he was transferred to the sky to become that planet. Hesperos, as Venus was known in its nature as the evening star, came to be personified (as did Heosphoros, representing the morning star, at an early period), but virtually nothing is recorded for him in the way of myth. The name of Mars as Pyroeis or 'Fiery' is explained quite neatly in relation to the mythology of its presiding god, although Hephaistos was not altogether successful in guarding his wife if the *Odyssey* (8.266 ff.) is to be believed. And finally, Hermes surely deserved to have his special star if he could be credited with the organizing of the heavens, as Eratosthenes had described in his lost poem about him.

48. THE MILKY CIRCLE

EPITOME 44. MILKY CIRCLE

THIS is one of the visible circles,* which goes under the name of Galaxia (the milky circle). It was not possible for sons of Zeus to have any share in the honours of the sky* unless they had been suckled at Hera's breast; and that is why Hermes, so they say, brought Heracles along after his birth and placed him at Hera's breast, for him to be suckled at it; but when Hera became aware of it, she thrust him away, and the rest of her milk spilled out accordingly to make up the milky circle.

HYGINUS

The Mythology

There is also a circle in the heavens which is white in colour, and which men have called the milky circle. Eratosthenes recounts in his *Hermes** that Hera unknowingly gave milk to the infant Hermes, but when she came to realize that he was Maia's son, she pushed him away; and that is why a bright trail of spilled milk can be seen among the stars. Others have said that Heracles was placed at Hera's breast while she was asleep, and she acted as has just been described when she woke up. Or according to other authors, Heracles was so greedy that he sucked in so much milk that he could not keep it in his mouth, and what spilled out from his mouth is shown in this circle. Others say that when Rhea presented Cronos with a stone* in place of her child, he told her to offer it some milk; and when she pressed her breast, the milk flowed out and formed the circle that we have just mentioned. (*Astronomy* 2.43)

COMMENTARY

(i) The favourite mythical explanation for the origin of the Milky Way was that it was formed from milk that had spilled from Hera's breast. There was a tradition that suggested that Hera had offered her breast to Heracles when he arrived on Olympos, to confer immortality on him, and doubtless also as a mark of reconciliation, because she had been hostile to him, as an illegitimate son of Zeus, during his earthly life; in images on Italian vases and mirrors, she can thus be seen offering her breast to him willingly when he is fully grown. But in another form of the myth, she was tricked into suckling him when he was still a baby, either on earth near his birthplace at Thebes (Pausanias 9.25.2), or on Olympos after he had been brought there by Hermes, as messenger of the gods. This last version provided an opening for the development of astral myths to explain the origin of the Milky Way: Hermes (or some other deity) applies him to her breast, but she pushes him away when she wakes up, or comes to realize who he is, and some of her milk spills out. Or in more humorous versions, Heracles was such a glutton even at that young age that he suckled too greedily, and could not hold all the milk in his mouth, or provoked Hera into pushing him away.

(ii) Or when Rhea gave Cronos a stone to swallow instead of his son Zeus (see Ap. 1.1.6 for the circumstances), she pressed some milk from her breast to show him that she really had given birth, and it formed the Milky Way.

(iii) It had been suggested that the milky circle might represent the path that the sun had burned out on its daily course, but the problem then arose that the circle does not correspond with the present course of the sun, as represented in the ecliptic. One solution could be found in the notion that the sun had once followed a different course, and a mythical explanation could then be put forward to explain why it had turned from its original course: the sun-god had been so appalled to see Thyestes serving his nephews up as a meal to their father Atreus (Ap. Epit. 2.10–14) that he had turned away in horror, to follow a new course from that time onward (Achilles, *Isagoga* 24). Or else, when his son Phaethon borrowed his chariot and drove it on an irregular course through the sky, he burned this new circle through the heavens (Diodorus 5.23.2, Manilius 1.735 ff.); or he displaced a star, and the milky circle marks its trajectory (Aristotle, *Meteorology* 1.8.1, ascribed to some Pythagoreans).

49. EQUULEUS, THE FOAL

OF all the canonic constellations of ancient origin, as catalogued by Ptolemy, this is the one of latest origin. Known neither to Aratus nor to Eratosthenes, it is mentioned by Geminos, who indicates that it was devised by Hipparchos, although that seems rather doubtful. No myths are recorded for it in any ancient source. Those that are sometimes ascribed to it were invented in the seventeenth century by Philip von Zesen, a German author who published a voluminous book on constellation myths in 1662, *Coelum Asronomico-poeticum*. According to a tradition from early epic, Cronos fathered the Centaur Cheiron by Philyra, daughter of Ocean (schol. A.R. 1554, citing the *Gigantomachia*), and it is stated in a later source that Rhea, the wife of Cronos, caught them in the act, prompting Cronos to make a rapid escape by turning himself into a horse (A.R. 2.1231–41). Zesen suggested that if Zeus had commemorated a similar episode by placing a swan in the heavens (see p. 20), there is nothing to prevent us from supposing that Cronos might have done the same by placing an image of a horse there. He cites Virgil's allusion to the episode in this connection (*Georgics* 3.92–4), but these lines naturally provide no direct support for his suggestion. As alternatives, he suggested that Poseidon might have set this horse in the sky to commemorate how he had caused the first horse, Scyphios, to spring forth from the earth by striking the ground with his trident, or that this is Cyllaros, a horse that one of the Dioscuri, Castor, who was a notable horseman, had received as a gift from Hermes. This was a game that could be prolonged without end, even in modern times.

50. CORONA AUSTRALIS, THE SOUTHERN CROWN

THE ring of stars under the forefoot of the Archer was noted from a relatively early period; it was mentioned by Aratus, and Eratosthenes referred to it under the name of the Boat (see p. 77), in accordance with a Mesopotamian conception. It is included in a list of constellations ascribed to Hipparchos, as the Crown beneath the Archer, and Ptolemy included it among his constellations under the name of the Southern Crown. Putting aside material in the Aratus scholia that is wrongly transferred from the other Crown, it can barely be said to have any ancient myth; at the most we have Hyginus's suggestion, which was put forward to explain the origin of the Archer, that this is the crown of Crotos, which he had thrown off as in play (see p. 78).

ARATUS, *PHAENOMENA*

I. THE CONSTELLATIONS

Proem

LET us begin with Zeus, whom we men never leave unnamed: filled with Zeus are all the streets and all the meeting-places of human beings, and filled too the seas and harbours; and everywhere all of us have need of Zeus. [5] For we are indeed his offspring, and he in his paternal kindness sends helpful signs to mortals, and rouses people to work by reminding them of life's demands, he tells us when the soil is most fit for oxen and for picks, he says when the right season has come for digging trees into the ground and sowing every kind of seed. [10] For it was Zeus himself who fixed the signs* of these things in the heavens by marking out the constellations, and arranged that the stars over the course of the year should provide men with most dependable signs of the passing seasons, so that everything may grow as it properly should. And thus it is that first and final homage is always addressed to him. [14] Hail Father, great marvel that you are, and great source of benefit to human beings, hail to you and to the prior race!* And to the kindly Muses, one and all! As for me, I who am praying to you to be able to tell fittingly of the stars, guide my song right through to the end.

The northern constellations and signs of the zodiac

[19] Numerous though they are and scattered in their different places, the stars are drawn along all alike in ceaseless movement with the sky, day after day, for all time. But the axis of the world does not shift to even the slightest degree, but remains firmly fixed forever; it holds the earth in equilibrium, running through its centre, and causes the sky to rotate around it.* At either end it is bounded by two poles, one of them invisible, while the other on the opposite side, to the north, rises high above the ocean.* [26] Around the axis two Bears rotate together; for that reason they are also called Wagons.* Each of them always has its head facing toward the flank of the other, and they always travel back to back, with their shoulders turned in opposite directions. [30] If the tale can be credited, they ascended to the heavens from Crete at the will of mighty Zeus, because long ago, when he

was still a child, they laid him in a cave on fragrant Dicton,* not far from Mount Ida, and nursed him there for a year, at the time when the Dictaean Curetes* were deceiving Cronos. [36] One is named as Cynosura, and the other as Helike.* It is Helike whom the Achaeans* take as their guide to know where to steer their ships, but it is in the other that the Phoenicians place their trust when sailing across the sea. [40] For if Helike is bright and easy to distinguish, shining out large from the beginning of the night, the other Bear, though small, is of greater value to sailors because she turns in her entirety in a narrower orbit, and by looking to her the Sidonians* are able to steer the straightest course.

Between the two Bears, like a river flowing on its way, winds that great wonder, the Dragon, coiled around at huge length, and on either side of its coil* travel the two Bears, taking care not to plunge into the dark blue ocean.* [49] It has the tip of its tail stretched out toward one of them, while it encircles the other with its coil: its tail ends near the head of Helike, but Cynosura has her skull within its coil, which winds right round her head and passes up to her foot, but then turns sharply back to run upward. The Dragon does not have just a single star on its head, shining all alone, but has two on its temples and two on its eyes, while another, set lower down, occupies the tip of this fearsome monster's jaw. [58] Its head is set aslant, and one has the impression that it is facing toward the end of Helike's tail; for its mouth and right temple stand in direct alignment with the tip of her tail. That head wheels at the very point where the ends of the settings run together with the beginnings of the risings.*

[63] Nearby there rotates a figure resembling a man engaged in toil. No one can say for sure who this is, or on what task he is bent, but people just call him the Kneeler.* He seems to be sinking to his knees under the burden of some effort, and from his two shoulders his arms are raised up, stretching out in opposite directions at full length; and he has the tip of his right foot set directly above the middle of the encoiled Dragon's head.

[71] In this region too the famous Crown, which Dionysos set there as a splendid memorial to the dead Ariadne,* circles under the back of the toil-worn figure. The Crown lies near his back, then, but beside the top of his head look out for the head of the Serpent-bearer, and starting from that, you can distinguish the gleaming Serpent-bearer himself, so brilliantly do his shoulders shine out below his head; they

are indeed visible even on a night of the full moon. But his arms are by no means as bright, for only a faint light runs along the one and the other; but all the same, they too can be seen, being not entirely dim. Both are struggling to keep a grip on the Serpent that winds around the Serpent-bearer's waist. [83] Maintaining a firm stance, the latter is trampling that huge beast the Scorpion under his two feet, standing upright on its eyes and thorax. The Serpent for its part is writhing in his two hands, just a little of it in the right, while it rises above his left hand at great length. [88] The tip of its jaw lies close to the Crown, and beneath its coils you may seek to distinguish the enormous Claws,* short of light though these are, and by no means brilliant.

[91] Behind Helike, as though driving her forward, comes the Bear-guard, whom men also call the Oxherd* because he seems to be whipping along the Wagon-Bear; he is very conspicuous throughout, and below his belt wheels Arcturus itself, a star brilliant above all.

[96] Below the two feet of the Oxherd you can observe the Maiden, who is holding the gleaming Ear of Corn* in her hand. Whether she is the daughter of Astraios,* who is said to have been the ancient father of the stars, or someone else's child, may she pass peacefully on her way. [100] But there is another tale in circulation among men, that she once lived on earth and approached human beings directly. She did not scorn the company of men and women in days of old, but took her seat among them, immortal that she was; and they called her Justice.* She gathered together the elders, in the market-place perhaps, or in some spacious thoroughfare, and exhorted them most urgently to pass judgements that would serve the good of the people. [108] In those days they were as yet unacquainted with ruinous strife, or malicious discord, or the din of battle, but lived a simple life. The sea and its perils lay far from their thoughts, and ships did not as yet bring in provisions from lands far away, but the ox and plough, and Justice herself, the sovereign of all and dispenser of what is right and good, provided in full measure for all their needs. [114] Things continued in that way as long as the earth still nourished the golden race, but with the race of silver she associated but little, and no longer with a willing heart, because she longed for the ways of the people of old. But all the same, even in the time of the silver race, she still remained present. [118] She would descend from the echoing mountains toward nightfall, all on her own, never approaching

anyone with gentle words. But rather, when she had filled the broad hills with crowds of people, she would assail them with threats and reproach them for their wickedness, declaring that she would no longer come to meet them even if invited: [123] 'How inferior are the offspring that your fathers of the golden race have left behind them! And you will bring into the world children who are viler still! And then there will be wars and murderous bloodshed among men, and sorrow will descend on them as a result of their transgressions!' [127] After speaking these words, she headed for the mountains, leaving the whole crowd still gazing after her. But when these people died in their turn, the race of bronze came into being, men who were even more pernicious than those who had gone before, being the first to forge the pernicious sword to commit murder on the highways, and the first to eat the flesh of the plough-ox; [133] Justice had nothing but contempt for this race of men, and fled up into the heavens and made her home in that place, where she still appears to human beings at night as the Maiden near the far-seen Oxherd.

[137] Above her two shoulders there circles a star on her right wing—it is known as the Vintager*—of the same size and endowed with the same brightness as that which can be seen below the tail of the great Bear; for the Bear is most splendid, and splendid too are the stars that lie near her, and once you have caught sight of them, you need not look for any other guide, so large and beautiful are the stars that circle in front of her feet, one in front of her forelegs, one in front of those that descend from her loins, and another under her hind knees. But all of them revolve singly, each in its separate station, without a name.

[147] Beneath the Bear's head lie the Twins, and beneath her waist the Crab, and beneath her hind feet the Lion shines forth in splendour. This is where the path of the sun is at its hottest in summer, and the fields can be seen to be bereft of their ears of corn when the sun first comes into conjunction with the Lion. [152] At this time too the roaring Etesian winds* come sweeping down on the broad sea, and it is no longer the season to venture out to sea under oar. To my way of thinking one should then take recourse to broad-beamed ships, and helmsmen should hold their vessels into the wind.

[156] If you have a mind to look at the Charioteer and his stars, and report has reached you of the Goat and her Kids, who have often looked down on men falling into distress on the storm-tossed sea, you

will see the whole body of the Charioteer stretched out at length to the left of the Twins, while the top of his head wheels on its way opposite Helike. [162] Attached to his left shoulder is the sacred Goat, who is said to have offered her breast to Zeus; the interpreters of Zeus call her the Olenian Goat.* Large she is, and brilliant, whereas her Kids on the wrist of the Charioteer shine with only a feeble light.

[167] At the feet of the Charioteer, look for the horned Bull that is crouching there. The signs are established in such a way as to make it easily recognizable—see how clearly its head is marked out; no other sign is needed to distinguish the head of the Bull because the stars themselves figure it forth as they turn on their courses on both sides of it. [172] Their name is mentioned very frequently, never does one cease to hear talk of the Hyades, which are distributed all along the face of the Bull.* The tip of its left horn and the right foot of the neighbouring Charioteer are occupied by one common star;* these are carried along together on a shared course, but the Bull always runs ahead of the Charioteer as they descend toward the horizon, even though it rises along with him.

[179] Nor will the sorely afflicted family of Cepheus, from the line of Iasos,* be passed by without mention; for their names too have ascended to the heavens, because they were closely related to Zeus.* Behind the Bear Cynosura, Cepheus appears in the likeness of a man who is holding his two arms outstretched. The line that extends from the end of the Bear's tail to each of his feet is equal in length to the distance between his two feet. And one has to direct one's glance only a short way beyond his belt to find the first coil of the huge Dragon. [188] In front of him wheels the ill-fated Cassiepeia, who shines out none too clearly on a night of the full moon; for she is lighted by only a few stars, set alternately, which sketch out her entire figure quite distinctly. [192] As in the key* that one applies to push back the bolts on a double door barred from the inside, so do the stars that make her up appear to be arranged, each set apart from the other. Formed in such a way, she holds her arms stretched out at full length from her shoulder; one would say that she was grieving over the lot of her daughter.

[197] For in that same region revolves the woebegone figure of Andromeda, shining forth beneath her mother.* I fancy that you will not have to peer around for long in the night sky before you catch sight of her, so clear is her head, and so clear are her shoulders on

either side and the whole of her girdle. And yet even up above she has her arms stretched out, and she is burdened by chains* even in the sky: her arms remain raised and outspread for all eternity.

[205] Up against her head there presses the gigantic Horse,* touching her with its belly; a common star gleams both on that creature's navel and on the crown of her head. Three others, standing apart, mark out lines of equal length on the flank and shoulders of the Horse; they are large and bright, but the same does not apply to its back, or to its neck, long though that is. The last star on its blazing mouth, however, could even rival the four preceding stars, which mark its outline most vividly. But not having all four legs, the sacred Horse wheels through the sky half-complete, cut off through the middle at the level of its navel. [216] This is the horse, so they say, that caused the fair waters of Hippocrene* to flow down lofty Helicon as a source of fertility; for the summit of Helicon was unwatered as yet by any spring, but the horse struck it, and water gushed forth from that spot in abundance at the blow of its front hoof. It was the shepherds who first gave the name of Hippocrene to this wellspring. It continues to well out of the rock, and never can you see it far from where the men of Thespiai* have their dwelling; but the Horse circles in the realm of Zeus where you can always see it.

[225] There too run the very swift paths of the Ram,* which rushes around the longest circle and yet does not fall behind the Bear Cynosura as it runs on its way. In itself it is faint and starless,* as though one were viewing it by moonlight, but you can track it down nevertheless by means of Andromeda's belt, because it is set no great distance below her. It treads through the central reaches of the vast heavens, where the tips of the Claws and the belt of Orion make their circuit.

[233] Near it is fixed yet another constellation, below Andromeda: the triangle is measured out on three sides, being recognizable as isosceles from its two equal sides; the other is not as long, but it is very easy to find, because it is more brightly starred than many constellations. The stars of the Ram lie a little to the south of the Triangle.

[239] Still further ahead, and approaching further toward the south, lie the Fishes; but one of them is always more prominent than the other,* and hears the North Wind better when it begins to descend. From the tails of both there stretch chains, so to speak, which run down in a continuous line from either side to join into one. [243] That

meeting-point is occupied by a single star, large and bright, which is known as the celestial Knot.* May the left shoulder of Andromeda be the sign that points you to the northern Fish, because it is set very close to that, while her two feet will guide you to her suitor Perseus, on whose shoulders they are forever carried.

[250] He passes in the north, taller than the other figures there. His right arm is stretched out toward the throne of his mother-in-law,* and as though pursuing something close in front of her, he hastens with long strides, all covered in dust, through the domain of his father Zeus.

[254] Near his left knee, all clustered together, the Pleiades follow their path; they are all contained within no great space, and are too dim in themselves to be easy to distinguish. They are renowned, however, among human beings as the stars on their seven courses, although only six of them are visible to our eyes. [259] No star at all, I think, has ever disappeared without trace from the sky of Zeus since human memory began, but that is how the story goes. These seven are named as Alcyone, Merope, Celaino, Electra, Sterope, Taygete, and the venerable Maia.* [264] Although they are small and faint one and all, renowned is their passage at morning and nightfall, through the will of Zeus, who has appointed them to signal the start of summer and winter, and the arrival of the time for the plough.

[268] And that tortoise-shell there is small too; Hermes was still by his cradle when he hollowed it out, and said that it should be given the name of Lyre.* And bringing it up into the sky, he set it in front of the unknown figure,* who, crouching down, draws close to it with his left knee, while the Bird's head circles around on the other side. The Lyre is thus fixed between the head of the Bird and that knee.

[275] Yes, it is true that a gleaming Bird* follows the heavens on their course, hazy in parts, but teeming with stars in others, not very bright, though by no means dim. Just like a bird on the wing in fair weather, it glides toward the far horizon, as though on a favourable breeze, with the tip of its right wing extended toward the head of Cepheus; and near its left wing lies the prancing Horse.

[282] Round the Horse that prances in the sky range two Fishes, and beside its head there stretches the right hand of the Water-pourer, who rises after Capricorn. And Capricorn for his part is set further ahead and lower down, where the mighty sun turns back again.* [287] In that month do not expose yourself to a battering from the waves

by venturing out into the open sea. Neither will you make much progress in the course of the day, because the days pass all too quickly then, nor will dawn come soon if you are overcome by fear at night, in spite of all your cries. Dreadful are the south winds that come rushing down at that time, when the sun enters Capricorn, and worse still the frost that descends from the sky on to the sailor benumbed with cold. Yet all the same, the sea surges beneath ships' keels throughout the year, and like diving seagulls, we keep peering around at the sea from the ships on which we are set, with our face turned toward the shore; but the wave-beaten strand is still far off, and only a thin plank of wood keeps death at bay.

[300] And even in the preceding month, after undergoing many a torment at sea when the sun scorches the Bow and the Archer who draws it, you should trust no longer in the night, but put to shore as evening falls. As sign for this season and this month, you may take the rising of the Scorpion as the night is drawing to its end. [305] For the Archer draws the string of his huge Bow close to the Scorpion's sting, and the Scorpion stands only a short way in front of him at its rising, while he himself rises soon afterwards. At that time of year also, the head of Cynosura* runs very high at the end of the night, while Orion sets in his entirety just before dawn, and Cepheus from his head to his waist.

[311] Further ahead there is another Arrow, on its own without a bow.* The Bird is stretched out beside it, nearer to the north, while nearby another bird is carried along by the wind, of lesser size but dangerous* when it rises from the sea at the end of the night; men call it the Eagle.

[316] The Dolphin, which is none too large, runs above Capricorn; it is hazy in the middle, but is outlined by four brilliant stars, set two by two on parallel lines.

[319] Such, then, are the stars that are scattered between the north and the sun's wandering path,* but there are many others that rise below, between the south* and the course of the sun.

Constellations south of the zodiac

[322] Aslant beneath the truncated figure of the Bull* lies Orion himself. Should anyone fail to catch sight of him set high up in the heavens on a clear night, he should not expect to behold anything more

splendid when he gazes up at the sky. [326] Look, furthermore, at the watch-Dog that appears under the towering back of Orion, standing up on its two hind legs; lit unevenly, it is not bright throughout, but is dark up to its belly as it wheels on its way; but the tip of its jaw is set with a blazing star, one that burns with searing heat, and people call it Sirius accordingly.* When Sirius rises with the sun, the vines can no longer outwit it by covering themselves with puny leaves, because its keen rays pierce through their ranks with ease, strengthening some, but destroying all the freshness of others. We also hear talk of it at its setting; but the other stars of the Dog, which are set around to mark out its limbs, are less brilliant.

[338] Below the two feet of Orion, the Hare is under constant pursuit for all time, while Sirius runs behind it forever, as though on its trail, rising just after it and keeping a close watch on it as it sets.

[342] Near the tail of the great Dog, Argo is hauled along stern-foremost. For her course does not accord with what is customary for a ship, no, she moves backwards, as do real ships when the sailors have already turned the stern around to run up to the moorings, and all of them quickly work together to back-paddle the ship, as she moves backwards to come to shore. [348] It is in such a way that Jason's Argo* is carried along stern-foremost. She is hazy and devoid of stars from her prow up to her mast,* but all the rest of her shines out brilliantly. Her steering-oar is detached and is set beneath the front feet of the Dog, which runs on ahead of her.

[353] Although lying quite some distance away,* Andromeda comes under threat from the huge Sea-monster as it advances against her. For she is exposed on her passage through the heavens to the blasts of the north wind from Thrace, while the south wind drives the aggressive Sea-monster against her, set as it is beneath the Ram and the two Fishes, and a little above the starry River.

[359] For down there, below the feet of the gods, wheel the remains of the Eridanos,* that river of many tears, which stretches out below the left foot of Orion. The celestial chains that connect the back ends of the two Fishes run down from their tails, in like fashion, to come together behind the back-fin of the Sea-monster, where they join into one, ending in a single star, which lies at the top of the monster's back.

[367] Some other stars, of no great size and endowed with no great brightness, circle between the ship's steering-oar and the Sea-monster, scattered below the flanks of the grey Hare, all without

name. For they are not laid out in such a way as to resemble the limbs of any distinct figure, like the many that travel in ordered ranks along unchanging paths as the years are completed, the constellations that someone from a departed generation* devised, undertaking to provide them all with names and a clearly marked form. For he would naturally have been unable to give a name to all the stars, or to distinguish them, if they were taken in isolation, because there are so many of them in every direction, and many are alike in their size and brilliance, and all circle through the sky in the same fashion. [379] And so he resolved to order the stars into groups, so that they would represent figures when set in due relation to one another. The constellations were thus devised under their respective names, and no longer does the rising of any star take us by surprise. But if most stars appear in that way, fixed into well-defined constellations, those that are set below the hunted Hare wheel ill-lit and without a name.

[386] Below Capricorn, under the blasts of south wind, there hangs a Fish, which faces toward the Sea-monster and is distinct from the previous Fishes; it is known as the Southern Fish. [389] Other stars, scattered below the Water-pourer, float halfway between the heavenly Sea-monster and the Fish, faint and nameless; and near them, running from the right hand of the glittering Water-pourer like a thin stream of water sprinkled this way and that, some pale and puny stars go circling round. [395] Among them move two which are more conspicuous than the others, neither far apart nor very close; one of them, beautiful and bright, lies under the two feet of the Water-pourer, and the other under the tail of the dark Sea-monster. All taken together, these stars are called the Water. But a few others below the Archer, under his front hooves,* revolve unknown, set in a circle.*

[402] Below the blazing sting of that huge monster the Scorpion, close to the south, there hangs the Altar. Although it remains above the horizon for only a short time, you will not fail to see it, because it rises opposite Arcturus; the paths of that star take it very high above the earth, whereas the Altar plunges back all too soon into the western sea. [408] And yet ancient Night,* in her sorrow for human sufferings, has set the Altar to be a noteworthy sign for storm at sea, because it distresses her to see men being battered by the waves. So I would have you pray, when out at sea, that in a sky enveloped everywhere else in cloud, you may not see this constellation shining alone, itself free from cloud and radiant, but with billowing clouds pressing down

on it from above, such as often beset it when the north wind piles them up in autumn. For this is a sign that Night herself employs to announce the south wind, as a favour to sailors in adversity. [420] And if they pay heed to her salutary warnings, and immediately make everything tight and firm, their troubles will soon be alleviated; but if a terrible squall suddenly descends from above on their ship against all expectation, and plays havoc with all the sails, they sometimes find themselves sailing wholly underwater, while sometimes, if Zeus comes to their aid in response to their prayers and lightning flashes out from the north, they will be able to look at one another on the ship once again after their many sufferings. At this sign, you should fear the south wind until you see the north wind flashing lightning.

[431] But if the Centaur's shoulder is as far from the western horizon as from the eastern, and that constellation is veiled by a slight haze, while behind it Night is revealing the same signs on the brightly shining Altar, you should no longer expect a wind from the south, but one from the east. [436] You will find this constellation of the Centaur below two others, because the part of him that resembles a man lies below the Scorpion, while his equine hind-parts are set below the Claws. He always looks, furthermore, as if he is stretching his right hand out toward the round Altar, while holding another constellation firmly gripped in his hand, namely the Beast,* for such is the name that our forefathers bestowed on it.

[443] But yet another constellation climbs above the horizon— they call it the Hydra. Like a living creature it constantly twists and turns; its head reaches to below the middle of the Crab, while its coils pass under the body of the Lion, and its tail hangs over the Centaur himself. [448] Halfway along its encoiled body there is set the Bowl, and toward the end of it the figure of a Crow,* which seems to be pecking at it with its beak.

[450] And last of all, Procyon* shines forth brightly below the Twins.

[451] Such are the constellations that you can see as the years pass by, all returning in due succession; for they all remain fixed unchangingly in the sky, as adornments of the passing night.

The five planets

[454] But mixed in among them are five other stars of a quite different

nature,* which circulate here and there through the twelve figures of the zodiac. In their case it is no longer possible for you to work out their position by looking at other stars, because all of them constantly change their position. [458] Long are the periods of their orbits, and far distant from one another the signs of their renewed conjunction,* and no longer do I have confidence in myself when it comes to them. May it suffice for me to tell of the circles of the fixed stars and the constellations that mark them out in the sky.

II. MEASURING OF TIME THROUGH OBSERVATION OF THE HEAVENS

Circles of the celestial sphere

[462] There are, in truth, four circles* there, like wheels, for which one has especial desire and need if one is seeking to measure the passage of the years. All of them are marked all around by numerous signs, all closely bound together from one end to the other. The circles themselves have no breadth, and all are fixed to one another, but in size two are matched with two.

[469] If ever on a clear night, when all the stars are displayed in their splendour to human beings by the heavenly goddess Night, and none is dimmed in its passage by the full moon, but all shine bright and clear through the darkness, if ever on such a night you are seized by wonder at seeing the sky cleft all around by a broad circle, and if someone at your side calls your attention to that wheel bejewelled with light—it is known as the Milk*—you should know that there is no other circle in the sky that matches it for colour, but that two of the four equal it for size, while the others turn in a much smaller orbit.*

[480] Of the latter circles, one lies close to where the north wind* comes down. On it there move the two heads of the Twins, on it are set the knees of the firm-set Charioteer, and the left leg of Perseus too, and his left shoulder. It crosses the middle of Andromeda's right arm above the elbow, while her palm lies above it, closer to the north, and her elbow inclines to the south. [487] The hooves of the Horse, the neck of the Bird up to the top of its head, and the handsome shoulders of the Serpent-bearer revolve on their way around this circle; but the Maiden passes a little to the south and does not touch it,

unlike the Lion and Crab. The two latter are set side by side, and this circle cuts through the Lion beneath its chest and belly as far as its genitals, and passes straight through the Crab below its shell, where you can clearly see it to be cut in two at such an angle that its eyes stand on either side of the circle. [497] If one divides it, as accurately as possible, into eight parts, five parts revolve above the earth in the light of day, and the other three below the horizon. On it lies the summer turning-point of the sun. The circle is fixed in the north at the latitude of the Crab.

[501] There is another circle set opposite in the south which cuts through the middle of Capricorn, and through the feet of the Water-pourer and tail of the Sea-monster. The Hare lies on it, but it does not lay hold of very much of the Dog, only the space occupied by its feet. On it lie Argo and the massive back of the Horse, and on it too the Scorpion's sting, and the Bow of the magnificent Archer. [507] It is to this circle that the sun last comes as it descends from the clear north wind to pass southward, and it is there that its winter turning-point lies. Three of the eight parts of its course revolve above the horizon, and the five others beneath the earth.

[511] Halfway between these two circles, as large as the circle of white Milk, there is one that curves below the earth in such a way that it seems to be cut in half.* On it the days are of equal length to the night twice in the year, at the end of summer and again at the beginning of spring. The signs that mark it out are the Ram and the knees of the Bull; the Ram is carried lengthwise along the circle, but of the Bull just the clearly visible bend of its legs. [518] On it also lie the belt of blazing Orion and the coil of the resplendent Hydra, and on it too the faintly lit Bowl and the Crow, and the not so very many stars of the Claws; and on it there travel the knees of the Serpent-bearer. It claims no share of the Eagle, but has the great messenger of Zeus soaring nearby; and along it wheel the head and neck of the Horse.

[525] These three circles run parallel to one another, and are set at right angles to the axis of the world, which holds all of them at the centre; but the fourth is gripped obliquely between the two trop-ics,* which hold it on either side of the equator, while the middle circle cuts it halfway between those two points. [529] In no other way would a man skilled in the handicrafts of Athena fix together revolving wheels* of such a kind and of such a size, to make them all turn round together; so likewise, these circles up in the heavens,

clasped together by the oblique circle, speed together from dawn to night through all time. [530] Three of the circles rise up and then go down again all parallel to one another, but each of them has its single point at which it sets and rises successively at each horizon. [537] The fourth circle for its part passes over as much of the water of the ocean as rolls round from the rising of Capricorn to the rising of the Crab, traversing the same distance in the whole of its rising as it does when descending to the other side. [541] As far as the ray cast by the glance of an eye would extend, a line six times that length would subtend this circle, and each sixth, if all are measured equally, intercepts two constellations. Men refer to it by the name of the circle of the zodiac.

[545] On it lies the Crab, and then the Lion, and under that, the Maiden; and after her, the Claws and the Scorpion itself, and the Archer, and Capricorn; and after Capricorn, the Water-pourer, and after him, the two star-studded Fishes, and after them, the Ram, and then the Bull and the Twins. [550] Through all these figures, twelve in number, the sun progresses as it brings the whole year to pass, and as it travels around this circle, all the seasons ripen, each with its fruit.

[553] The arc of this circle that plunges below the hollow of the ocean is equal in length to that which rises above the earth; and each night, six twelfths of the circle always set while the same number rise. Every night always extends for the same length of time as it takes for half of the circle to rise above the earth from the beginning of the night.

Simultaneous risings and settings

[559] It is by no means unprofitable, if one is watching for daybreak, to observe when each sign of the zodiac rises, because the sun itself always rises with one of them. You can recognize them best by looking for the constellations themselves, but if they are obscured by cloud or hidden by a mountain at their rising, you must provide yourself with fixed signs that point to their arrival. Now the ocean itself, on both horizons, will furnish you with such signs in ample number, through the constellations with which it crowns itself as it brings up each sign of the zodiac from below.

[569] They are not the faintest, the circling stars that, at the rising of the Crab, lie around the horizon to east and to west, some setting while others rise from the opposite horizon. Setting is the Crown, as

is the Fish as far as its back; half of the setting Crown can still be seen in the sky, but half has already been taken beneath the edge of the world. [575] As for the backward-turned kneeling figure, the lower parts of him up to his belt have yet to set, but his upper parts are moving in darkness. The Crab also drags the wretched Serpent-bearer down from his knees to his shoulders, and the Serpent too, almost to its neck. No longer does the Bear-guard stretch out at length on both sides of the horizon, less of him is above while the greater part of him is already in darkness. [581] For the time that it takes the Oxherd to be received by the ocean is equivalent to that which is taken by four signs of the zodiac, and when he has finally had his fill of light, at the time of year when his setting coincides with the setting of the sun, it takes him more than half of the passing night to unloose his oxen. These nights are named after his late setting. [586] So these constellations go down, while opposite them no mean figure, but one brilliant for his belt, brilliant for his two shoulders, Orion, trusting in the might of his sword, stretches out along the other horizon, bringing all of the River along with him.

[590] At the coming of the Lion, all the constellations that were setting with the Crab go down completely, as does the Eagle. As for the Kneeling figure, he has already set for the most part, except that his knee and left foot are not yet under the surging ocean. But the Hydra's head is rising, as are the bright-eyed Hare and Procyon, and the forefeet of the scorching Dog.

[596] They are not few, indeed, the constellations that the Maiden sends beneath the edges of the earth at her rising. The Cyllenian Lyre* and the Dolphin go down then, as does the finely fashioned Arrow; and with these, the Bird is cast into shadow from its first feathers up to its very tail, and so are the farthest reaches of the River. [601] The Horse's head goes down, and its neck too, but the Hydra rises still further, up as far as Bowl, while the Dog, rising ahead, brings up his other feet, dragging behind him the stern of many-starred Argo; and that ship runs across the earth, cut off right at the mast, as soon as the Maiden is completely above the horizon.

[607] Nor can the coming of the Claws pass unnoticed, although they shine but faintly, because that mighty constellation the Oxherd rises all at once in its entirety, marked out by Arcturus. Argo is wholly above the horizon by now, but the Hydra, stretching as it does at great length across the sky, still lacks its tail. The Claws bring up

only the right leg, as far as the knee, of the one who remains forever kneeling, forever crouching, beside the Lyre, that unknown being among the heavenly figures, whom we often see setting and then rising from the other horizon on the very same night. Only his leg can be seen at the rising of the Claws, while he himself, head downward and facing in the other direction, is still waiting for the rising of the Scorpion and Drawer of the Bow; for it is those that bring him up. The Scorpion brings up his waist and the rest of him, except for his left hand and his head which are brought up by the Bow. He is thus raised up bit by bit, in three portions. Half of the Crown and the very end of the Centaur's tail are also brought up by the Claws at their rising. [627] At this time too, the Horse sets, after its head has already departed, and the tail-tip of the previously vanished Bird is dragged under. The head of Andromeda also sets. That most terrifying creature, the Sea-monster, is incited against her by misty south, but opposing it from the north, Cepheus raises his mighty arm to warn it off. And while the Sea-monster, leaning downward toward its back-fin, goes down as far as that, Cepheus sets with head and hand and shoulder.

[634] The winding River will sink down into the fair streams of the ocean as soon as the Scorpion arrives, and its appearance also puts mighty Orion to flight. [637] May Artemis grant us her pardon! There is a tale told by our forebears, who said that brawny Orion seized her by her robe* at the time when, on Chios, he was striking down all the wild beasts with his massive club, as he strove to gain the favour of Oinopion* through his exploits in the hunt. [641] But the goddess immediately incited another beast against him, breaking the hills of the island in two through the middle to send forth the Scorpion, which stung and killed him, mighty though he was, showing itself to be mightier still, because he had committed an outrage against Artemis herself. It is for that reason, so they say, that when the Scorpion ascends above the horizon, Orion flees round the boundary of the earth.*

[647] Nor do the remains of Andromeda and of the Sea-monster fail to take heed of the rising of the Scorpion, but they too take flight with all speed. At that time Cepheus for his part grazes the earth with his belt, as he dips all the upper parts of his body into the ocean, but the rest he may not—the Bears themselves forbid it*—his feet and knees and loins. [653] The unfortunate Cassiepeia herself hurries

after the image of her daughter; no longer do they shine forth in a fitting posture from her throne, her feet and knees set uppermost, no, she plunges headfirst like a diver, undergoing her full share of distress, for she could not claim to rival Doris and Panope* without suffering grave consequences. [659] She is carried, then, toward the other horizon, but there are other constellations that the eastern sky brings up from below, the second curve of the Crown, and the tail of the Hydra; and it also brings the body and head of the Centaur, and the beast that the Centaur is holding in his right hand. But the forefeet of the horseman-beast await the arrival of the Bow.

[665] At its coming, there rise up the coils of the Serpent and the body of the Serpent-bearer, but their heads are brought up by the rising of the Scorpion itself, which also raises up the hands of the Serpent-bearer and the foremost coils of the star-encrusted Serpent. As for the Kneeler, since he always rises upside down, other parts of him then ascend above the horizon, namely his legs and waist, and the whole of his chest, and his shoulder with his right hand; but his head and other hand do not emerge until the rising of the Bow and the Archer. [674] Along with them the Lyre of Hermes, and Cepheus, as far as his chest, ride up from the eastern ocean, while the great Dog sets in all its brilliance, and Orion goes down in his entirety, as does the whole of the Hare which is subjected to never-ending pursuit.* [679] But on the Charioteer, the Kids and Olenian Goat do not disappear all at once, they still shine forth on his huge arm, and are marked out above all other parts of him for raising storms when they come together with the sun. Some of him, however, his head and other arm and waist, is sent down by the rising of Capricorn, whereas all the lower parts of him descend with the Archer. Neither Perseus nor the stern of many-starred Argo remain above, but Perseus sets except for his knee and right foot, and the ship as far as the curve of its stern. Argo goes down wholly at the rising of Capricorn, at the time when Procyon also sets, and other constellations rise, the Bird, the Eagle, the stars of the winged Arrow, and the sacred Altar located in the south.

[693] When the Water-pourer has risen as far as his waist, the Horse wheels his legs and head above the horizon, while opposite the Horse, starry Night draws the Centaur down by its tail, but cannot yet swallow down his head or broad shoulders together with his chest; she does bring down the coiled neck of the gleaming Hydra, however,

and the whole of its face; although much of the Hydra still remains behind, Night engulfs that too in its entirety, along with the Centaur, when the Fishes rise. With the Fishes comes the other Fish that is located below dim Capricorn, but not wholly, because a small part of it waits for the next sign. [704] So too the piteous arms, knees, and shoulders of Andromeda stretch out all divided, partly ahead, and partly behind, when the two Fishes first emerge above the horizon; her right side is drawn up by the Fishes themselves, but her left side is brought up from below by the rising of the Ram.

When the Ram comes up, you can also see the Altar in the west, while Perseus can be seen rising on the other horizon, though only his head and shoulders; as to his belt, it is questionable as to whether it appears at the end of the rising of the Ram or at the rising of the Bull, with which he wheels completely into view. Nor is the Charioteer left behind when the Bull rises up, their courses being closely connected; and yet he does not rise completely with that sign, it is the Twins who bring him up fully and wholly. [718] But the Kids, and the sole of his left foot, and the Goat herself too, travel together with the Bull, at the time when the back-fin and tail of the celestial Sea-monster rise up from below. By that time the Bear-guard is already setting along with the first of the four signs that bring him down, all except his left hand, which circles below the great Bear.

[724] May the sight of the Serpent-bearer setting right up to his knees be a sign for you that the Twins are rising above the opposite horizon. At that time none of the Sea-monster is divided any longer by the horizon as it is drawn on its way, you can now see it in its entirety. [728] Now too, on a clear night at sea, a sailor can see the first bend of the River rising up from the sea, as he waits for Orion himself to provide him with some indication of the length of his night or voyage. For everywhere the gods send these many messages to men.

Days of the month and times of the year

[733] Don't you see? When the moon shines forth with slender horns from the west, she tells us that a new month is beginning; when the first rays are shed from her that just suffice to cast a shadow, she tells us that she is entering on her fourth day; when half-full, she is at eight days; when full-faced, at mid-month. As she constantly turns

different faces toward us in her different phases, she tells us which day of the month is coming around.

[740] To announce the endings of the nights, the twelve signs of the zodiac serve very well. But as regards the seasons of the great year, the time to plough the fallow field, the time to plant, all of that is already indicated everywhere through signs from Zeus. And out at sea too, on a ship, one can recognize the coming of a hard-beating winter storm by taking note of dread Arcturus,* or other stars that emerge from the ocean at dawn or when the night is just beginning. [748] For in truth the sun passes through them all in the course of the year as he drives his huge furrow, and runs up against one and then another, now at his rising and now at his setting, and so it is that different stars look down on different days. [752] The things that I am saying here you know for your own part too; for they have come to be widely celebrated, the nineteen cycles* of the radiant sun, and all that the night brings round, from the belt of Orion to the last of Orion and to his fierce Dog, and the stars which, seen in the realm of Poseidon or that of Zeus himself,* provide human beings with well-established signs.

III. WEATHER SIGNS

The value of signs

[758] Study them, then, and if you ever entrust yourself to a ship, make sure that you discover all the signs that are set down to give notice of storm-winds and tempests at sea. The effort is trifling, but huge is the benefit that a man soon draws from his attentiveness if he is always on his guard. In the first place, he is safer for his own part, and he can be of great help to others too through his advice when a storm is brewing up in the neighbourhood. [765] For often a man will prepare his ship against danger on a calm night for fear of what the sea will bring at dawn; but sometimes the peril strikes on the third day, sometimes on the fifth, and sometimes it comes along unexpectedly. For we human beings have not as yet acquired knowledge of all things from Zeus, there is much that is still hidden from us that Zeus, if he so wishes, will reveal to us at some future time; for he plainly does come to the aid of the human race, revealing himself on all sides, and displaying his signs everywhere.

Signs from the Moon

[773] Some things the moon will tell you when she is half-full as she is waxing or waning, or again when she is full, and other things the sun will urge on you, at his rising, or again at nightfall. And there will be other signs that you can draw from other sources regarding both night and day.

[778] Pay attention first of all to the horns on either side of the moon. For the evenings as they pass constantly paint her with a different light, and at different times her horns assume different forms as she begins to wax, one form on the third day, another on the fourth; from those forms you can gain information about the month that is beginning.

[783] If she is slender and clear on the third day, she is a sign of good weather; if slender and very red, she is windy; if thicker with blunted horns from the third day to the fourth, it is the south wind or the approach of rain that is making her so blunt. If on the third day one sees her two horns neither bent forward nor leaning back, but rather curving straight up on both sides, winds will blow in from the west after that night. [792] But if she is still standing just as upright on the fourth day, she is then warning that a storm is brewing up. If her upper horn is inclined well forward, you should expect the north wind, and if it is leaning backward, the south wind. But if on the third day she is fully encircled by a halo, red throughout, she then foretells a storm, and the more fiery the red, the fiercer the storm.

[799] Look at her when she is full, and when she is half-full on either side of her full state, as she is either waxing or returning to her crescent form; and from her colour, draw evidence about the weather of each month. If she is clear all over, you can infer that the weather will be fine; if red all over, you can expect that wind will be on the way; and if dark in patches, you should expect rain.

[805] But the signs do not all remain valid for every day of the month. Those that are manifested on the third or fourth day hold good until the first half-moon; those at the half-moon, right up to the full moon; then likewise from the full moon to the waning half-moon; and next comes the fourth day from the end of the month, and finally the third day of the following month.

[811] When haloes fully encircle the moon, whether she be surrounded by three, or two, or one alone, expect either wind or calm if

there is only a single halo, wind if it is broken and calm if it is fading away; and if there are two haloes running around the moon, you can expect a storm; while a triple halo will bring a more severe storm, and worse still if it is dark, and worse again if it is broken.

These, then, are the signs for the month that you can learn from the moon.

Signs from the Sun

[819] Pay heed to the sun too at either end of his daily course; the signs connected with the sun are particularly clear, both at his setting and when he is rising above the other horizon.

[822] May his disk not be mottled as he begins to strike the earth with his rays, when you have need of a fine day, no, may he be clear of any mark and appear entirely unblemished. And if he remains as pure when the hour comes for the oxen to be unyoked, and he sets unclouded at dusk with a gentle glow, he will again bring fine weather at dawn on the following day. [828] But not when he looks hollow as he rises up again, nor when his beams are divided, some striking north and others south, while his centre shines bright, since his course will then take him through rain or through wind.

[832] Examine, if his beams permit, the sun himself, since that is the best manner of observation, to see if a blush is running across him, for he often reddens here and there when clouds trail over him or he is in some way obscured. May such darkening be a sign to you of approaching rain, and any trace of redness a sign of wind. But if he is tinged with both colours at the same time, he will bring rain and also run through wind. [840] If when he rises, or again when he sets, his rays run together and collect into a single point, or if he is shrouded by cloud as he passes from night to day or from day to night, his course will be accompanied on those days by pouring rain. When a small cloud rises ahead of him, and he himself rises after it shorn of his beams, do not fail to expect rain.

[847] But when a broad circle of cloud around him seems to broaden out, as though melting, when the sun first rises, and then narrows again, he will be passing on his way in fine weather, and so too if in winter-time, he turns pale when setting. But if there has been rainfall in the course of the day, examine the clouds afterwards, looking in the direction of the setting sun, and if the sun is shrouded by

a cloud that seems to be turning dark, while on either side of him, his rays are divided this way and that as they move between, you will surely still have need of shelter until the following day. [858] But if he sinks cloudless into the western ocean, and the clouds that stand nearby turn red as he goes down, you need have no fear at all of rain on the morrow or during the night, although you should fear it if the sun's rays suddenly seem to die away as they strain down from the sky, just as they fade out when the moon overshadows them when standing between the earth and the sun.

[866] When the sun is late in showing himself, and reddish clouds appear here and there before dawn, the fields will not remain unwatered on that day. And if, when the sun is still below the horizon, the rays that he sends out ahead of him seem to be dimmed by shadow before dawn, do not fail to realize that rain or wind will be on their way. [872] The more that his rays come enveloped in shadow, the more they should be seen as a sign of rain; but if only a light veil of darkness covers them, such as gentle mists are liable to bring, the darkness that enwraps them is a sign of oncoming rain. [877] Nor do dark haloes near the sun give sign of good weather; the nearer they are to the sun and the more consistently dark, the worse are the storms that they foretell; and if there are two haloes, the storms will be fiercer still.

[880] Watch out to see, when the sun is rising or again when it is setting, whether the clouds known as parhelia* turn red to the south or north or on both sides, and do not carry out that observation without proper care; for if these clouds hold the sun between them on both sides at once, close to the horizon, a storm will come down from the heavens without delay; but if there is only one cloud shining red to the north, it will bring storm-winds from the north, or if to the south, from the south, or perhaps drops of rain will come pelting down. Pay particular heed to these signs when they come from the west, for if they come from there, they are always equally dependable.

Signs from the Manger

[892] Keep an eye too on the Manger.* Like a small patch of mist in the north, it leads the way under the Crab. On either side of it travel two stars that shine with a dim light, neither far apart nor very close, but seeming to be separated by about a cubit; one is to the north,

while the other inclines toward the south. They are known as the Asses, while between them lies the Manger. [899] If all of a sudden, when the sky as a whole is clear, the Manger suddenly disappears from view, while the stars that travel on either side look to be close together, the fields will be drenched by a storm of no mean strength. [903] Or if, when the Manger darkens, the two stars remain just as they were, they foretell rain. But if the Ass to the north of the Manger shines feebly, being somewhat hazy, while the Ass to the south gleams brightly, expect wind from the south; while you should watch out, on the contrary, for wind from the north if it is the southern Ass that is hazy and the northern that is bright.

Signs for wind

[909] Take for a sign of wind also a swelling sea, and beaches that roar from afar, and seashores that resound in fine weather, and the moaning of mountain-peaks. And if a heron comes to dry land from the sea, flying in an erratic fashion with many a scream, it will be moving ahead of a wind that is blowing up over the sea. [916] And on occasion too, when petrels are flying around in fair weather, they will flock together to face winds that are due to arrive. Or often wild ducks, or gulls that roam the seas, come and beat their wings on the dry land; or a cloud lengthens out on the mountain-peaks. [921] It has been noted too that seed-fluff, the down of the white thistle, serves as a sign of wind when it drifts in large amounts on the surface of the dumb sea, some ahead and some behind. And from the direction from where, in summer, the thunder and lightning-flashes come, it is from there that you may expect the wind to come blowing in. [926] When through the dark night shooting stars fly in swift succession, leaving bright trails behind them, you may expect a wind to come blowing in on the same course; and if others shoot in the opposite direction, and others again from other parts of the sky, you should be on your guard then for winds coming in from all quarters, those winds being exceedingly irregular, blowing too chaotically for men to predict.

Signs for rain

[933] When lightning flashes from the east and south, and sometimes

the west and sometimes the north, the sailor out at sea then begins to grow afraid, fearing that he may get caught by the sea on the one hand and rain from heaven on the other; for it is with rain that so much lightning comes flashing from every side. Often, before the coming of rain, clouds appear that look very like tufts of wool, or a double rainbow arches over the broad sky, or perhaps some star is ringed with a dark halo.

[942] Often birds of the lake or sea wet themselves over and over again by plunging into the water, or swallows dart for long periods around a lake, grazing the rippling water with their breast, or those wretched creatures that are a blessing to water-snakes, the fathers of tadpoles, croak more loudly than usual from the water itself, or a solitary tree-frog pipes out its song to the dawn, or perhaps a chattering crow on a jutting shoreline ducks its head when a wave comes into land, or else dips itself into a river from its head to the top of its shoulders, or even plunges in completely, or keeps walking back and forth by the water-side, croaking hoarsely all the while.

[954] And before rain comes down from the heavens, cattle sniff it out in the air, looking up toward the sky; and from their hole in the ground, ants hastily bring up all their eggs; and hosts of millipedes are seen climbing up the walls, and earthworms are seen wandering about, those creatures that men call entrails of the dark earth. [960] And the domestic fowl born of the cock carefully clear themselves of lice and cluck at the top of their voice, making a sound like raindrops dripping down in swift succession. Sometimes families of ravens too, and tribes of jackdaws, can be a sign that rain is due from the sky of Zeus, when they appear in flocks and screech like falcons. [966] And crows too imitate with their cry the heavenly drops of rain that are on the way, and sometimes they croak twice over in a deep tone and then make a loud whirring noise by repeatedly flapping their wings. [970] Domestic ducks, furthermore, and jackdaws that live under our roof, come in under the eaves, clapping their wings, or the heron hurries out over the waves with shrill screams.

[973] Never fail to heed any of these signs when you are on your guard against rain, nor if the flies are biting more than usual and are yearning for blood, nor if snuff collects around the wick of a lamp on a moist night, nor if, in winter-time, the flame does not always rise up straight and even, but sparks sometimes fly from it like weightless bubbles, nor if the beams of light from it flicker, nor if the island

birds fly around in dense flocks in high summer. [983] And do not fail to take note if a pot or tripod standing over the fire is surrounded by an unusual number of sparks, or if in the ashes of glowing charcoal there are spots shining out here and there like millet-seed, but watch out for all of this too if you are looking around for signs of rain.

Signs for fair weather and change of weather

[988] If a misty cloud is stretched out along the base of a high mountain while the uppermost peaks look clear, you should then have very fine weather. You will also have good weather when low cloud appears above the broad sea, not rising up to any height, but pressed down right there like a flat sheet of rock.

[994] When you have fine weather, watch out all the more for signs of rain, and when it is stormy, for signs of calm. You should look with special care at the Manger, which is carried around near the Crab, as it grows clear from below of all the mist that is covering it; for it clears up when storms are drawing to their end.

[999] And may the unruffled flames of lamps and the gentle hooting of the night-owl be a sign for you that a storm is subsiding, and so too the crow when it cries gently in the evening in constantly changing tones, and rooks too when, on their own, they utter two solitary cries, followed by loud screams in rapid succession, or when, flocking together in larger numbers, they think of going off to roost and sing at the top of their voice. One would suppose that they are full of joy, seeing how they call out in resonant tones, often around the foliage of a tree, or sometimes on the tree itself, at the place where they roost, and flap their wings as they return home. [1010] And cranes, before a gentle calm, will strain steadily onward on a single course, all flocked together, and as long as weather is fine, will fly on their way without turning back.

[1013] But when the clear light of the stars is dimmed, although not obstructed by banks of cloud, and no other source of darkness stands in the way, and no moonlight either, but the stars suddenly turn dim of their own accord, you should no longer regard this as a sign of calm, but rather look out for a storm. The same applies too when some clouds remain in the same position, while others move up toward them, some overtaking them and others lagging behind.

[1021] And geese hurrying to their pasture with many a cry is a sure sign of a coming storm, and so too the nine-lived crow* crying out at night, and the chaffinch chirping at dawn, and all the seafowl flying in from the sea, and the wren or robin slipping into a hollow, and hosts of jackdaws leaving rich pastures to return to their evening roost. [1028] When a fierce storm is brewing, the buzzing bees no longer fly far afield in search of wax, but labour at home at their honey and building-work; and in the sky above, long lines of cranes no longer strain forward on the same course, but wheel round to fly back home. [1033] And when, in windless weather, airy cobwebs are flying loose, and the flames of the lamp flicker weakly, or fires and lamps prove hard to light although the weather is fine, you can surely expect a storm to be on the way. Why recount for you all signs that are available to human beings? For even in the ugly clumping of ashes, a sign of snowfall can be seen, and a sign of snow in your lamp too when spots like millet-seeds form a circle all around the burning wick; and in live coals a sign of hail, when the coal itself is seen to burn brightly, but something like a faint mist appears at its centre amidst the burning fire.

Seasonal signs from vegetation

[1044] Nor are the holm-oaks* laden with fruit untried, or the dark mastic,* and the cultivator never stops peering around on every side for fear that the summer may slip from his hands. When the holm-oaks carry a moderate load of clustering acorns, they are telling you that the winter will be harsher than usual; but hope that they may not be weighed down too heavily all over, and that the fields may thus bring forth good crops of grain far removed from any drought. [1051] Three times the mastic buds, and three times it produces its fruit: and each growth provides in its turn signs for the field-work. For men divide the growing-season into three periods, the middle one and the two at either end; and the first fruiting is the sign for the first sowing, the middle for the middle sowing, and the last of all for the final sowing. [1057] To the degree that the richly-blooming mastic brings forth its finest crop, so also will the ploughing yield the richest harvest of grain: the most modest crop points to a poor harvest, and a middling crop to a middling harvest. [1060] Likewise, the stalk of the squill* flowers three times over, and one can see there too the signs of a corresponding harvest; all the signs that the farmer observes in the mastic crop, he can find again in the white flower of the squill.

Signs for the forthcoming winter and summer

[1064] When in autumn wasps come swarming down everywhere in large numbers, one can tell that winter will arrive even before the setting of the Pleiades, such are the whirls and eddies that suddenly develop among the spiralling wasps. [1068] And when sows, ewes, and she-goats never stop coupling, and repeatedly mate again after having received every attention from the males, they foretell a long winter just as the wasps do. But if the goats, ewes, and sows mate late in the season, this is a source of joy to the poor man who finds it hard to keep warm, because their mating indicates that the weather will be good that year. [1075] The farmer who carries out his work in a timely fashion also rejoices to see the flocks of cranes arriving at the proper time, and the untimely farmer to see them arriving late: for winter comes along at the same time as the cranes. When they come early and largely flocked together, winter will come early; but when they arrive late without gathering into flocks, over a longer period and not in large numbers at any one time, the delayed farm-work will benefit from the delay in the arrival of winter.

[1082] If cattle and sheep dig at the ground after fruit-laden autumn and stretch their heads out against the north wind, very stormy will be the winter that the Pleiades bring at their setting. And may they not dig excessively, because if they do, the winter will be exceptionally long and favourable neither to trees nor to crops. May an abundance of snow cover the broad fields, lying over the young shoots when they are undeveloped as yet and still short, such that the hopeful man may enjoy prosperity.

[1091] May the stars up above always remain unchanged, and may there not be one or two or more with a comet's tail, for a large number of comets is the sign of a dry year.

[1094] When a man on the mainland sees flocks of birds come in from the islands to swarm down on to his fields in large numbers at the start of summer, he is none too happy, because he has very grave fears for his harvest; he is afraid that the corn will come as empty ears and chaff, spoiled by drought. The goatherd rejoices, however, to see these same birds in moderate numbers, because he may hope after that to have a good year for milk. [1101] So it is that we poor inconstant human beings make our livings in our different ways, but all of us are ready to pay heed to the signs that we find in front of us and to adopt them for the present.

Signs of bad weather from the behaviour of animals

[1104] Shepherds recognize from their sheep that bad weather is on the way when they run to pasture with unusual haste, while some animals from the flock, now rams, now lambs, amuse themselves on the way by butting one another with their horns; or when, here and there, they jump up into the air, the young agile ones with all four feet off the ground, the horned ones with two, or when the shepherds are moving them from the flock in the evening, driving them home against their will, and they keep biting at the grass all the way, although urged along by being pelted with many a stone.

[1113] From their cattle too, farmers and herdsmen learn that a storm is blowing up; for when cattle lick around their front hooves with their tongue, or stretch themselves out on their right flank to sleep, the experienced ploughman expects a delay in the ploughing. [1118] Or when the cows never stop lowing as they gather together to make their way home in the evening, the disgruntled heifers are giving sign that they will be grazing all too soon on storm-beaten pastures. Nor is it a sign of good weather when goats chew eagerly at the prickly holm-oak, or sows dig away at their bedding in a frenzied manner. [1124] And when a lone wolf howls for a long time, or when, showing little concern about the farmers, it comes down into cultivated land, as though in search of shelter close to human company, to set up its lair at that very spot, you may expect a storm before three days are out. [1129] And so too, from other signs that have come before, you can tell that there will be wind or storm or rain on that very day, or on the following day, or again on the day after next. [1132] For even mice when they squeaked louder than usual in fair weather, and leaped around as if they were dancing, did not pass unnoticed by our forebears, nor did dogs; for a dog digs at the ground with both front paws when it senses that a storm is on the way, and those mice too act as weather-prophets in such circumstances. [1138] Indeed, even a crab will leave the water to come on to dry land when a storm is about to descend, and mice will throw their litter around in the daytime, wanting to nestle down at the appearance of signs of rain.

Concluding remarks

[1142] Don't fail to heed any of these warnings. It is a good idea to examine one sign after another, and if two are in accord, your expectation is confirmed, while if there is a third, you can have confidence. [1145] As the year progresses, constantly review and compare the signs to see whether, at the rising or setting of a star, the day indeed shows itself to be as the sign had foretold. The surest results can be achieved by observing the last four days of the old month and the first four days of the new; for these enclose the boundaries of the converging months, when the sky is more deceptive than usual on eight nights for want of the bright-faced moon.

[1153] Keep a close eye on these signs, all taken together, throughout the year, and you will never draw an ill-founded conclusion from what you see in the sky.

APPENDIX

EXTRACTS FROM GEMINOS, *INTRODUCTION TO THE 'PHAENOMENA'*

The Zodiac

The circle of the signs [zodiac] is divided into twelve parts, and each of these sections is described by the general name of twelfth-part (*dodekato-morion*), and by a name which is specific to each sign, in accordance with the stars that it contains, which give each its particular form. The twelve signs are as follows: Ram, Bull, Twins, Crab, Lion, Maiden, Scales, Scorpion, Archer, Capricorn, Water-pourer, and Fishes.

The term sign can be understood in two senses: in one sense it is the twelfth part of the circle of the zodiac, that is to say a certain stretch of space marked off by the stars or points, while in the other sense it is an image formed from stars, in accordance with resemblance and the position of the stars.

The twelfth-parts are thus equal in size, because the circle of signs can be divided into twelve equal parts by use of the *dioptra* [an optical instrument]; but the constellation-signs are neither equal in size nor made up of the same number of stars, nor do they always fill the space belonging to each twelfth-part. But rather, some fall short, such as the Crab which takes up only a small part of the space that belongs to it, while others stretch out beyond, taking up part of the preceding and following signs, as in the case of the Maiden. Furthermore, certain of the twelve signs do not even lie wholly within the circle of the zodiac, but some extend north of it, such as the Lion, and others south, such as the Scorpion. . . . [from Chapter 1]

The Constellations

The constellations are divided into three classes, for some lie on the circle of the zodiac, and some are said to be northern, and some are described as southern.

Those that lie *on the zodiac* are the twelve signs, whose names we have already mentioned. And in these twelve signs, there are some stars that have been thought worthy of being given particular names because of the indicators associated with them. Thus in the Bull, some stars lying on its back, six in number, are called the Pleiades, while some lying on the head of the Bull, five in number, are called the Hyades. The leading star in the foot of the Twins is called Propous (Forefoot). The stars in the Crab that resemble a patch of mist are called the Manger; and the two stars that lie next to it are called the Asses. The bright star that lies on the heart of the Lion is named after the place in which it is set, being called the Heart of the Lion; but it is also called Basiliskos (Little King) by some people, because those who are born in this region seem to be of kingly nativity. The star that lies at the tip of the left hand of the Maiden is called Stachys (Ear of Corn); and the small star that lies on the right wing of the Maiden is called Protrygetor (Announcer of the Vintage). The stars that lie at the end of the right hand of the Water-pourer are called the Jug. The stars that lie in a row starting out from the tail parts of the Fishes are called the Cords. In the southern Cord there are nine stars, and in the northern, five. The bright star lying at the end of the cord is called the Knot.

The *northern constellations* are those that lie to the north of the zodiac. They are the following: the Great Bear and the Small, the Dragon that lies between the Bears, the Bear-guard, the Crown, the Kneeler, the Serpent-bearer, the Serpent, the Bird, the Arrow, the Eagle, the Dolphin, the Forepart of a Horse according to Hipparchos, the Horse, Cepheus, Cassiepeia, Andromeda, Perseus, the Charioteer, the Triangle, and the constellation later established by Callimachus, Berenice's Lock of Hair.

In these constellations once again, some stars have particular names because they have important indicators associated with them. The bright star which lies between the legs of the Bear-guard is called Arcturus. The bright star lying by Lyre is called by the same name as the constellation as a whole. The midmost of the three stars in the Eagle is called likewise by the same name as the constellation. The stars that lie at the tip of the left hand of Perseus are called the Gorgon's Head, while those that lie at the tip of the right hand of Perseus, massed together and small, are arranged to form the image of the sickle. The star that lies on the right shoulder of the Charioteer is called the Goat, while the two little stars at the tip of his [left] hand are called the Kids.

The *southern constellations* are those that lie to the south of the zodiac. They are the following: Orion and Procyon, the Dog, the Hare, Argo, the Water-snake, the Bowl, the Crow, the Centaur, the Beast that the Centaur is holding, and the Thyrsos-lance that the Centaur is holding according to Hipparchos, the Censer, the Southern Fish, the Sea-monster, the Water coming from the Water-pourer, the River flowing from Orion, the Southern Crown, which some call the Canopy, and the Caduceus according to Hipparchos.

And again, in these constellations, some stars have names of their own. The bright star in Procyon is called Procyon. The bright star on the mouth of the Dog which seems to bring the burning heat is called by the same name as the constellation as a whole. The bright star that lies at the tip of the steering-oar of Argo is named Canopos. At Rhodes it is hard to see, or can only be seen at all from high ground, but in Alexandria it is fully visible, because it appears almost a quarter of a sign above the horizon. . . . [from Chapter 3]

The Circles of the Sphere

Of the circles of the sphere, some are parallel, some oblique, and some pass through the poles.

The parallel circles are those that have the same poles as the cosmos. There are five parallel circles: the arctic circle, the summer tropic, the equator, the winter tropic, and the antarctic circle.

The *arctic circle* is the largest of the circles that are always visible, it touches the horizon at one point and lies wholly above the earth. The stars that lie within it neither rise nor set, but can be seen throughout the night revolving round the pole. In our part of the world, this circle is traced out by the forefoot of the Great Bear.

The *summer tropic* circle is the northernmost of the circles that are marked out by the sun during the rotation of the cosmos. When the sun is on this circle, it brings the summer solstice, on which the day is the longest of all the days of the year, and the night is the shortest. For the summer solstice, however, the sun is no longer seen to be progressing toward the north, but it turns toward the other side of the cosmos, which is why this circle is called a tropic [turning point].

The *equator* is the largest of the five parallel circles. It is bisected by the horizon, so that one semicircle is situated above the earth, while the other lies below the horizon. When the sun is on this circle, it brings about the equinoxes, namely the vernal and the autumnal.

The *winter tropic* is the southernmost of the circles that are marked out by the sun during the rotation of the cosmos. When the sun is on this circle, it brings about the winter solstice, on which the night is the longest of all the nights of the year, and the day is the shortest. After the winter solstice, however, the sun is no longer to be seen progressing toward the south, but it turns back toward the other side of the cosmos, which is why this circle too is called a tropic.

The *antarctic circle* is equal in size to the arctic circle and runs parallel to it, touching the horizon at one point, and being situated wholly beneath the earth; the stars that lie within it always remain invisible to us.

Of the aforementioned five parallel circles, the equator is the largest, while the tropics are the next largest, when viewed from our part of the world. One must think of these circles as being without breadth, and as being perceptible to reason alone, in so far as they are established by the positions of the stars, through observations made through the dioptra, and through the exercise of our own thought. For the only circle in the cosmos that is visible is the milky circle, whereas the others are only perceptible to reason.

Through the poles pass the circles that some call *colures*; they are characterized by the fact that they have the poles of the cosmos on their own perimeters. They are called colures because certain parts of them lie out of sight. For the other circles can be seen in their entirety during the rotation of the cosmos, but a certain part of the colures cannot be seen, that which is cut off below the horizon by the antarctic circle. These circles pass through the solsticial and equinoctial points, and so divide the circle that passes through the middle of the signs [i.e. the ecliptic] into four equal parts.

The *circle of the twelve signs* [the zodiac] is an oblique circle. It is itself made up of three parallel circles, two of which are said to mark off the width of the zodiac, while the other [the ecliptic] is called the circle through the middle of the signs. The latter touches upon two parallel circles of equal size, the summer tropic at the first degree of the Crab, and the winter tropic at the first degree of Capricorn; and it bisects the equator at the first degree of the Ram and first degree of the Scales. The zodiac is called oblique because it cuts the parallel circles.

The *horizon* is the circle that separates, for us, the visible part of the cosmos from the invisible, and bisects the whole sphere of the cosmos, so that one hemisphere lies above the earth, and the other below it. . . .

The *milky circle* is an oblique circle. This circle stretches obliquely, in a fairly wide band, through the tropic circles; it is made up of a cloudlike mass of small elements and is the only visible circle in the cosmos. It is not of consistent width, but is broader in some sections and narrower in others. For that reason, the milky circle is not inscribed on most celestial globes. This too is one of the greatest circles, these being the circles that have the same centre as the sphere. These greatest circles are seven in number: the equator, the zodiac with the circle through the middle of the signs, the circles through the poles [i.e. the colures], the horizon at each specific place, the meridian, and the milky circle. [from Chapter 5]

EXPLANATORY NOTES

The notes concentrate on points which have not already been discussed in the editorial commentaries in the main text, or elucidated within the translated narratives themselves (for if something seems unclear or obscure in the Epitome, further information may often be found in the corresponding narrative by Hyginus, which is usually fuller). Special attention has naturally been paid to mythological matters.

The following *abbreviations* are used:

Ap.	Apollodorus, author of the *Library*, a very useful mythological compendium dating to the 1st or 2nd century AD; there are translations in the present series and in the Loeb series. The latter part of the work survives only in summary form, and the reference is then given as Ap. Epit., i.e. Apollodorus, Epitome.
fr.	fragment
Hes. fr.	Hesiod, fragment; these fragments come from writings such as the *Catalogue of Women*, an important mythographical work, or the *Astronomy*, which were of later origin than the genuine works of Hesiod, the *Theogony* and *Works and Days*. The references are to the standard edition by Merkelbach and West, Oxford 1967.
Hes. *Theog.*	Hesiod, *Theogony*
Il.	Homer's *Iliad*
Isthm.	Pindar's *Isthmian Ode*
Nem.	Pindar's *Nemean Ode*
Od.	Homer's *Odyssey*
Ol.	Pindar's *Olympian Ode*
Phaen.	Aratus's *Phaenomena*
Pyth.	Pindar's *Pythian Ode*
schol.	scholion; scholia are marginal notes by ancient or medieval scholars to ancient works, which can be a valuable source for mythographical information.
schol. Arat.	scholion to Aratus
schol. Germ.	scholion to Germanicus. These are not actually scholia in the proper sense: see Introduction, p. 25; Germanicus was the author of a Latin version of Aratus's *Phaenomena*.
Serv. Ecl.	Servius on Virgil's *Eclogue*

Dates: all dates are BC unless otherwise indicated.

Sources cited by the Epitome and Hyginus: these are often quite obscure, sometimes so obscure indeed that little information can be offered about them; when a note is required, it is inserted only on the first occasion on which the source is cited.

THE MYTHOLOGICAL NARRATIVES

3 *Hesiod says*: in fr. 163 MW, probably from the Hesiodic *Catalogue*, written well after the lifetime of Hesiod; for the first part of the story only, ending with the birth of the child.

daughter of Lycaon: Callisto.

inviolable sanctuary of Zeus: the sanctuary of Lycaean Zeus in south-western Arcadia. No one was allowed to enter it, and it was said that any-one who did would die within a year (Pausanias 8.38.6). There was assur-edly no law to prevent animals from entering, and in other respects too the Epitome and Hyginus cannot be taken as reliable sources for Eratos-thenes' narrative (see pp. 10–11).

son . . . Arcadians chased after her: it can be assumed that in the original narrative, Arcas tried to hunt down his bear-mother in ignorance of her identity, and that the Arcadians then chased after both of them because Arcas was pursuing her into the sanctuary.

Amphis: author of comedies who wrote at Athens in the 4th century BC; a fittingly humorous version of Callisto's story.

4 *one that stands higher*: the Small Bear, being closer to the pole.

uppermost circle: i.e. the arctic circle. If the position of that circle is deter-mined by whether observable stars are seen never to set, its latitude will naturally vary according to the latitude on earth from which the observa-tions are made; when viewed from the southern Aegean the Bear as a whole never sets, and could thus be said to lie wholly within the arctic circle, but now that the arctic circle has been fixed universally at 66.6 degrees N, some of its principal stars lie outside the circle.

pole star: not our pole star, alpha Ursae Minoris, which is the brightest star in the constellation, but epsilon Ursae Minoris, which was closest to the pole at that period.

the Choreutes: alpha and delta Ursae Minoris.

arktos . . . Arcas: because of the similarity in sound, it could be suggested that he had been given that name because his mother was in the form of a bear when she gave birth to him.

5 *Aetolians*: this reflects a misunderstanding of the Greek source: *aipoloi*, herdsmen, are confused with *Aitoloi*, Aetolians (people who lived far away from Arcadia, north of the Gulf of Corinth).

sanctuary of Lycaean Zeus: near the summit of Mount Lykaion in south-west Arcadia; there was a large ash-altar on the summit with a retaining wall, and a sacred precinct nearby (see Pausanias 8.38.6–7).

Arctos: the Greek word was sometimes used in Latin in connection with the constellations, rather than Ursa, the usual Latin word for a bear; Hygi-nus uses it here because the constellation Bootes was called Arctophylax (a Greek word that was also used as a loan-word in Latin) in so far as it was viewed in relation to the Bear.

Hera in her anger: as the consort of Zeus, Hera resents his dalliances with mortal women, and often takes action against them or against their children.

Araithos of Tegea: an Arcadian author who wrote about the mythical history of the province, perhaps in the latter part of the 3rd century.

Ceteus . . . Kneeler: on the varying traditions about Callisto's parentage, see Ap. 3.8.2; Ceteus was a son of Lycaon, Callisto would originally have had no connection with Lycaon or his family. The Kneeler is the constellation now known as Hercules.

6 *Septentrio*: in Latin the stars of the Bear or, more precisely, of the Plough, were known as the Septentriones, or Seven Plough-Oxen, hence Hyginus's use of the singular to refer to the Bear.

8 *Phoenike*: i.e. the Phoenician, because the Phoenicians steered by it.

Artemis held her in high regard: Callisto, not Phoenike (see p. 4).

Aglaosthenes: a local historian of Naxos of unknown date.

9 *Histoi . . . Nicostratos*: Histoi was a typical port name, here a harbour-town in Crete; Nicostratos was the son of Menelaos and Helen, so this refers to a foundation myth.

Our people: the Romans; Hyginus occasionally mentions the Latin name of a star or star-group.

wagon . . . Hamaxa: this being the Greek name for a wagon.

Aratus says: inferred from *Phaen.* 25–35 and 91–3.

Parmeniscos: Alexandrian scholar who wrote about astronomical matters and much else besides; author of a commentary on Aratus.

under the name of Bootes: the name Bootes was originally applied to the bright star Arcturus alone, which could be pictured as being an ox-driver driving the Wagon, but it was later transferred to the constellation which was constructed around Arcturus. The name Arctophylax, which would indeed have been of later origin, was applied to the constellation alone.

both the Bear and the Wagon: see *Il.* 18.487, and *Od.* 5.273; for Homer the constellation under either name would have consisted of the seven bright stars alone (our Plough); it was only later that astronomers drew in other stars to create the more elaborate constellation-figure mentioned shortly before.

Bootes . . . Arctophylax: it is true that Homer never mentions the name Arctophylax (Eudoxos in the 4th century is the first author who is definitely known to have used it), but 'late-setting Bootes' in *Od.* 5.272 would surely have been the star Arcturus rather than the constellation.

10 *Herodotus of Miletos states*: in his *Histories* 1.70; cf. Diogenes Laertius 1.22;

the historian came from Halicarnassos, it was the philosopher-scientist Thales who was a citizen of Miletos. Thales may have 'measured out the little stars of the constellation' (Callimachus fr. 191), but there is naturally no truth in the suggestion that the Phoenicians first learned about the constellation from him.

12 *Hesperides*: already known to Hesiod (*Theog.* 215–16) as daughters of Night who protected the apples; they were thought to live in North Africa, in the farthermost West, as their name, 'daughters of Evening', would suggest. Atlas was commonly placed in the same area, hence the name of the Atlas mountains.

at her bidding: in the usual tradition Heracles was obliged to confront the dragon because Eurytheus told him to fetch some of the apples, as one of the last and most dangerous of his labours; it is not clear whether Hyginus is referring to a divergent account or has misinterpreted his Greek source.

Pherecydes: of Athens, mythographer of the 5th century, one of the main sources for the surviving compendium by Apollodorus; he was cited by Eratosthenes for this detail alone; in his version of the myth Prometheus was said to have fetched the apples on Heracles' behalf.

14 *set in fourth place*: i.e. this constellation was the fourth to be discussed in the original treatise by Eratosthenes.

according to Euripides: Euripides wrote a famous play about this myth, the *Andromeda*, now lost; it is unlikely that portrayals of the myth in Attic tragedy contained any catasterisms.

same distance: this is in no way true.

16 *Polydectes*: the king of the island of Seriphos, where the young Perseus was living with his mother Danae. Polydectes had fallen in love with Danae, and wanted to get Perseus out of the way to prevent him from obstructing the marriage. For the story of how Perseus fetched the Gorgon's head, see Ap. 2.4.2–3.

adamantine: adamant was a mythical metal of extreme hardness.

the Graiai: three sisters of the Gorgons who acted as their protectors. Their name means 'Old Women'; Hesiod says that they were grey-haired from birth (*Theog.* 270–1; here there are only two them), and they are pictured in later accounts of the myth as being old and largely toothless. For a fuller account of the myth of Perseus and Medusa, see Ap. 2.4.2–3.

Tritonis: a large mythical lake set somewhere in North Africa. Although Hesiod placed the Gorgons even further to the west, beyond the ocean (*Theog.* 274–5), Aeschylus evidently set this story in the westernmost reaches of Africa in his lost play.

17 *sickle*: I have omitted the following paragraph, which discusses the meaning of a Greek word in Aratus's description of this constellation.

conceived in a most unusual manner: Zeus transformed himself into a shower of gold to have intercourse with his mother, Danae (Ap. 2.4.1); but the crucial point here is that Perseus was a son of Zeus.

helmet of Hades: Homer mentions how Athena once wore the *Aidōs kuneē* to render herself invisible, *Il.* 5.844–5, and in the Hesiodic *Shield*, 227, Perseus is said to have used it for the same purpose. This 'cap of the Invisible one' was properly a cap of invisibility rather than a cap or helmet that was the personal property of Hades as god of the Underworld, and he is never mentioned in surviving sources as either making use of it or giving it to those who do use it. At most there is the suggestion by Apollodorus (1.2.1) that the Cyclopes provided him with the cap for use in the war against the Titans, when they armed Zeus with his thunderbolt and Poseidon with his trident.

a deed . . . not described in any writings: a surprising observation, since the decapitation of Medusa was described by the early mythographer Pherecydes, 3F11, and later sources, e.g. Ap. 2.4.2, add further details which were surely not of late invention; the episode is already mentioned by Hesiod, *Theog.* 280 ff.

our Genealogies: Hyginus is presumably referring to an edition of his *Fabulae* or *Mythical Tales* rather than a wholly separate work; see *Mythical Tale* 51.

Athena who killed the Gorgon: since she wore the Gorgon's head on her aegis, it could easily be suggested that she had killed Medusa herself (rather than acquiring her head from Perseus as in the usual story); but Euhemerus would have offered a rationalized account of the myth which was not relevant to astral mythology. Hyginus does not return to Euhemerus' story in what remains of his works.

18 *the same star*: the binary star Alpharetz, alpha Andromedae, was also identified as delta Pegasi until the modern constellation boundaries were established; cf. Aratus 206–7.

19 *rival the Nereids in beauty*: fifty sea-nymphs who were daughters of the primordial sea-god Nereus and Doris, daughter of Ocean (Hes. *Theog.* 240 ff., cf. *Il.* 18.38 ff.); Amphitrite, the consort of Poseidon (see pp. 106–7), belonged among them, as did Thetis, the mother of Achilles, but only three of them had any individual destiny; they were otherwise imagined as being a group of sisters who lived together in the sea. When Cassiepeia insulted them, it was naturally the sea-god Poseidon who exacted vengeance.

20 *as the poet Cratinos reports*: when developing this myth of Zeus and Nemesis into an astral myth, Eratosthenes followed the version developed by this Athenian author of comedies from the 5th century, rather than the original version from early epic (see pp. 21–2).

21 *threw it into Leda's lap*: if Helen was the daughter of Nemesis, as the *Cypria* suggested (see p. 21), it had to be explained how she came to be connected with Sparta and the Spartan royal family; according to

another suggestion, a shepherd found the egg in a forest and took it to Leda (Ap. 3.10.7). It is not known how the difficulty was resolved in the *Cypria*, but Apollodorus's account may well have been derived from an early source because Nemesis is said to have turned into a goose there, rather than a swan as was normal in the later tradition.

23 *from a tortoise and the cattle of Apollo*: Hermes used a tortoise-shell to make the body of the lyre, and gut from sheep or from the stolen cattle of Apollo to make the strings.

daughters of Atlas: because Hermes' mother, Maia, was a daughter of Atlas, as Hyginus explains.

Helios . . . Apollo: as a god of light, Apollo was sometimes identified with the sun-god.

24 *Pangaion*: on the north-eastern fringes of Greece, between Macedonia and Thrace.

Aeschylus recounts: in his lost tragedy, the *Bassarids*; Bassarids was another name for Maenads (see p. 26).

Leibethroe: in Pieria, a district of Macedonia lying on the northern slopes of Mount Olympos; cf. Pausanias 9.30.5.

to the shell like arms: the body of this lyre is formed from a tortoise-shell, and it has two wooden arms fitted into one end, with a cross-piece at the top, from which the strings are stretched to run across the underside of the shell. A normal lyre in historical times would have a wooden body with a flat sounding-board.

to the Underworld: after the death of his wife, Orpheus descended to the Underworld to recover her. Hades was so enchanted by his music that he agreed to release her, on condition that Orpheus never looked back to see if she was following him; but he could not resist the urge to do so, and she had to turn back (Ap. 1.3.2, Ovid, *Metamorphoses* 10.8 ff.; earliest allusion to the story in Euripides, *Alcestis* 357–62).

Oineus forgot Artemis: Oineus was king of Calydon in west-central Greece, and Artemis punished his oversight by sending the Calydonian boar to ravage his land, which gave occasion for a boar-hunt which attracted leading heroes from all parts of Greece (Ap. 1.8.1–3).

25 *his daughters*: i.e. the Muses, who were his daughters by Mnemosyne (Memory personified).

a wand: his *caduceus* in Latin or *kerykeion* in Greek, a herald's staff which became one of his special attributes; he would carry it when performing his customary activities, such as acting as messenger of the gods or guiding the dead.

cithara: a more elaborate form of lyre, used especially in public performances.

entrusted with Adonis: Ap. 3.10.4 is our main source for this myth; in that version, Zeus himself decrees that Adonis should spend a third of the year with each of the goddesses, and a third by himself; but he chooses to spend his third with Aphrodite, so she gets the best of the bargain. This is merely an alternative account of the death of Orpheus; it is not directly relevant to the astral myth.

head . . . island of Lesbos: the Hellenistic poet Phanocles described how the head of Orpheus was carried across the sea to Lesbos along with his lyre (Powell, *Collectanea Alexandrina* (1925), 107), cf. Ovid, *Metamorphoses* 11.49 ff.; but in the present context the lyre has a different destiny. Lesbos, the homeland of Sappho and Alcaeus, was renowned for its lyric poets.

26 *to the love of boys*: a notion apparently introduced by Phanocles in the 3rd century; cf. Ovid, *Metamorphoses* 10.64 ff. and 11.1 ff.

27 *serpent . . . guard*: see p. 12 ff.; it becomes the constellation of the Dragon.

28 *Panyasis*: of Halicarnassos, poet of the 5th century, author of a long epic poem about Heracles, now lost.

Aratus claims: Phaen. 64–70.

as we remarked above: see p. 5.

Ellopian sword: Ellopia was a place in northern Euboea (Strabo 10.1.3 ff.); the island was noted for the quality of its metal-work, Chalchidian swords being particularly famous.

Anacreon: not the famous lyric poet from the 6th century, but an Alexandrian poet who wrote about astronomical matters.

31 *Dia*: of uncertain location; some scholars identified it with a small island mentioned in the *Odyssey* (11.323, with Eustathius on 324); but this was often thought to be just another name for Naxos, a wine-rich island which was specially associated with Dionysos.

lock of hair . . . Ariadne: this is the group of stars that was identified as the Lock of Berenice (see pp. 69–72); it would be interesting to know whether it had been identified as Ariadne's lock before that constellation was devised.

Cretan Tales: attributed to the semi-mythical sage and seer Epimenides of Crete.

32 *Argolica*: a lost prose-work about matters of Argive myth and cult, originally written by a certain Argis.

Semele . . . from the Underworld: Dionysos was a son of Zeus by a mortal woman, Semele, daughter of Cadmos, king of Thebes; Zeus inadvertently killed her when she asked him to visit her in his full divine form, but Dionysos later descended to the Underworld to recover her, and she then became immortal as the goddess Thyone.

Polymnos asked: Hyginus discreetly indicates that Polymnos wanted the youthful deity to promise to yield to him as a sexual partner. Clement of Alexandria (*Exhortation to the Greeks* 2.30) is more explicit, and states that Dionysos found the man, here called Prosymnos, dead on his return, and fulfilled his vow symbolically at his grave by use of a fig-tree phallus; a bizarre aetiological myth that was offered to account for the carrying of phallic symbols in the Argive cult of Dionysos.

33 *showed him the way down*: through the Alcyonian Lake near Lerna in the Argolid, which was bottomless, a fact that would later be confirmed experimentally by Nero (Pausanias 2.37.5).

Kneeler . . . Theseus: see p. 28.

with seven maidens and seven boys: as tribute to Minos, the Athenians had to send that number of young people every so often to serve as food for the Minotaur; Theseus volunteered to go on this occasion with the intention of killing the Minotaur, or else he just happened to be included on the list.

Theseus . . . son of Poseidon: although he was conventionally regarded as the son of Aigeus, king of Athens, by the Troezenian princess Aithra, it was also claimed that he was of semi-divine birth as a son of Poseidon, as might seem fitting for such a great hero; Pausanias (2.33.1) reports a Troezenian tradition to that effect. Some mythographers reconciled the conflicting traditions by suggesting that Aithra had slept with Aigeus and Poseidon on the same night (Ap. 3.15.7, Hyginus, *Mythical Tales* 37).

Thetis: daughter of Nereus, the sea-goddess who married Peleus to become the mother of Achilles, but later returned to the sea to live with her Nereid sisters; Theseus was also said to have received the crown from Amphitrite, the consort of Poseidon (see p. 34).

35 *served him to Zeus*: this famous story, which is recorded in many conflicting versions, is not directly relevant to the astral myth, but it is drawn in as being central to the mythology of Lycaon; the child is quite often anonymous (e.g. Ap. 3.8.1), as was probably the case in the earliest tradition.

Trapezous: it is suggested that this Arcadian town acquired its name because Zeus upset the table there, *trapeza* being the Greek word for a table.

set among the constellations: at a later time of course, the Vatican Fragments supply the missing story.

as Hesiod recounts: fr. 163 MW, from the Hesiodic *Catalogue* or *Astronomy*, written well after the lifetime of Hesiod himself.

served him at table: although this gruesome tale is not directly relevant to the catasterism, it is drawn into the overarching narrative through the suggestion that Lycaon took this action because he knew that Zeus had raped his daughter. It is not clear whether he was aware that Arcas was the child who had been born as a result of that. The child was usually said to have been served up to Zeus to test whether he was really a god, either by Lycaon (e.g. Ovid, *Metamorphoses* 1.211 ff.) or often by his sons (e.g. Hyginus, *Mythical Tales* 176); in Apollodorus's version (3.8.1) they apparently undertook this action as a deliberate act of impiety. The child is usually left unnamed, and we may be sure that Arcas was introduced into the story at a secondary stage, after Callisto, who originally had no connection with Lycaon, came to be identified as his daughter.

36 *had intercourse with his mother*: this is unexpected, to say the least, but the same suggestion can be found in the Germanicus scholia; I think this must be an error (the two sources belong to the same line of transmission) rather than an alternative tradition, and that one must look to Hyginus for the only reliable account of the present story, in which Arcas incurs this trouble from the Arcadians because he pursues his bear-mother on to forbidden ground.

on his belt: Arcturus was represented as being on the belt of Bootes in the Aratean tradition (following *Phaen.* 94), but more usually as lying between his knees.

really was a god: that was the traditional explanation, but there is reason to think that Eratosthenes presented the story rather differently, connecting Lycaon's action to his knowledge of Zeus's rape of his daughter (see p. 35 and note).

an Aetolian: properly, a herdsman; an error resulting from a misunderstanding of the Greek source.

37 *already stated*: see p. 5.

Eratosthenes . . . goat: this is a quotation from the *Erigone*, Eratosthenes' lost poem about Icarios and Erigone; the story of the goat provided an explanation for the practice known as *askōliasmos*, in which people participating in grape-harvest festivals in Attica would try to dance on a greased wine-skin. Icarios presumably told his companions to try to dance *on* it in the original narrative.

Maira by name: derived from a name for the dog-star (see p. 117).

38 *Greeks call it Procyon*: this sentence, which may well be an interpolation, is misleading; the dog Maira became the dog-star specifically (see p. 117). Although Canicula (Little Dog) was primarily the Latin name for the dog-star, it could also be applied to the constellation of the small Dog in accordance with its literal meaning.

annual rite: this explains the origin of a practice at the Anthesteria at Athens, an annual festival held in honour of Dionysos, namely the rites of the Aiora or 'Swinging', in which girls would be swung on something resembling modern children's swings. On the same day, girls would sing a song known as the Aletis or Wanderer, and Aletides was an alternative name for the rites. Erigone originated as a heroine associated with the Aiora, and it was only at a secondary stage that she was identified as the daughter of Icarios and introduced into his story. She was also identified with Erigone, daughter of Aigisthos and Clytemnestra.

Canicula . . . heat: the dog-star, Seirios in Greek, was thought to bring heat because its early rising announces the hottest time of year (see p. 117).

39 '*requested*': a strained etymology in which the name is derived from the Greek verb *aitein*; in fact these were quite literally 'annual' winds.

Hermippos: of Smyrna, an author of the 3rd century who belonged to the school of Callimachus.

Homer: *Od.* 5.128.

Petellides of Cnossos: a Cretan author, otherwise unknown; the catasterism may well have been added by Hermippos.

Parion: a Greek city in Mysia in Asia Minor; this seems to have become the accepted account of its foundation.

accompanied by . . . Erigone: this is probably an error: in the original story Erigone stayed at home until the dog led her to her father's corpse.

40 *whom we call Justice*: by reference to Aratus's tale about the origin of the constellation (see pp. 141–2).

Arcturus: Icarios became the constellation Bootes, not the star Arcturus; the name Arcturus was sometimes applied to the constellation in Roman literature, but is not clear that Hyginus is using it in that sense here.

41 *in imitation of Helios*: the sun-god was pictured as driving across the vault of the sky by day in such a chariot, and returning around the encircling ocean by night in a golden cup.

Euripides reports: in a play of unknown title (not his *Erechtheus*).

42 *Hephaisteion*: in Athens to the west of the Agora; Hephaistos is honoured there in conjunction with Athena at a temple dating from the Periclean period.

Panathenaia: annual festival held in honour of Athena, in which there was a splendid procession up to the Acropolis, apparently illustrated in the Parthenon sculptures; from 566/5 a grander festival, the Great Panathenaia, was celebrated every four years, and athletic and musical contests were held in connection with that.

dismounter: *apobates* in Greek, who participated in a special form of chariot-race, in which someone partially dressed like a warrior would jump off, run alongside for a while, and then jump back in; a contest peculiar to Attica and Boeotia, illustrated in the Parthenon frieze.

Goat and the Kids: the star Capella (alpha Aurigae) with the smaller zeta and eta as the Kids.

Musaeus: a legendary sage and musician to whom apocryphal writings were attributed, including poems with mythical content.

entrusted him to Themis: a primordial goddess, daughter of Sky and Earth, who was the personification of justice and order; although she was associated with Zeus as symbolizing an aspect of his rule, the present role is not ascribed to her in any other source.

Amaltheia: a Cretan nymph.

goat's hide as a weapon: the aegis (see p. 47).

at the level of his knees: thus Eudoxos (cf. Aratus 482), but later astronomers observed more accurately that it is his feet that touch the tropic.

43 *a single star*: the star Elnath, beta Tauri, was also identified as gamma Aurigae until the modern constellation boundaries were established.

casket . . . Mysteries: the sacred chest, *kistē*, associated with the Eleusinian Mysteries, containing sacred objects whose nature was known only to initiates.

44 *Orsilochos*: this seems to be an error: he is called Trochilos in Greek sources (see p. 45).

Melisseus: 'Bee-man', his name was evidently inspired by traditions in which the infant Zeus was said to have been fed by bees or on honey. Apollodorus tells the same story (1.1.6), naming his daughters as Adrasteia and Ida. Or else they were called Amatheia and Melissa (Lactantius, *Divine Institutes* 1.22), but that is less appropriate in the present context, because Amaltheia is given as the name of their goat, as in Apollodorus's account. Apollonius (3.132 ff.) and Callimachus (*Hymn* 1.46 ff.) mention Adrasteia as the nurse, without indication of parentage, the latter saying that she fed the infant on milk from the goat Amaltheia and sweet honeycomb.

Cleostratos of Tenedos: astronomer born in the latter part of the 6th century, credited with having introduced the zodiac and solar calendar.

45 *Euhemerus*: of Messene, fl. *c*.300, author of an imaginative work in which the gods were presented as having been historical figures who only came to be venerated as gods at a later time.

49 *According to Aratus*: 216 ff.

50 *Centaur . . . Cheiron*: see pp. 119–20.

51 *Bellerophon*: the story of how Bellerophon came to be sent out to confront the Chimaira is already recounted in similar terms in the *Iliad* (6.152 ff.), but without any mention of Pegasos; the horse appeared in the story from an early period nonetheless, because Hesiod mentions in the *Theogony* (225) that they worked together to kill the Chimaira. See also Ap. 2.3.1–2. Bellerophon, son of Glaucos, was a grandson of Sisyphos, the founder of Ephyra/Corinth.

Iobates: across the Aegean, in Lycia, in the south-western corner of Asia Minor, hence the value of the winged horse Pegasos as a means of transport.

sometimes called Stheneboia: she is Anteia in the *Iliad*, 6.160, but she was called Stheneboia in Attic tragedy (Euripides wrote a play of that name) and quite often in the later tradition too.

Chimaira: a three-headed fire-breathing monster, with a lion's head at the front, a goat's in the middle, and a dragon's behind (Hes. *Theog.* 319–22, *Il.* 6.179–82); Iobates would have thought that he was sending Bellerophon to certain death.

51 *tried to fly up to the heavens*: it is only now that we arrive at the element in the story that is directly relevant to the catasterism; this tale (without the catasterism) is first mentioned by Pindar (*Isth.* 7.43–8), and is attested for the lost *Bellerophontes* of Euripides.

divulging the plans of the gods: this was the version in Euripides' *Melanippe Sophe*; Zeus turned her into a horse because she sang oracular songs to mortals, telling them of cures, and of means by which they could relieve their pains (fr. 48 Kannicht, 13–17). Euripides wrote two Melanippe plays; Eratosthenes evidently made use of the other as the basis for his astral myth.

53 *Hyperboreans*: a mythical people of the far north who lived a life free from all toil and worry in an ideal climate.

temple made from feathers: according to Delphian tradition, the second temple of Apollo at Delphi had been constructed by bees from bees' wax and feathers, and had been sent by Apollo from the land of the Hyperboreans (Pausanias 10.5.6).

Heracleides of Pontos: a philosopher and astronomer of the 4th century.

54 *Prometheus . . . created men*: a relatively late notion, not attested before the 4th century; he modelled them from clay (Ap. 1.7.1, Hyginus, *Mythical Tales* 144, Ovid, *Metamorphoses* 1.82–7).

same fire: the classic account of the origin of these sacrificial practices can be found in Hesiod's *Theogony*, 536–60. Since it was the normal practice at a sacrifice for the participants to eat the meat from the victim, while the offal was burnt on the altar from the gods, this arrangement which apparently works to the disadvantage of the gods (if they are imagined as actually consuming the vapours rising from the altar) is explained as having been established as the result of a deception that was worked on Zeus. Like much else in this chapter, none of this is directly relevant to the astral myth.

fennel stalk: from the giant fennel, *Ferula communis*, not belonging to the same genus as ordinary fennel; its stalks have soft white pith at the centre.

shaking a torch: torch races were held at some ancient athletic festivals, such as the Panathenaic and Panthessalic Games; the runners would compete, either individually or as part of a team, to be the first to light the flame on an altar.

favour . . . woman: in the original story this was intended as a punishment rather than a favour (Hes. *Theog.* 567 ff.); the woman is described as a 'beautiful evil' (585). Hesiod returns to the story of the first woman in his *Works and Days* (60–105); it is there that she is first named as Pandora (81).

according to . . . Aeschylus: in his lost play *Prometheus the Fire-Bringer* (schol. to *Prometheus Bound* 94): as against only thirteen generations in *Prometheus Bound* (840–1).

55 *outshine that of his father*: Thetis, who was a Nereid, finally married a mortal, Peleus, to become the mother of Achilles, who would outshine his father as the greatest of warriors at Troy.

Prometheus ... reported it to Zeus: this story was again recounted by Aeschylus, in his *Prometheus Unbound* (Philodemus, *On Piety*, p. 41 Gomperz). It was probably invented by Aeschylus himself; in the earliest tradition, Prometheus was delivered from the eagle but not from his bonds (Hes. *Theog.* 613–16).

the apples of the Hesperides: see pp. 12–13.

58 *Anaplades*: this should perhaps be Anubis.

Acheloos: a great river of the western mainland of Greece, on the eastern boundary of Aetolia, far away from Egypt where the story ends.

Amythaonia in Egypt: Amythaonia was actually in Elis in the western Peloponnese (much closer indeed to the river Acheloos); it would seem that one or other of these names is incorrect.

59 *Hippolytos*: the son of Theseus, who met his death at Troezen as a result of action taken by Poseidon (see p. 46); Capaneus, Lycourgos, Tyndareus, Hymenaios, and Glaucos are also named in a list preserved in the text of Apollodorus (3.10.3).

60 *the tip of his knee . . . the equator*: his knees actually stretch some distance below the equator, which is more at waist-level.

Anguitenens: this simply means Serpent-bearer like Ophiouchos in Greek; we now use the Latinized form of the latter as the name for the constellation.

61 *Polyzelos*: local historian of Rhodes, writing in the early 3rd century or thereabouts.

65 *touches the equator with its feet*: the lesser Dog actually lies wholly within the northern hemisphere, if no great distance above the equator.

66 *the hydra*: the Lernaian hydra, which lived in Lerna, a coastal region of the southern Peloponnese south of Argos which was rich in springs. 'Hydra' simply means water-snake, but this one was exceptional as a monstrous child of Typhon and Echidna which was reared by Hera to present a threat to Heracles (Hes. *Theog.* 313–15). It was commonly pictured as being many-headed. Heracles was sent to kill it as his second labour (Ap. 2.5.2).

Heracleia: a 5th-century epic account of the exploits of Heracles, which Eratosthenes also cited in connection with that hero's confrontation with the dragon of the Hesperides (see p. 28).

the Manger: a star-cluster between the Asses which resembles a patch of mist, now more familiar as the Beehive; the Greeks used it as a weather-sign (see p. 28).

67 *Thesprotia*: a coastal region of Epirus in north-western Greece.

67 *oracle of Zeus at Dodona*: an oracle in Epirus associated with the mother-goddess Dione, identified there as the consort of Zeus, and also with Zeus himself. Pherecydes said that the nurses of Dionysos were nymphs of Dodona, (see pp. 87–8), but Dionysos had no ancient connection with the place.

Satyrs and Seilenoi: beings with some equine or caprine features who belonged to the retinue of Dionysos; Hephaistos, who can also be seen as a rather comical figure, could be imagined to be riding on an ass because he was lame.

Triton's horn: a minor sea-god (Hes. *Theo*g. 90–3); it was with him that the conch-shell horn was originally associated; he is often depicted with it in vase-paintings.

69 *Peisandros of Rhodes*: or Peisander in Latinized form, the author of a lost epic poem, the *Heracleia*, about the exploits of Heracles, probably 6th century; he was supposed to have been the first author to describe Heracles as wearing a lion's skin and carrying a club, rather than being dressed and armed like a normal warrior. Heracles acquired the lion's skin by killing the Nemean lion as the first of his labours; it could be used in place of armour because it was impenetrable to weapons, the lion having been invulnerable.

Lock of Berenice Euergetis: Berenice (267/5–221 BC) was the wife of Ptolemy III Eurgetes, king of Egypt (see further on pp. 71–2); Eratosthenes presumably explained how the constellation came to be devised at that relatively late period, as in the corresponding passage from Hyginus's *Astronomy*. It was not accepted as one of the canonic constellations in ancient times, although it has been adopted in the modern era. This group of stars was also identified as the Lock of Araiadne (see p. 31).

70 *Zephyrion*: the temple lay at the tip of Cape Zephyrion, north of Alexandria.

Berenice . . . Olympic Games: not otherwise recorded, but members of the Ptolemaic dynasty sent horses and chariot-teams to the Olympic Games (and other main festivals) over a long period of time, winning a number of victories; Callimachus wrote a poem to celebrate a victory that Berenice won at the Nemean Games.

Callimachus called her great-souled: *magnanimam* in Hyginus's Latin, indicating that she was a woman of spirit and courage. Although Callimachus doubtless did use such language of her—it appears in Catullus 66 (26) which was based on his poem about the Lock of Berenice—it need not be assumed that it was in connection with the preceding story, of a rather dubious nature, which is reported by Hyginus alone.

Lesbian girls: this passage seems muddled. It seems likely that Eratosthenes referred to an alternative name for this star-group, in which they were described as star-maidens, and identified with figures from legend, perhaps the seven girls from Lesbos mentioned in the *Iliad* (9. 128 ff. and 270 ff.). If that is correct, Berenice has been introduced into the story by error. In the corresponding reference in the Germanicus scholia, it is merely indicated that there was a tradition that suggested that the stars represent some maidens who perished at Lesbos.

72 *Hesiod says . . . Justice*: *Theogony* 901–2, but for the genealogy alone; it was Aratus who first identified this figure with the constellation, and the story that he tells about her in that connection was wholly of his own invention (except in so far as it refers to Hesiod's myth of the gold, silver, and bronze races).

73 *Aratus . . . daughter of Astraios and Eos*: Aratus merely suggested this as a possibility (98–9), by way of a joke, because Hesiod had described Astraios ('Starry') and Eos (Dawn) as being the parents of *all* the stars (*Theog.* 378–82).

spoken about above: see p. 37 ff.

74 *between two signs*: of the zodiac, because the constellation-figures in it were supposed to mark twelfth-parts of the circle (see p. 169); the sign in front of the body of the Scorpion was identified either as the Claws or as the Scales.

Chios . . . sting Orion: this is Aratus's account of the death of Orion (635–44), which was usually set in Crete; on this body of myth, see pp. 104–5. Eratosthenes would also have recounted the original version in which Earth sent forth the scorpion, as is confirmed by the Vatican Fragments, which give that version alone.

75 *symbol of that event*: i.e. the present constellation commemorates the fact that Earth had caused the death of Orion by sending forth the scorpion.

76 *tail like that of the Satyrs*: these beings, nature spirits who were associated with Dionysos, had tails like those of a horse; in early representations in particular they may also have legs like those of a horse, and the question under dispute is thus whether the Archer should be pictured as a Satyr of that form or as a Centaur.

Eupheme: apparently a nymph of Mount Helicon. Pausanias (9.29.3) mentions that there was a relief statue of her there; her name is suggestive of good repute—and thence acclamation, as is relevant to the present tale— or of reverent silence.

Sositheos: an author of tragedies from the 3rd century who seems to have been particularly famous for his Satyr plays (see *Palatine Anthology* 7.707), which contained a strong element of burlesque; and it was from a play of that kind that Eratosthenes drew the present story about Crotos, who was presumably invented by Sositheos himself.

77 *the Boat*: this is the group of stars later known as the Southern Crown (see p. 135).

Centaur's crown: another reference to the Southern Crown, here seen as a crown, but not yet regarded as a separate constellation.

79 *modelled on him*: a rather free translation, but that is surely the meaning of

the Greek phrase, which has sometimes been misinterpreted as implying that Capricorn was born or descended from Aigipan. The constellation-figure resembles Aigipan (i.e. Goat-Pan: see p. 80) in so far as it has goat-like features; its fish-like features are explained separately at the end of the narrative.

79 *the Goat*: the goat that suckled Zeus was said to have become the star known as the Goat (Aix, or Capella in Latin) in the constellation of the Charioteer (see p. 42).

80 *Typhon*: a primordial monster who revolted against Zeus and the gods after they had defeated the Titans, rivalling the Giants as their most fearsome enemy. According to Hesiod (*Theog.* 820 ff.), who calls him Typhōs, he was a son of Tartaros and Earth, and a thousand fire-breathing snakes' heads sprang from his shoulders. Although Zeus defeats him on his own in Hesiod's account, by striking him down with a thunderbolt, the struggle becomes longer in later accounts, and the other gods too become involved (there is a full narrative in Ap. 1.6.3, which includes the following Egyptian tale among much else).

Hermes . . . cat: the best account of this myth is that provided by Antoninus Liberalis (28, following Nicander); it explains why the Greek gods were represented in animal or part-animal form, Hermes being identified with Thoth, who was often depicted with the head of an ibis, Apollo with Horus, who was depicted as a hawk or with a hawk's head, and Artemis with Bastet, who was depicted with a cat's head.

81 *cite the poet Homer as a witness*: *Il.* 20.232–5.

83 *large Fish*: the Southern Fish (see p. 128).

84 *whom we mentioned above*: see p. 80.

86 *Euripides . . . in his Phrixos*: one of the two plays that Euripides wrote under this title must have made some reference to the myth of Europa, even if that was not the main subject of the play.

cut-off: apotomē, where the constellation-figure is cut short at the back.

six of them had liaisons with gods: the daughters of Atlas stood at the head of the Atlantid genealogies, which accounted for the origin of the Laconian and Trojan royal families, among others; Maia stood somewhat apart as the mother of the god Hermes, and Merope was the wife of Sisyphos, founder of Ephyra/Corinth.

88 *Lycourgos . . . put them to flight*: in the earliest account of this famous myth, this Thracian king puts the nurses to flight and causes Dionysos himself to seek refuge under the sea with Thetis (*Il.* 6.130–41, cf. Ap. 3.5.1). It seems almost certain that this story, which is also mentioned in another source for Pherecydes' account of the adventures of the young Dionysos (schol. *Il.* 18.486), formed no part of Pherecydes' narrative, and it is thus irrelevant to the astral myth. Hyginus explicitly names another author as his source.

Asclepiades: of Tragilos, a mythographer from the 4th century who was a pupil of Isocrates.

fifteen daughters: this is an error, there should be twelve; see further on pp. 93–4.

greater number . . . Pleiades: it is suggested that they were called the Pleiades because they were more in number, *pleious* in Greek; but see p. 89 for the correct version of this story.

Alexander: Alexander Polyhistor, a Greek scholar of the 1st century BC who resided in Italy; Hyginus had studied under him.

of Hyas and Boeotia: the Hyades are here seen as daughters of a Hyas who was the eponymous founder of a Boeotian tribe, the Hyantes, who were said to have been some of the earliest inhabitants of Boeotia (Pausanias 9.5.1).

89 *through Boeotia . . . Orion*: although his adventures also took him to the Aegean islands, Orion was primarily associated with Boeotia in east-central Greece, the land of his birth.

Vergiliae . . . ver: this is a folk etymology: the name is thought to be derived from *verga/virga*, meaning a twig.

Suculae: i.e. Piglets; the name was not of popular origin but originated from a misinterpretation of the Greek name Hyades, as though it were derived from *sus*, a pig.

Lycourgos . . . Naxos: Lycourgos was a Thracian king, and he is normally said to have driven the nurses from his own region of Thrace; perhaps an error for Nysa, where the episode is said to have taken place in Homer's account (*Il.* 6.129 ff.).

94 *Nephele*: i.e. Cloud, a minor goddess; she was the first wife of Athamas, a Boeotian king, but he later married Ino, who plotted to cause the death of Nephele's son Phrixos by causing the grain-harvest to fail by roasting the seed-corn, and then making people believe that an oracle had demanded the sacrifice of Phrixos as the only possible remedy. But Nephele sent him away on the wondrous ram along with his sister Helle. See Ap. 1.9.1. But there were conflicting accounts, and Hyginus also reports a wholly different version.

Hesiod and Pherecydes report: fr. 68 MW and fr. 99 Fowler respectively.

95 *Paion*: he was the eponym of Paionia, which lay somewhere in Thrace, and thus not all that far from the Hellespont; this is the only source for this tradition. The Edonos mentioned as alternative offspring by Hyginus was the eponym of the Edonians, who also lived in Thrace.

land of Aietes: he was king of Colchis, which lay at the far end of the Black Sea.

on the equator: Hipparchos and later astronomers placed the Ram above the equator, as we do, with only the star on its front feet stretching below it.

95 *Cretheus married Demodike*: she was named by Pindar as the new wife of Athamas (fr. 49 SM), but the following narrative, in which she is the aunt of Phrixos rather than his stepmother, follows a totally different pattern, that in which a woman makes a false accusation after failing to seduce a man (as found, for instance, in the story of Bellerophon: see pp. 51–2). There is nothing to indicate the original source of this narrative, which probably contained no catasterism in any case.

96 *Ammodes*: 'Sandy'; a connection with the name of Ammon is presumably implied.

to that spot: i.e. the oasis of Siwa some 350 miles east of Cairo, where the oracle temple of Amun, identified by the Greeks as Zeus Ammon, was located.

Leon: of Pella, 4th-century historian and theologian, who put forward rationalistic explanations for the gods and their myths, on the same lines as Euhemerus, claiming that they had been human beings who were subsequently deified; Dionysos is presented accordingly as a mighty king, and Ammon as an agricultural innovator.

97 *in memory of him*: since Dionysos would have been presented as mortal in Leon's account, the constellation-figure would have been devised by astronomers in memory of him. There is no evidence to show that Leon himself ever set out to explain the origin of this or any other constellation.

98 *heads are separated*: although Eudoxos placed the summer tropic at around the level of the head of the Twins (cf. Aratus 481), later astronomers represented it as running through their waist, as we do.

99 *already mentioned*: see pp. 60–1.

Aphidnai: Castor and Pollux attacked this town in Attica with a force of Spartans because Theseus had abducted their young sister Helen, and had left her there in the care of his mother; they were usually said to have recovered her without coming to any harm.

under attack from Idas and Lynceus: see Ap. 3.12.2. Castor was usually said to have been killed by Idas; the story of this conflict, which goes back to early epic, is recounted in different ways in different sources. None of this is directly relevant to the catasterism.

According to Homer: in the *Odyssey* (11.301–4) it is merely said they live (i.e. among the gods) and are dead (i.e. are in the underworld) on alternate days; Pindar explains (*Nem.* 10.55 ff.) that Pollux, who was a son of Zeus, asked to be allowed to die along with his brother, who was wholly mortal as a son of Tyndareos, and Zeus said that he could either enjoy full immortality on Olympos, or else share it with his brother, so that each of them would spend half their time above and half below. Since it is stated in the *Odyssey* (11.298–300) that both were sons of Tyndareos and Leda, the following lines about their shared immortality could well have been inserted at a later period.

shine on alternate days: this seems to make little sense.

101 *Hesiod says*: fr. 148a MW, in the Hesiodic *Catalogue*, written well after the lifetime of Hesiod himself.

raped Merope, daughter of Oinopion: Apollodorus, who offers a similar account of the life of Orion, states that Oinopion got him drunk and blinded him when he sought the hand of Merope, without mentioning the rape; according to Parthenios (*Sorrows of Love* 20) Orion asked to marry her, clearing the island of beasts as a service for the king and gathering booty as a bridal gift, but finally raped her when the king constantly postponed the wedding. Oinopion was a son of Dionysos, as might seem fitting for the primordial king of a wine-rich island which was closely associated with the god of wine. In one version of this story, Oinopion sought the help of Dionysos after his daughter was raped, and the god sent his Satyrs to put Orion to sleep and tie him up, so that the king was thus able to blind him while he lay in a helpless state (Servius on *Aeneid* 10.763).

Lemnos . . . Hephaistos: the island was specially associated with the divine blacksmith, who was supposed to have a forge there; Chios lies further south, just off the coast of Asia Minor, about halfway down.

Helios . . . cured by him: the sun-god could be seen as an appropriate person to cure him of his blindness; his home was thought to lie near the sunrise in the farthermost east.

Artemis and Leto: Leto was the mother of Artemis; she is regularly described in astral mythology as hunting in the company of her daughter, although there is no indication of that elsewhere.

102 *Iphiclos*: son of Phylacos, king of Phylace in Thessaly; according to the Hesiodic *Catalogue* (Hes. fr. 62 MW) he could run over the fruit of the asphodel and not break it, and over ears of corn without damaging them.

a certain Hyrieus: founder and ruler of the city of Hyria in Boeotia; his two sons, Lycos and Nycteus, went to Thebes and rose to power there. Hyrieus was a son of Poseidon by the Pleiad Alcyone (Ap. 3.10.1), which may help to explain why he was mixing on familiar terms with the gods.

shed their semen: literally, urinated; in the original Greek narrative, the name of Orion was derived from the verb *ourein*, which could be used in a euphemistic sense.

103 *Istros*: Alexandrian poet of the 3rd century, a follower of Callimachus.

106 *fled to Atlas*: i.e. to the ocean in the far west.

the Nereids: her sisters; they were the fifty daughters of Nereus, a pre-Olympian sea-god, and the Oceanid Doris. Only three of them were said to have married and had children.

107 *head . . . Pegasos*: as the constellation-figures are drawn in that area nowadays, the Dolphin is by no means close to the muzzle of Pegasus; but stars

that originally formed part of the head of Pegasus were later transferred to Equuleus, when it was inserted between Pegasus and the Dolphin.

107 *one called Delphinus*: the searcher is described as a human being here, through a misunderstanding of the Greek source rather than through any deliberate alteration of the myth.

Tyrrhenian shipmasters: in the *Homeric Hymn* 7, to Dionysos (7–8), the god is said to have been abducted by Tyrsenian pirates (this being another form of the same name). Although these would have been people from somewhere in the Aegean area (it is uncertain exactly where), it subsequently came to be assumed that the abductors of Dionysos were Etruscans from as far away as Italy, these being known to the Greeks as Tyrrhenians.

citharode: someone who sang to the cithara, an elaborate form of lyre which was used in public performances. Arion would have sung poems of his own composition.

Tainaron: Cape Matapan, the southernmost point of the Peloponnese.

108 *statue of Arion*: cf. Herodotus 1.24.8, Pausanias 3.25.7.

Pyranthus: i.e. Periandros, tyrant of Corinth, born in 625, who was Arion's patron.

109 *the dolphin's monument*: it is implied that this was at Corinth, and of considerable size, whereas it was in truth a small memorial which was located far to the south at Tainaron.

should be crucified: this Roman punishment is obviously out of place in this story set at quite an early period in Greece.

111 *Aristotle . . . On Animals*: = fr. 343 Rose; there is no reference to the supposed thirst of crows in Aristotle's surviving treatises on animals.

112 *Coronis*: a daughter of Phlegyas, king of the Lapiths in Thessaly, who aroused the love of Apollo. Pindar (*Pyth*. 3.8–46) tells the story at some length without mentioning the crow, although he seems to allude to it (27); it was mentioned as the informant somewhere in the Hesiodic corpus (fr. 60 MW), and a scholiast (schol. *Pyth*. 3.52b) cites a certain Artemon, probably Hellenistic, for the just-so story of how the crow was turned black.

Phylarchos: of Athens or Naucratis, historian of the 3rd century.

Protesilaos: son of Iphicles, the first Greek warrior to disembark at Troy; he soon died, at the hand of Hector, as the first Greek to land was fated to do. He was honoured in hero-cult at his supposed tomb in Elaiousa, opposite the Troad, as is first mentioned by Herodotus (9.116).

114 *given to Europa*: by Zeus, after he abducted her from Phoenicia to Crete to become his mistress (see p. 86).

the lance: a wondrous lance or javelin which always struck its target, just as the dog was fated always to catch its prey. Minos came to possess both of them as the eldest son of Europa.

the fox: the savage Teumessian fox or vixen, which caused such trouble to the Thebans that they were obliged to appease it by exposing one of their citizens to it each month (Ap. 2.4.6–7); it had been sent against them by Dionysos for some unstated reason (Pausanias 9.19.1). This was an ancient myth already recounted in early epic.

115 *Minos . . . was cured*: his wife Pasiphae had put a spell on him which caused him to bring death to any other woman who slept with him; Procris found a solution, by magical means or practical ingenuity, and became his mistress for a while (Ap. 3.15.1, Antoninus Liberalis 41). Hyginus offers a rather bowdlerized account of all of this.

Cephalos . . . went to Thebes: in the version from early epic he went there to be purified after accidentally killing his wife, but it was also said that he was specifically invited to bring his dog.

turned both of them to stone: referring to a Hellenistic poet for a version of the myth in which there was no catasterism, Hyginus fails to mention that the dog was transferred to the stars in the astral myth instead of being turned to stone.

dog of Icarios: see pp. 37–8.

116 *on its head another star*: this is strange because the Greeks located Sirius on the tongue or muzzle of the dog, and identified it with the dog-star; Greek and Egyptian material seems to have become mixed up together here, to confusing effect.

118 *thunderbolt*: the Cyclopes forged the thunderbolt of Zeus (see p. 53), but it is not clear how this is connected with the altar.

120 *Antisthenes*: an immediate follower of Socrates, born in the middle of the 5th century, who favoured an austere and ascetic way of life; regarded as the founder of the Cynic/Stoic strain in the Socratic tradition.

122 *Aristotle . . . On Animals*: he refers to this phenomenon, known as superfetation, in his *History of Animals* (524b, 579b–580a, 585a), and *On the Generation of Animals* (774a).

123 *Callimachus . . . blood of hares*: in his third *Hymn*, to Artemis, Callimachus states at the very beginning that she devoted herself to archery and the shooting of hares. The poem is humorous in tone.

Leros: a small island of less than thirty square miles in the southern Aegean quite close to Asia Minor.

125 *because of her speed*: *argos* means swift in Greek; this was probably the true origin of the name.

Argos was her builder: a son of Phrixos, who is said to have built her under the guidance of Athena (Pherecydes 3F111, Ap. 1.9.16).

Pindar . . . Demetrias: not in any surviving poem, although there is an account of the voyage of the *Argo* in *Pythian* 4.

according to Callimachus: in *Aetia* 18.13; Hyginus is not necessarily citing him for the following etymology, which does not appear in the remnants of his works. From his time onward Pagasia was regularly named as the point of departure.

125 *Athena attached a piece of timber*: Aeschylus fr. 20 Radt, cf. A.R. 1.526–7, Ap. 1.9.14.

126 *according to Aratus*: line 360. See p. 127.

128 *Bambyke*: a city in Syria lying north-east of Aleppo, later known to the Greeks as Hieraopolis (the Holy City), a centre for the worship of the Syrian goddess; see p. 85.

129 *Ctesias*: an author born in the late 5th century who wrote about Assyria, Persia, and India; see further on p. 85.

130 *takes its name from Helios*: phaethōn was an epithet that was applied to the sun-god from an early period (*Il.* 11.735, *Od.* 4.579), in reference to the radiance of the sun, thus providing an appropriate name for his ill-fated son, who was mentioned by Eratosthenes in connection with this planet, as we know from Hyginus. Although the name is here applied to Saturn, and the name Phainon (which means much the same) to Jupiter, this is the reverse of the usual practice.

Pyroeides: or *pyroeis*, both meaning 'fiery', in allusion to the reddish or orangey colour that makes Mars so easy to distinguish. It has that appearance because of the iron oxide (rust) in the rocks on its surface.

that which is found in the Eagle: alpha Aquilae, known as Altair, the twelfth brightest star in the sky; that it should be described as being red in appearance is surprising—it does not appear red nowadays and is not described as such in ancient astronomical writings.

Hesperos . . . Phosphoros: i.e. the Evening star and, as the morning star, Light-bringer; in the latter capacity, this planet was also called Heosphoros, Dawn-bringer.

Stilbon: the verb in question was used to describe the twinkling of the fixed stars, which scintillate (as small points of light) in a way that distinguishes them from the planets; e.g. Aristotle, *On the Heavens* 290a; but because of its smaller apparent size and the relatively unfavourable conditions at which it is viewed, at a low altitude, Mercury appears to scintillate more than the other planets.

Hermes . . . ordering of the heavens: this was a theme developed by Eratosthenes himself in his lost poem, the *Hermes*.

Heracleides of Pontos: philosopher and astronomer of the 4th century, a pupil of Plato.

131 *that of Helios*: the idea that Saturn is the star of the Sun or Sun of the night was a notion that was ultimately of Babylonian origin.

son of Cephalos and Eos: Cephalos was a lover of Eos (Dawn), who bore a son Phaethon (Hes. *Theog.* 986–7) or else Tithonos (Ap. 3.14.3) to him; Apollodorus calls him a son of Hermes and Herse, and he was not originally the same person as the Athenian Cephalos (see p. 114 ff.), who was sometimes identified with him. Some authors evidently thought that these were suitable parents for Hesperos.

132 *one of the visible circles*: the Milky Way was usually regarded as the only visible circle, the others being accessible to reason alone; perhaps the horizon is envisaged here as a sort of visible circle.

share in the honours of the sky: i.e. this was necessary if sons of Zeus by mortal women, specifically Hermes and Heracles, were to become immortal and live among the gods on Olympos.

133 *in his Hermes*: a lost poem by Eratosthenes, in which he seems to have offered an account of the life and adventures of Hermes, and then to have described how he ordered the heavens.

Rhea presented Cronos with a stone: because Cronos, knowing that his son was fated to be mightier than he was, swallowed his children, she hid away the new-born Zeus, and gave Cronos a stone wrapped in swaddling clothes instead.

ARATUS, *PHAENOMENA*

139 *Zeus himself who fixed the signs*: Aratus is talking in mythical terms in this context; he would naturally have considered the constellation figures to be of human invention (cf. 374 ff.).

the prior race: of disputed meaning, perhaps best taken as a reference to the gods in general, as against the human race, which was of later origin.

axis . . . rotate around it: the earth is to be imagined as standing at the centre of the universe, with the celestial sphere, on which the stars are set, revolving around it; the fixed axis of the universe thus runs through the earth from north to south.

ocean: since the ocean was envisaged as encircling the earth, this was regularly used as a term for the horizon in an astronomical context.

also called Wagons: Wagon, *Hamaxa*, was originally and properly a name for the Great Bear alone, suggested by the shape of the pattern of stars that form the Plough.

140 *Dicton*: commonly taken as another form of the name of Mount Dicte in Crete, where the infant Zeus was sometimes said to have been reared; it was in fact by no means close to Mount Ida, which was an alternative location for this tale of the infancy of Zeus.

Dictaean Curetes: when Cronos was searching for his son Zeus with the intention of killing him, they beat their spears against their shields outside the cave in which the infant was hidden, to drown out his cries.

Cynosura . . . Helike: for these names and the preceding myth, see pp. 9–11.

the Achaeans: here used as a name for the Greeks in general, as in the *Iliad*.

Sidonians: i.e. Phoenicians, Sidon being one of their main cities at the

eastern end of the Mediterranean. It was better to navigate by the smaller
Bear because it lay closer to the pole, hence its tighter orbit.

140 *on either side of its coil*: they actually lie on either side of its tail.

not to plunge into . . . ocean: because they lie near the north pole, they never
set below the horizon.

settings run together with . . . the risings: stars within the arctic circle never
set, those just south of it set only very briefly; so passing northward toward
the pole, the setting and risings draw ever closer together.

Kneeler: the constellation Engonasin, now known as Hercules; on Aratus's
attitude to it, see p. 29.

Dionysos . . . Ariadne: the price that the god paid for marrying a mortal was
to feel the pain of her death; see further on pp. 31–5.

141 *enormous Claws*: because the Scorpion was so large, it was divided to make
up two signs of the zodiac, the Scorpion and Claws; this sign is now identified as Libra, the Scales.

Oxherd: Bootes in Greek, which remains the modern name for the constellation; if the Great Bear is pictured as a wagon instead, he can be seen
to be driving along the oxen that are pulling it. The Oxherd was originally
just Arcturus, the brightest star in the constellation that was subsequently
constructed under that name. In so far as the constellation was viewed
in connection with the Bear, it was described as Arctophylax, the Bear-
guard.

Ear of Corn: Stachys in Greek, Sopica in Latin; alpha Virginis, a star of the
first magnitude.

Astraios: 'Starry'; since Hesiod referred to him as the father of all the stars
(*Theog.* 370), it is humorously suggested that he may be the father of the
star-Maiden.

Justice: Dike, righteousness personified, described by Hesiod as a daughter of Zeus and Themis (*Theog.* 901–2). Aratus develops an allegorical tale
in which the stages of her withdrawal are aligned to the deterioration of
successive early human races, as described by Hesiod in his myth of the
gold, silver, and bronze races (109–55; he omits any reference to Hesiod's
next race as not being relevant to his purpose).

142 *on her right wing . . . Vintager*: this line is generally regarded as an early
interpolation, since Aratus could not have regarded the constellation-
figure as being winged; the star (epsilon Virginis) acquired that name,
Protrygetor in Greek, Vindemiatrix in Latin, because its early rising
marked the start of the wine-harvest.

Etesian winds: 'annual' winds from the north that moderated the heat in
the dog-days of summer (see pp. 38–9).

143 *Olenian Goat*: a phrase apparently of double meaning: see p. 47.

Hyades . . . face of the Bull: unlike other star-groups associated with the main constellations, the Hyades form part of the constellation-figure, marking out the face of the Bull. On this star-cluster, see p. 86.

one common star: beta Tauri.

family of Cepheus . . . Iasos: Cepheus was the father of Andromeda, who was rescued from a sea-monster by Perseus (see p. 14 ff.); he was descended from Iasos, son of Argos—a primordial king of Argos—through Io (Ap. 2.1.3).

related to Zeus: the family of Cepheus was descended from a son whom Zeus had fathered by Io (Ap. 2.1.4); and Perseus, who became connected with the family by marriage, was a son of Zeus by Danae (Ap. 2.4.1).

key: a Greek temple-key, consisting of a long metal rod with two bends in it, so that it ran upwards for a short way before bending back to run parallel to its original course. This describes the position of the stars that represent Cassiepeia herself (as against those that make up her chair), two stars, epsilon and delta, and then two others, gamma and alpha, further along and at a different level. As a rough parallel, one can imagine how the stars would sketch out someone seated in a chair, viewed from the side.

her mother: Cassiepeia, whose boast had prompted Poseidon to send the monster (see p. 19).

144 *burdened by chains*: she still looks as she was when she was chained up to be exposed as prey to the sea-monster.

the gigantic Horse: not yet identified as Pegasos.

Hippocrene: for this myth, see p. 52.

Thespiai: a Boeotian city that lay below Mount Helicon; the waters of the spring can only be seen in the immediate neighbourhood, but the horse that created it can be seen from everywhere.

swift paths of the Ram: irrespective of the latitude at which they lie on the celestial sphere, stars complete their circuit within the same space of time; since the Ram lies near the equator while the Bear lies near the pole, the Ram has a much greater distance to traverse, and so has to run faster.

faint and starless: a consistent theme in Aratus and the Aratus literature, but somewhat exaggerated; there are two stars of second magnitude in the Ram's head. The Triangle was also cited as a marker (see p. 48).

more prominent than the other: I have followed Kidd's interpretation and translation here, that the northern Fish is 'superior' in so far as it stands higher, and so is more prominent for an observer at Greek latitudes.

145 *celestial Knot*: alpha Piscium.

his mother-in-law: Cassiepeia.

Alcyone . . . Maia: these were the daughters of Atlas. Maia is presumably singled out because she was the mother of the god Hermes; for the Pleiades and their myths, including those that were put forward to explain why one of them is 'missing', see pp. 86–92.

145 *Hermes . . . Lyre*: see pp. 23–6.

unknown figure: i.e. the Kneeler (Hercules).

gleaming Bird: now known as Cygnus, the Swan.

where . . . sun turns back again: Capricorn marks the southernmost point reached by the sun on its annual course, and thus the tropic or 'turning point' which we know as the Tropic of Capricorn. The sun arrives there at the winter solstice, on 22 December, hence the danger of storm that Aratus goes on to speak about.

146 *Cynosura*: the Small Bear.

on its own without a bow: the large arrow that is formed by the stars of this constellation is contrasted with the arrow that can be imagined as being the bow drawn by the Archer (Sagittarius).

dangerous: the Eagle gave sign of storms at its early rising in December.

north . . . wandering path: i.e. between the north pole and the ecliptic.

the south: i.e. as far south as could be seen at Greek latitudes, those near the south pole being permanently invisible.

the truncated figure of the Bull: only the front half of the bull is shown in the constellation-figure.

147 *people call it Sirius accordingly*: Seirios means 'the Scorcher'; for the dog-star as a heat-bringing star, see p. 117.

Jason's Argo: the heavenly ship was identified as the ship of the Argonauts from an early period; see pp. 124–6.

devoid of stars . . . to her mast: the front part of the ship is not represented at all in the constellation-figure, but it is cut off some way in front of the mast.

quite some distance away: the Sea-monster is the only constellation of the Perseus–Andromeda group to be set in the southern hemisphere; Andromeda lies some way north of the equator, the Tropic of Cancer cuts through her.

remains of the Eridanos: see pp. 126–7; it was a river of sorrow because Phaethon had plunged down into it.

148 *someone from a departed generation*: to ascribe the invention of all the constellations to a single person is just a manner of speaking—we are not meant to take this literally.

under his front hooves: Aratus follows Eudoxos in identifying this figure as four-footed, rather than two-footed as in Eratosthenes' conception (see pp. 76–8).

set in a circle: these form what would later be known as the Southern Crown (see p. 135).

ancient Night: a goddess who was brought to birth at an early stage in the development of the world (Hes. *Theog.* 123). Although personified as a goddess, she is to be viewed as an aspect of Zeus, who is to be interpreted in turn in Stoic terms; so in ascribing such an action to her, Aratus is speaking in figurative rather than straightforward mythical terms.

149 *the Beast*: now known as Lupus, the Wolf; the Beast could be pictured as a sacrificial victim that the Centaur is bringing to the Altar (see pp. 119–22).

Hydra . . . Bowl . . . Crow: because these three constellations seem so closely interconnected, a joint myth was put forward to explain their origin (see p. 110 ff.).

Procyon: the 'Fore-dog', i.e. the Small Dog, called by that name because it rises ahead of the large one and runs ahead of it. The name Procyon is now applied to the brightest star in the constellation.

150 *stars . . . different nature*: the five planets that were known to the ancient Greeks; this is a transitional passage leading up to Aratus's description of the circles on the celestial sphere.

renewed conjunction: a reference to the 'great year' or 'Platonic year', the period that elapses before the sun, moon, and five planets return to exactly the same positions as they had originally held in relation to one another.

four circles: as the end of the sentence shows, time measurement will be the theme of this section of the poem, and only the four circles relevant to that will be described, namely the ecliptic, equator, and the two tropics. The polar circles are omitted.

the Milk: the Greeks referred to the Milky Way as the Milk or milky circle; Aratus starts with it because it is a visible circle, by contrast to those that have to be pictured in the mind or through reference to diagrams.

equal it . . . smaller orbit: the equator and ecliptic are two large circles of equal size set aslant to one another, while the two tropics, lying further toward the pole on either side, are inevitably smaller (although not actually so very much smaller).

one lies . . . north wind: Aratus begins with the summer tropic (tropic of Cancer), before passing on to the winter tropic (tropic of Capricorn).

151 *seems to be cut in half*: the celestial equator is bisected by the horizon, and the spring and autumn equinoxes occur when the sun crosses it in its annual course, as marked by the two points at which the ecliptic cuts across the equator.

gripped obliquely between the two tropics: since the two tropics are imaginary circles drawn round the highest latitude that the sun reaches to the north and south on its annual course, they can naturally be visualized as gripping the oblique circle of the ecliptic between them; and halfway between its northernmost and southernmost points, the ecliptic is cut by the equator.

revolving wheels: Aratus may have intended his readers to think of armillary spheres that were constructed to illustrate these matters.

153 *Cyllenian Lyre*: i.e. the lyre that Hermes invented and then placed in the

sky (Aratus 268–71); Hermes was supposed to have been born on Mount Cyllene in north-eastern Arcadia.

154 *Orion seized her by her robe*: for this myth, see pp. 103 and 105.

Oinopion: a primordial king of Chios. Orion hoped to gain his favour, and perhaps his daughter's hand, by clearing his island of wild beasts, but things turned out badly (see further on p. 101). Orion was usually said to have become a hunting-companion of Artemis at a later time on Crete, and to have met his death on that island rather than on Chios.

flees round the boundary of the earth: sets below the opposite horizon.

the Bears themselves forbid it: as main polar constellations, they are presented as guarding it, and thus ensuring the stars inside it do not set.

155 *rival Doris and Panope*: Cassiepeia offended the Nereids, fifty beautiful sea-nymphs, by claiming to rival them in beauty (see pp. 19–20); by citing the names of two of them (from Hes. *Theog.* 250), Aratus refers to the group as a whole.

Hare . . . pursuit: as part of the hunting-scene in the heavens, the hare is under pursuit from Orion and his Dog.

157 *dread Arcturus*: the brightest star in Bootes, its heliacal rising in September marked the arrival of the time of year when stormy weather could be expected at sea.

nineteen cycles: referring to the system devised by Meton of Athens, 5th century, to adjust the lunar calendar to the solar year.

realm of Poseidon . . . of Zeus himself: of uncertain meaning; since many of the constellations of the southern hemisphere have marine or aqueous associations, Aratus is perhaps distinguishing that as the realm of Poseidon.

160 *parhelia*: mock suns or sun dogs, bright spots on either side of the sun, often accompanied by a halo.

the Manger: now known as the Beehive, a star-cluster in the Crab between the Asses which resembles a patch of mist.

164 *the nine-lived crow*: crows were thought to be exceptionally long-lived, as in more recent Greek folklore; Aratus is doubtless referring to some Hesiodic verses (fr. 304.1–2 MW) which state that a crow lives for nine human generations.

holm-oaks: or holly oak, Quercus ilex, an evergreen oak of the Mediterranean region.

the dark mastic: Pistacio lentiscus, a resinous evergreen shrub; there is no truth in the notion, below, that it flowers and fruits three times over.

squill: Scilla, a bulbous plant; the notion that it flowers three times over is again untrue, although it may give the impression of doing so because different species flower at different times of year.

INDEX

The index covers all references to *characters from myth* in the main text, both in the translated material and in the editorial commentaries (except in the case of Zeus, who is mentioned so frequently in different connections that only the passages of greatest interest have been included). Genealogical indications have been added, usually in the form of a patronymic, and other information that might be useful, irrespective of whether anything of the kind is to be found in the translated texts.

The index refers to *ancient authors* only in so far as they are explicitly cited as sources in the translated texts.

As regards *constellations and heavenly bodies*, the index is selective, referring to the accounts and discussions of their myths, and to Aratus's main references to them in his description of the heavens.

Main entries are printed in bold type.

Greek and Latin names

Although Hyginus, as a Roman author writing in Latin, naturally refers to mythical figures under their Latin or Latinized names, Greek forms have consistently been used in the preceding translations, because these are Greek myths derived from Greek sources; on this point, see further on p. xxxv. In a few cases, familiar Anglicized forms have been retained.

In most cases the differences between the original Greek names and the Latin versions are not very great, and they are not usually of such a nature as to cause confusion. It should be noted that the Greek diphthongs *ai* and *oi* will thus be found rather than the Latin forms *ae* and *oe* (thus Aigeus and Oinopion rather than Aegeus and Oenopion), and that the Greek digraphs *ei* and *ou* are not transliterated into long *i* and *u* as in Latin usage. For primarily aesthetic reasons, however, a *c* has generally been used as in Latin usage, rather than a *k*, to transliterate Greek kappa; this is properly a hard *c*, but where it seems natural in English, it may often be pronounced as a soft *c* (as for instance in the name Eurydice).

Because the Romans liked to identify Greek deities with deities of their own, Hyginus used completely different names in this connection, referring to

Aphrodite	as	Venus
Ares		Mars
Artemis		Diana
Cronos		Saturn
Demeter		Ceres
Dionysos		pater Liber
Eros		Cupid
Hephaistos		Vulcan
Hera		Juno

	Hermes		Mercury
	Poseidon		Neptune
and	Zeus	as	Jupiter.

In such cases, cross-references are included in the index.

Pronunciation of Greek names

In ordinary speech, it is usual for English speakers to pronounce Greek names in a way that seems natural without attempting to reproduce the exact pronunciation of the ancient Greeks. This conventional (or compromise) pronunciation presents no great problems if a few rules are observed:

VOWELS There are no mute vowels. In particular, a final *-e* and the *e* in final *-es* should always be sounded, as in familiar names like Aphrodite and Socrates.

In Greek *ae*, *oe*, and *oo* are never diphthongs, and each vowel should be sounded separately (e.g. in Danae, Theonoe and Bootes).

Of diphthongs, *ai* may be pronounced as in *high*, *au* as in *how*, and *oi* as in *boil*; and *eu* is commonly pronounced as in *eulogy*, or when followed by an *r*, as in *Europe*.

In names, *ei* is usually a digraph which may be pronounced as in *pay* (e.g. in Cassiepeia or Cheiron).

Greek chi, which represents an aspirated *k*, is transliterated as *ch*; it may be pronounced like a *k*.

G is properly hard as in *gallery*, but when it seems natural in English, it may often be pronounced as in *gin* (as e.g. in Aigeus).